STAFFORD COUNTY, VIRGINIA

ORDER BOOK ABSTRACTS

1664-1668
1689-1690

Ruth and Sam Sparacio

The Antient Press Collection
from

Colonial Roots
Millsboro, Delaware
2016

Colonial
Roots

Helping You Grow Your Family Tree

ISBN 978-1-68034-089-1

CONTENTS

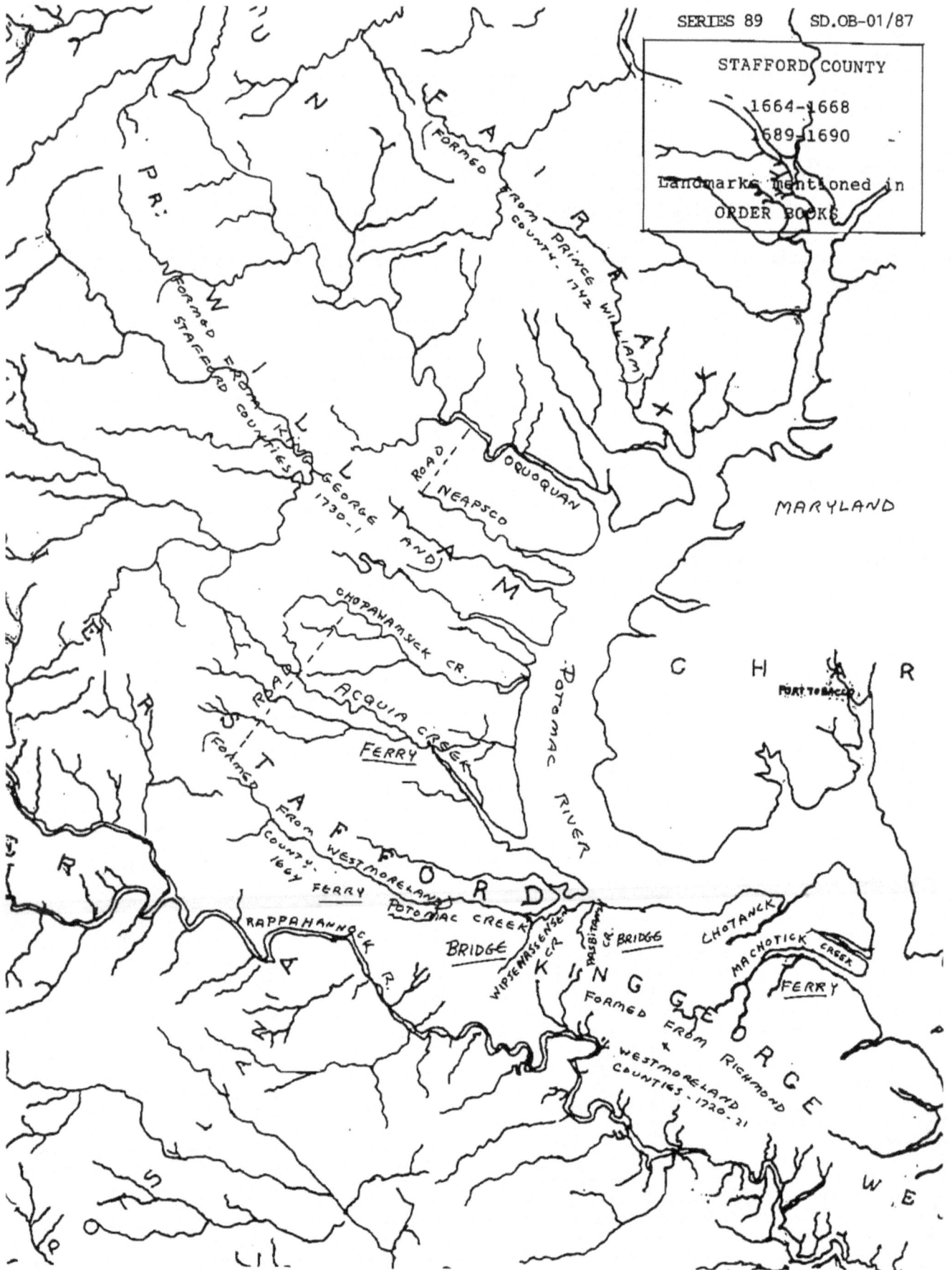

SERIES 89   SD.OB-01/87

STAFFORD COUNTY

1664-1668
1689-1690

Landmarks mentioned in
ORDER BOOKS

PRI.

FAU

FORMED FROM PRINCE WILLIAM COUNTY 1742

WILLIAM AND MARY

FORMED FROM STAFFORD COUNTIES KING GEORGE 1730-1

ROAD

NEAPSCO

OQUOQUAN

MARYLAND

CHOPAWAMSCK CR.

ACQUIA CREEK

FERRY

POTOMAC RIVER

CHAR

FORT TOBACCO

RA

STAFFORD

FORMED FROM WESTMORELAND COUNTY 1664 FERRY

POTOMAC CREEK

BRIDGE

WIPJEMASSENSE CR.

PASBITOWN CR. BRIDGE

CHOTANCK

MACHOTICK CREEK

FERRY

RAPPAHANNOCK R.

KINGGEORGE

FORMED FROM RICHMOND

WESTMORELAND COUNTIES - 1720-21

P O S

WE

STAFFORD COUNTY, VIRGINIA

ORDER BOOK

1664 - 1667/8

Page 1.   At a Court held for the County of Stafford 27th May 1664

PRESENT

1.   Lt. Colo. Robert Williams   Mr. Roger Perfitt
       Capt. John Alexander   Mr. Richd. Fossaker   Justices
       Mr. Richd. Heaberd

2.   Colo. JOHN DODMAN was sworne Sheriff for this County for this year
       as Mr. Secretary LUDWELL signified by his Letter to the Court that
it was the Governours Pleasure the said Colo. Dodman being enter'd into Bond
to perform the said office.

3.   ANTHONY P---DGES was this day sworne Clerke of this County by grant
       of the Secretary of Virginia.

4.   The Court doth order that Capt. JOHN ALEXANDER shall forthwith presse
       Six men of Horse & go to the Manfatters Indians to see if he can dis-
cover what Indians they were that had lately committed that Murther above at
Potomeck.

5.   Let noe will be proved (if any made) nor administration granted of
       the Estate of JACOB PORTER deceased unless JOHN WHITSON principall
creditor of the said deceased be first called.

Adjourned 14th June 1664 this Caveat was entered.

6.   At a Court held for the County of Stafford the 15th of June 1664

PRESENT

       Lt. Colo. Robert Williams   Mr. Roger Perfitt
       Capt. John Alexander   Mr. Richd. Fossaker   Justices
       Mr. Richd. Heaberd

7.   The Court doth adjudge JOS^h HAYWARD to be about the age of fourteen
       years & therefore he is exempted from paymt of Levies till he be of
age according to the Act of Assembly.

8.   Whereas THOMAS SPEEDY was imployed on a Messadge to the Honble ye
       Governor about the Indians the Court doth therefore order the said
Speedy shall be 400 lb Tobo out of ye next levies.

Page 2. Court held 27th May 1664

9.   Whereas it doth appear unto the Court that GARRARD FFORD doth owe
       unto Colo. JOHN DODMAN one quarter cask of Sack by Bill the Court
doth therefore order that the said fford shall make paymt of the said Quarter
Cask of Sack unto the said Colo. Dodman ye 10th of February next with charges
of Court alias Execution.

10.   The Court doth order GARRARD FFORD shall be fined 500 lb Tobo to the
       use of the County for his unlawful gaming to be paid ye 10th of 9ber
next with charges of the Court alias Execution.

11.   To the worshipful Justices of the Peace of the County of Westmoreland
       the humble petition of Mr. JAMES CLIFTON sheweth that Capt. GEORGE
MASON doth unjustly detain a servant maide of your Petitioner & hath delivered

Page 2 (contd).   Court held 15th June 1664.

her soe 5 weakes this Verry day Wherefore your Petitioner humbly praies that
he may have an order of this Court against the said Capt. Mason to restore the
said Servant & to satisfy for the time the said Servant hath bin out of you
Petitioners imployment & Service & that he may pay the charges of Court unto
your Petitioner and he shall pray
                                    Vera Copias Teste   Thos. Willford Cl Cur

   It is the verdict of the Jury that the maid Servt in controversy is Capt.
Masons.

(blank) Wells	John Michams
Richd. Hope	Steph. Norman
Henry Aldy	Hugh Donding
Ffran. Grey	Phill Carpenter

   The Court doth order that the Verdict of the Jury shall be enter'd for the
Judgmt & that Capt. GEORGE MASON shall keep & possess the maid servant called
ELLEN FFELT which he bought of the said Mr. JAMES CLIFTON And the Court doth
further order that the said Mr. Clifton shall pay

Page 3.   Court held 15th June 1664

the said Capt. Mason the charges of Court the 10th of 8ber next alias Execution.

12.   The Court doth order that a Commission of Administration shall be granted
      unto ANN PORTER of the Estate of JACOB PORTER her late Husband Deceased
the giving in an Inventory & Secretary to the Court for the same.

13.   The Court doth order that HUGH DONGDING, ROBT. BUTTERFEILE, JOHN WILLIAMS
      & STEPHEN NORMAN shall make appraisal of JACOB PORTERS Estate they having
taken their oaths to that purpose.

14.   The Court doth adjudge SUZANAH HOMAN to serve her Matter Colo. JOHN DOD-
      MAN or his assigns five years according to Act of Assembly from this Day.

15.   The Court doth adjudge JOHN NELSON to serve his Master Colo. JOHN DODMAN
      or his assigns Twelve years according to Act of Assembly from this day.

16.   The Court doth adjudge WM. HITCHIN to serve his Master WILLIAM WITHERS
      or his assigns Eleven years according to Act of Assembly from this day.

   The Court is adjourned to ye first Wednesday in Sept next for to be held at
Mr. TOWNSENDS at Choctanck.

17.   At a Court held for County of Stafford ye 7th 7ber 1664

                              PRESENT

Lt. Colo. Robt. Williams	Mr. Roger Perfitt
Capt. John Alexander	Mr. Richd. Fossaker Justices
Mr. Richd. Heaberd	Mr. Hugh Donding

18.   Mr. HUGH DONDING Sworne one of the Justices of the Peace for this County
      of Stafford.

19.   Whereas HENRY ALDY hath arrested JOHN WILLIAMS to this Court and doth
      not appear to prosecute his action the Court doth order that the said
Aldy be nonsuited & pay 50 lb of Tobo with costs of Suit the 10th of October
next alias Execution.

Page 4. Court held ye 7th 7ber 1664.

20. WILLIAM GREEN & VINCENT YOUNG Sworne Churchwardens of Potomack Parish THOMAS GRIGGS sworne Constable ye bounds and from Colo. PETER ASHTONS upwards.

21. Whereas HENRY ALDY dies supenia WM. RUSH to this Court the Court doth order that Henry Aldy pay unto Mr. Rush 40 lb Tobo ye 10th 8ber etc.

22. Whereas FRANCIS HALES did profer himself to be Security for the Widow PORTERS administration of Estate of JACOB PORTER her Husband deceased the Court doth order the said Hales to enter into Bond & that administration be thereupon to the said Widow granted.

23. Whereas FRANCIS WILLFORD hath written out the Acts of Assembly with several presidents for the use of this County the Court doth order that the said Mr. Willford have out of the next levies for this county (blotted out by smudge) of Tobo.

24. Whereas GARRARD FFORD arrested Capt. GEORGE MASON to this Court & hath not cause of Accon the Court doth order that the said fford be nonsuited & pay 50 lb Tobo with costs of Suite the 10th 8ber next alias Execution.

25. Whereas MICHAEL PHILLIS arrested GARRARD FFORD to this Court doth not appear to (blank) his Accon the Court doth order that the said Phillis be nonsuited & pay 50 lb Tobacco with costs of Suit the 10th of 8ber next alias Execution.

26. The Court doth order Mr. ROGER PERFITT & MR. RICHARD FOSSAKER to take the Estate of ROBERT MOSLEY into their possession.

27. Whereas FRRANCIS HALES Ent a petition against the Estate of ROBERT MOSLEY the said Mosley being returned the Court doth order that the said Hales be first satisfied according to Law wth costs of Suite.

28. Whereas Mr. HUGH DONDING Ent a petition against the Estate of JACOB PORTER deced for 424 lb Tobo & Cask & that it did appear that a Steere of the sd Porter was in possession of said Donding the Court doth order the said Steere to be in full satisfaction of the sd Bill etc.

Page 5. Court held ye 7th 7ber 1664.

29. Whereas Colo. VALLENTINE PEYTON did sue ANDREW WATSON for a certain quantity of Tobacco upon Bill the said Watson proving the afsd Bill Paid the Court doth order that the said Bill be delivered up to the said Watson & that Collo. pay the costs of Suite.

30. Whereas it doth appear unto this Court that JACOB PORTER deced did owe unto FFRANCIS HALES 330 lb Tobo & Cask the Court doth therefore order that a Judgment be ent against the Est of said Porter in the behalf of the said Hales else Execution.

31. Whereas it doth appear unto this Court that Colo. HOAKE doth owe unto Captain HOSKINS 1750 lb Tobo & cask the said Colo. Hoake did acknowledge judgment for the same with forbearance and costs of Suite to be paid the 10th 8ber alias Execution.

32. The Court doth order that THOMAS BLAXLEY & JOHN PALMER remain in the Sheriffs hands until they put in the sufficient security to Ffra. JORDAN for the payment of (blank) Tobo & cask.

Page 5 (contd) Court held ye 7th 7ber 1664.

33. Whereas it doth appear to the Court that ROBERT MOSLEY doth owe unto Capt. Brent (Capt. GILES BRENT in margin) 800 lb Tobo & cask & that a Estate Inventus is returned the Court doth order that an attachment against the Estate of the said Moseley for soe much with costs of Suite.

34. Whereas a difference in this Court doth depend between JOHN MATHIES & GARRARD MASTERS the Court doth order that it be referr'd to next Court.

35. Whereas Mr. DANIEL HUTT did arrest Mr. HENRY MEESE to this Court & doth not appear to prosecute his account the Court doth order that the said Hutt be nonsuited & pay 50 lb Tobo with costs of Suit the 10th 8ber alias Execution.

36. It is the Verdict of the Jury that the horse was shot with Shott after PHILLIP CARPENTER shott him with Salt & soe hand found the horse by Evidence.

Page 6. Court held ye 7th 7ber 1664.

Capt. Geo. Mason	Wm. Howard	Christopher Lund
Thomas Humphries	Tho: Sharpe	Thomas Griggs
John Williams	Wm. Rush	John Heaberd
Stephen Norman	(blank) Pate	Robt. Butterfeile

37. Whereas it doth appear to the Court that EDMOND NANFEN doth owe unto HENRY ADAMS 350 lb Tobo & Cask the Court doth order that the said Manfen pay soe much to the said Addams the 10th 8ber next with costs of suite alias Execution.

38. Whereas CHRISTOPHER LUNN did arrest JNO. COLCLOUGH to this Court & hath no cause of Accon the Court doth order that the said Lunn be nonsuited & pay 50 lb Tobo with costs of Suite the 10th 8ber alias Execution.

39. The Court doth committ HENRY PARNHAM into the Sheriffs hands in Suspittion of Felony to be tried before the Governor & Councill at a General Court the 26th day of Novr next.

40. The Court doth order that WILLIAM GREEN prosecute.

41. The Court doth order that the fine of GARRARD FFORD of 500 lb Tobo & Cask fined the last Court be remitted.

42. Whereas Colo. GARRARD FFOOKE hath made oath that noe land hath bin taken up from 31 persons transported into this county The Court doth order that certificate be granted unto Colo. Ffooke for 1550 acres of land etc.

43. EDMOND NANFEN doth acknowledge judgment to Capt. FFENDALL of Maryland for 4000 lb Tobo and cask.

The Court is adjourned to the second Wednesday in 8ber next to be held at the house of Colo. Ffooke at Parsbitansy.

Page 7. At a Court held for the County of Stafford the 12th of October 1664

44. PRESENT

Lt. Colo. Robt. Williams	Mr. Hugh Donding	
Major Geo. Mason	Mr. Roger Perfitt	Justices
Mr. Richd. Heabeard	Mr. Richd. Ffossaker	

45. The Court doth order that OLIVER BALFE, ROBT. STREETE & THOS. DOVACKE be Surveyors of the highwais from Capt. ALEXANDERS to the extent of the county.

Page 7 (contd) Court held 12th of October 1664.

46. The Court doth order that JOHN MATHIES & MICHAEL HILL be surveyors of
    the highway from the head of Potomack to Capt. BRENTS.

47. The Court doth order that JOHN AXTON & THOMAS ROWLAND be surveyors of
    the highway from Parsbitansy to the head of Potomack.

48. Whereas it doth appear unto this Court that THOMAS BLAXLEY stands indebted
    to JOHN PALMER 558 lb Tobo and cask & that the said Blaxley hath abensented
himself the Court doth order the said Palmer have an attachment against the
Estate of said Blaxley.

49. Whereas it doth appear unto this Court that ELIZABETH PARNHAM hath abused
    in Languadge WILLIAM GREEN and his wife the Court doth order that the said
Elizabeth Parnham ask the said Greene forgiveness alias be whipt.

50. Whereas Colo. Ffooke sold a certain tract of land to JOHN COLCLOUGH &
    to dell pattent for the same the Court doth order that said Colclough
pay unto Colo. Ffooke 400 lb Tobo & that thereon Colo. Ffooke dell the pattent
to the said Colclough.

Page 8. Court held 12th of October 1664.

51. Whereas it doth appear to this Court that Mr. JAMES CLIFTON doth sue unto
    Capt. Brent 1000 lb Tobacco and cask the Court doth order the said Brent
have Judgment for the same to be paid the 10th of 8ber 1665 & that the said
Clifton perform the condition & dell the mare the 28th August next.

52. Whereas it doth appear unto this Court that JOHN MATHIES bought a cow
    of the wife of GARRARD MASTERS the Court doth order that the said Garrard
Masters forthwith dell the said cow to the said Mathies & pay all charges of
Court.

53. The Court doth order that JOHN MATHIES unto DIXY WARD four days atten-
    dance 30 lb Tobo according to Act of Assembly.

54. The Court doth order that JOHN MATHIES unto WALTER CANNON four days at-
    tendance 30 lb Tobo according to Act of Assembly.

55. Whereas it doth appear to this Court that RICHD. DUKE did kill a horse
    of OLIVER BALFE the Court doth order that Richard Duke after Expiration
of his time with Colo. JOHN DODMAN serve Oliver Balfe 2 years for satisfaction
of the said horse.

56. The Court doth order that GARRARD MASTERS pay unto WM. LANE and his wife
    60 lb Tobo for a days attendance according to Act of Assembly.

57. The Court doth order that by consent of both parties Mr. JAMES CLIFTON
    pay to Mr. GILES BRENT 1800 lb Tobacco and Cask with Court charges &
they both shall give general acquittances one to mower from the beginning of
the world to this day Excepting only the Judgment of Court for HANAH WORFLEYS
hire and condition & Bills for 3000 lb Tobacco & cask 1500 lb Tobacco appear
wherein the said Mr. Clifton stands bound to the said Mr. Brent whereof 1300
lb of the 1800 lb Tobo to be paid this year.

Page 9. Court held 12th of October 1664.

58. Whereas JOHN MATHIES did arrest JOSHUA EDWARDS to this Court and had noe
    cause of action the Court doth order that the said Mathies pay to the
said Edwards 30 lb Tobacco for Nonsuit forthwith with charges of Court alias
Execution.

Page 9 (contd) Court held 12th of October 1664.

59. The Court doth order that FRANCIS JORDAN forthwith pay unto NICHOLAS
VAUS 100 lb Tobo alias Execution.

60. Whereas it doth appear unto this Court that JOHN MATHIES doth owe unto
Capt. BRENT 1000 lb Tobacco and cask The Court doth order that the said
James Mathies and DIXY WARD pay unto Capt. Brent the sd some the 22d October
next with Court charges alias Execution.

61. Whereas it doth appear to this Court that DIXY WARD do owe to JO: EDWARDS
650 lb Tobacco & Cask the Court doth order that the said Dixy Ward forthwith pay the said some to Jo: Edwards with Court charges alias Execution.

62. The Court doth adjudge JOHN CONEY to serve his Master WILLIAM LANE and
MICHAEL HILL according to the custom of the country.

63. Whereas it doth appear to this Court that ROBERT MOSLEY doth owe to Capt.
GILES BRENT 697 lb Tobo and cask the Court doth order that the Estate
of the said Mosley forthwith pay unto the said Brent the said some with Court
charges alias Execution.

64. Whereas it doth appear to this Court that DIXY WARD doth owe to JOHN
MATHIES 2000 lb Tobacco and cask the Court doth order the said Dixy Ward
forthwith pay to John Mathies the said some with Court charges alias Execution.

65. Capt. MASON was this day sworne for this County.

66. The Court is adjourned till the second Tuesday in 9ber next to the house
of Colo. FFOOKE at Parsbitansy. Then Court is adjourned till the 15th
Sept.

Page 10. At a Court held for the County of Stafford the 15th 9ber 1664.

Present

67. Lt. Colo. Robt. Williams   Mr. Hugh Donding
     Major Geo. Mason   Mr. Richd. Heabeard   Justices
     Capt. John Alexander   Mr. Richd. Ffossaker

68. Whereas Mr. JOHN TOWNSEND Attorney of Mr. BROWN Merchant creditor of the
Estate of Mr. HENRY ADDAMS deced did put for administration on the Estate of the said Addams The Court doth order that the said Townsend forthwith
have a comicon of administration on the sd Addams Estate Major JOHN WASHINGTON
being Security.

69. Whereas HENRY POOLY hath absented himself out of his Master JOHN WIL-
LIAMS Service severall months and that the said Master hath bin at great
charge in the obtaining him against the Court doth order that Henry Pooly serve
his Master John Williams after the expiration of his time with him by Indenture
or Custome of the County three whole years for satisfaction of his loss &
charges.

70. The Court doth order that Mr. RICHD. HEABERD, THOMAS HUMPHRIES, WILLIAM
GREENE and DAVID COLLINS be appraisers of Estate of Mr. HENRY ADDAMS deceased.

71. Whereas it doth appear to this Court that JOHN PALMER stands indebted to
FFRA. JORDAN 2600 lb Tobacco and cask for a tract of land the Court doth
order that the said Palmer forthwith pay unto the said Jordan the some of 2600
lb Tobacco and cask with charges of Court or redeliver the said land and chattle into the possession of the said Jordan alias Execution.

Page 10 (contd)   Court held 15th 9ber 1664.

72.   Whereas EDWARD BULLOCK petitioned this Court for administration of Estate of HENRY RAMSEY deced the Court doth order the said Bullock have administration JOHN COLCLOUGH being Security.

Page 11.   Court held 15th 9ber 1664.

73.   The Court doth order that WILLIAM GREEN, THOMAS HUMPHRIES, JOHN KEECH and RICHD. ROSSAY be appraised of the Estate of HENRY RAMSEY deced.

74.   Whereas the Sheriff did return CHARLES WOOD arrested to this Court at the Suit of J: EDMONDS and that the said Wood did not appear The Court doth order that if the Sheriff bring not the body of the said Wood to this Court the next Court which shall be on the 2d Tuesday in Jany that then Judgment pass against the said Sheriff for the said Debt.

75.   JOHN MATHIES did acknowledge Judgment to JO: EDMONDS for 770 lb Tobacco and cask with charges of Court to be paid forthwith alias Execution.

76.   Whereas it doth appear to this Court that Mr. THOS SOLEY owed unto JOHN KEECH 400 lb Tobacco and cask The Court doth order that Mr. ANT. BRIDGES who married the relict of the said Soley forthwith pay unto the said Keech the sd 400 lb Tobacco & cask with charges of Court alias Execution.

77.   Whereas it doth appear to this Court that THOMAS BLAXLY owed unto Mr. STORKE 749 lb Tobacco and cask the Court doth order that the said Storke be payd the said some forthwith out of the Estate of the said Blaxly alias Execution with for Barance and Costs of Sute.

78.   The Court doth order that JAMES PRICE, ANDREW WATSON, SAMUEL HEARND and SAMUEL SPOONER be appraised of the Estate of THOMAS BLAXLY.

79.   PHILIP CARPENTER did acknowledge forthwith to pay unto Mr. WM. STORKE 824 lb Tobo & Cask als Ex.

80.   Whereas the levies of the County & Parish amt to 95 lb Tobo per poll the Court doth order that Colo. JOHN DODMAN high themselves the said levies.

81.   The Court doth order that WILLIAM GREENE have attachment against the Estate of HENRY PARNHAM for 400 lb Tobo in the said Greenes hands.

Page 12.   Court held 15th 9ber 1664.

82.   Whereas many sad accidents have happened by the Indians hunting in the woods as by firing the same and that particular persons harbor them Then the Court doth order that noe Indian by any person whatsoever shall be suffered to him in any place of the English habitation such only excepted as by Public Order are allowed to find out the residence of the Murtherers on the forfeiture of 500 lb Tobacco & cask & it is further order'd that the grand jury present all such offenders to be prosecuted accordingly.

83.   At a Court held for Stafford County the 10th Jany 1664/5
                                 PRESENT

Lt. Colo. Robt. Williams	Mr. Richd. Heabeard	
Major George Mason	Mr. Roger Perfitt	Justices
Capt. John Alexander	Mr. Richd. Ffossaker	

Then the Court adjourned till the 2d Tuesday in January

Page 12 (contd)   Court held the 10th Jany 1664/5

84. Whereas it doth appear unto this Court that Colo. DODMAN doth owe unto
Mr. RICHD. RANDOLPH 430 lb Tobo and cask as Security for THOMAS DUTTON
the Court doth order the said Colo. Dodman forthwith pay unto the said Randolph
430 lb Tobo & cask with costs of Suite alias Execution.

85. Whereas ROBT. MOSLEY did arrest NICHOLAS RUSSELL to this Court and had
noe cause of action the Court doth order that the said Mosley forthwith
pay unto the said Russell 50 lb for nonsuit with charges of Court alias Execution.

86. Whereas NICHOLAS RUSSELL did arrest ROBT. to this Court and had noe cause
of action the Court doth order that the said Russell be nonsuited &
forthwith pay unto Robt. MOSLEY 50 lb Tobo with costs of Suit alias Execution.

87. Whereas Mr. STORKE (WM. in margin) did arrest GARRARD FFORD to this Court
and did not prosecute his action the Court doth order that the said Storke
be nonsuited and pay 50 lb Tobo with costs of Sute alias Execution.

Page 13. Court held the 10th Jany 1664/5.

88. Whereas JOHN MATHIES did disburse in funerall church 650 lb Tobacco the
Court doth order JOHN TOWNSEND Att of Mr. WILLIAM BROWNE forthwith pay
to the said Mathies the said some ali Execution.

89. The Court doth order that Mr. ROBT. WILLIAMS Att of Mr. ROBT. TOWNSEND
Att against the Estate of WILLIAM WILLMS for 883 lb Tobacco and cask with
costs of Sute as Security of JAMES LINDSEY ali Execution.

90. Colo. FFOOKE Att of GARRARD MASTERS Mr. JOHN STONE ditto the cause depending between Garrard Masters and JOHN MATHIES is refer'd by consent
to the next Court.

91. Whereas JOHN MADDER ali MATHER and WILLIAM RUSHTON warnether Mr. HENRY
MEESE to this Court for their freedome acknowledging they had noe Indenture The Court doth order that the said Servants serve to the full period of
5 years from the first arrivall.

92. Whereas Mr. ROBT. MOSLEY did acknowledge Judgment to Colo. FFOOKE the
said Ffooke did now in Court acknowledge satisfaction for the same.

93. JOHN WILLIAMS, ROBERT STREET, ROBERT BUTTERFEILE, Mr. HUGH DONDING the
Court doth order appraisers of the Estate of JOHN GILES deceased.

94. The Court doth order as Order of Vestry that Colo. JOHN DODMAN Sheriff
pay the dues to the readers of the Estate Wednesday in February.

95. JOHN MATHIES did acknowledge Judgment for 253 pounds Tobacco and cask
Capt. JOHN ALEXANDER and Mr. RICHARD FOSSAKER.

The Court is adjourned to the Last Wednesday Feb: I 1664/5. The Court is
adjourned to the first Wednesday in April 1665.

Page 14.   At a Court held for the County of Stafford 5th April 1665.
PRESENT

Lt. Colo. Robt. Williams	Mr. Richd. Heabeard
Majr. Geo. Mason	Mr. Roger Perfitt Justices
Capt. John Alexander	Mr. Richd. Ffossaker
Mr. Hugh Donding	

Page 14 (contd)   Court held 5th April 1665.

96. Whereas RICHARD CORDWELL in his lifetime did count that into the hands
    of NICHOLAS BRULY the care of his Daughter GRACE CORDWELL the said Cord-
well being now dead The Court doth order that the said Grace doe remain with
the said Bruly till she be twenty one years of age.

97. Whereas Colo. JOHN DODMAN did arrest WM. STORKE to this Court at the
    Sute of Lt. Colo. ROBERT WILLIAMS & that the said Storke did not appear
The Court doth order that the said Dodman bring forth the body of the said
Storke on the first Wednesday in June next being the next Court to answer the
said Sute or pay the debt which is two men servants.

98. The Court doth order that the said Sheriff Colo. DODMAN have an attach-
    ment against the Estate of the said Storke for non appearance.

99. Whereas it doth appear to this Court that HENRY WALKER bought of THOMAS
    BLAXLEY 3 head of cattle which JOHN PALMER did attach the Court doth
order John Palmer forthwith deliver the said cattle to Henry Walker ali Exe.

100. Ordered against JOHN SAMWAIDS under Sheriff for non appearance of
     THOMAS DUTTON.

101. Ordered that the said Sheriff have attachment agst the Estate of THOMAS
     DUTTON .

102. Whereas an order from the Genl. Court did this day appear to this Court
     to stop the Escheat of the land of STEPHEN NORMAN nuncupative will being
proved & an heir found thereby the Court doth order that JOHN WILLIAMS, OLIVER
BALFE, ROBT. BUTTERFEILE & JNO. WELLS be appraised of the Estate of the sd
Norman & that Mr. HUGH DONDING sweare the said appraisers the April 1665.

page 15. Court held 5th April 1665.

103. Whereas it doth appear unto this Court that MASON GEORGE doth owe unto
     the Widdow BOOKE 400 pounds of Tobacco and cask the Court doth order
that the said Mason paid the said some to the said Beeze with costs of Suite
to the said BAYLY the 10th 8ber ali Exe.

104. Whereas Mr. HENRY MEESE did arrest HUMPH. BAYLY to this Court & did not
     appear to prosecute his accon the Court doth order that the said Mr. Meese
be nonsuited and pay 50 pounds of Tobacco with costs of Suite to the said
Bayly the 10th 8ber ali Execution.

105. Ditto CARPENTER agst Mr. WILLIAM BROWN.

106. Ditto ARCHDALE COMBS agst Ditto Brown.

107. Ditto JOHN WITHERS against Ditto Brown.

108. The Court doth order that Mr. JAMES CLIFTON pay to the use of the poor
     for proclaiming the name of God 80 pounds to Tobacco the 10th 8ber ali
Execution.

109. Whereas it doth appear to this Court that Mr. JAMES CLIFTON stands in-
     debted to Capt. JOHN ASHTON 400 lb Tobo the 10th 8ber ali Execution.

110. Whereas it doth appear to this Court that HENRY SNEAD stands indebted to
     THOMAS BUTLER have attachment against the Estate of said Snead for said
Debt with cost of Suite.

Page 15 (contd) Court held 5th April 1665

111. Whereas it doth appear that the Widdow Beeze hath bin in the house of
      JOHN MATHEIS the Court doth order that the said Mathies have 500 lb To-
bacco & cask out of the Estate of the WIDDOW BEEZE the 10th 8ber with costs
of Suite ali Execution.

112. Major GEORGE MASON Sworne High Sheriff. JOHN CLARK Sworne under Sheriff.

      The Court adjourned to the 6th June 1665.

Page 16. At a Court held for the County of Stafford the 6th June 1665.
                              PRESENT
113.   Colo. John Dodman   Mr. Roger Perfitt
          Capt. John Alexander   Mr. Richd. Ffossaker
          Mr. Hugh Donding   Mr. Edwd. Sanders

114. Whereas it doth appear to this Court that THOMAS DUTTON stands indebted
      to HENRY ALDY by Bill 626 lb Tobacco and Cask the Court doth order that
the said Dutton pay to the said Aldy the said some the 10th 8ber next with
charges of Court else Exe.

115. JOHN SAMWAIDS & THOMAS BLAXLY committed to the Sheriffs hands till they
      put in sufficient security to appear the next Court.

116. Whereas it appears to this Court that THOMAS BLAXLY sold to HENRY WALKER
      two cows & a yearling the which was put a jury

          Wm. Howsing   Jno. Williams   Wm. Greene
          Robert Butterfield   Wm. Howard   Jno. Chiles
          Wm. Bullock   Tho: Bourne   Wm. Wells
          Robt. Streete   Stephen Lund   Archdale Combs

      It is the verdict of the jury that Henry Walker injoy the cattle according
to the Bill of Sute having the first Bill of Sale The Court doth order that
the Verdict of the Jury be ent'd for Judgment and that Henry Walker enjoy the
cattle bought of the said Blaxly and doth further order that the said Blaxly
pay the charges of Court the 10th 8ber next else exe.

Page 17. Court held 6th June 1665.

117. The Court doth order that GEORGE JENKINS and his wife and JOHN COLCLOUGH
      have paid unto them by THOMAS BLAXLEY 60 pounds of Tobacco apeece for
three comeing to an attendance of the Court the 10th 8ber next else Execution.

118. Whereas it doth appear unto this Court that THOMAS BLAXLY doth owe unto
      JOHN PALMER 900 lb Tobo & Cask the Court doth order that Thomas Blaxly
pay unto John Palmer the said some the 10th 8ber next & charges of Court else
Exe.

119. Whereas it doth appear unto this Court that JOHN SAMWAY stands indebted
      to Mr. HUGH DONDING 4400 lb Tobo and cask the Court doth commit the said
Samwaids into the Sheriffs hands till he hath put in good security for the payment of the said debt the 10th 8ber next with charges of Court etc.

120. Reference between THOMAS SPEDY & THOMS. CHAEWRIGHT the Court doth order
      that ANDREW WATSON have of Thomas Speedy 60 lb Tobo for charges at his
Sute agst Thos. Shaewright.

121. Whereas it doth appear to this Court that JOHN CHILES arrested JOHN MILLS

Page 17 (contd)   Court held 6th June 1665.

and had no cause of accon the Court doth order the said CHILES be nonsuited
and pay to JOHN MILLS 50 lb Tobo with costs ye 10th 8ber next ali Execution.

122. The Court doth order Mrs. FRANCES WILLIAMS administratrix of the Estate
      of Mr. ROBT. WILLIAMS deced doth on the 10th 8ber next pay unto THOS.
BUNBURY 240 lb Tobo & cask for eight days use of a Shallop.

Page 18. Court held 6th June 1665.

123. Whereas it doth appear to this Court that NICHOLAS BRULY Churgion did
      attend on Mr. ROBT. WILLIAMS deceased did administer to him & pay to
the said Bruly 800 lb Tobo & Cask the 10th 8ber next else Exe.

124. The Court doth order that JOHN CHILES pay unto JAMES LAMBE 60 lb Tobacco
      being on his petition to this Court the 10th 8ber next ali Exe.

125. The Court doth order Mr. HENRY MEESE have 400 lb Tobo out of the next
      levy being for two wolves killed by Cheeticke.

126. The Court doth order Mrs. FFRANCIS WILLIAMS administratrix of Estate of
      ROBT. WILLIAMS deceased to pay to CHARLES WOOD 350 lb Tobo and cask the
10th 8ber next being for the said Williams Coffin & other things else Exe.

127. Whereas Mr. WILLIAM HORTON did arrest Mr. JOHN MATHEIS JUNR. to this
      Court & did not appear to prosecute his accon the Court doth order that
the said Horton be nonsuited and pay to the said Matheis 50 lb with costs of
Sute 10th 8ber next else Exe.

128. Whereas etc the Court doth order that Mr. WILLIAM HORTON be nonsuited
      & pay to OLIVER BALFE 50 lb wth charges of Court the 10th 8ber next else
Execution.

129. Whereas Colo. NATH: BACON did arrest WM. THOMAS to this Court & did not
      prosecute his accon the Court doth order that the said Bacon be nonsuited
and pay 50 lb Tobo to the said Thomas 10th 8ber next else Execution.

Page 19. Court held 6th June 1665.

130. Whereas it doth appear to this Court that Mr. ROBERT WILLIAMS did owe to
      WILLIAM THOMAS 400 lb Tobacco and cask the Court doth order Mrs. FRANCES
WILLIAMS administratrix of the Estate of Mr. Robert Williams deceased pay to
the said Thomas 400 lb Tobacco and cask the 10th 8ber next else Exe.

131. The Court doth order that WILLIAM THOMAS pay to THOMAS DERRICKE 60 pounds
      Tobacco being sub: at his Sute the 10th 8ber next else Exe.

132. Whereas it doth appear to this Court that Mr. ROBERT WILLIAMS deced did
      owe to Capt. SAML. WILLIAMS 12760 lb Tobacco and cask the Court doth
order that Mrs. FFRANCES WILLIAMS administratrix of the Estate of Mr. Robert
Williams the sd some of 12760 lb Tobacco & cask else Exe.

133. Whereas it doth appear unto this Court by two Depositions that Mr.
      ROBERT WILLIAMS stood indebted to Mr. HENRY MEESE 4142 lb Tobacco & cask
the Court doth order that Mrs. FFRANCES WILLIAMS administratrix of Estate of
Mr. Robert Williams pay to Mr. Henry Meese the said some of 4142 lb Tobo &
Cask the 10th 8ber else Exe.

134. A reference is granted between RICHARD WELLS & Mrs. FFRANCES WILLIAMS.

Page 19 (contd)   Court held 6th June 1665.

135.   Whereas it doth appear unto this Court that Mr. VINCENT YOUNG stands
       indebted to Mr. FFRAS. HALES 4000

Page 20.   Court held 6th June 1665.

pounds Tobacco in goods the Court doth order that the said Young forthwith pay
the said some of 4000 lb Tobacco in goods to the sd Hales with charges of
Court else Exe.

136.   Whereas it doth appear unto this Court that WM. LAMBE sold a cow to
       EDWARD HUGHS & hath not dell it the Court doth order the said Lambe forth-
with dell the sd cow & pay the charges of Court else Exe.

137.   Whereas it doth appear unto this Court that HENRY ALDY doth owe Mr. HUGH
       DONDING 2400 lb Tobo & cask the Court doth order that the said Aldy
forthwith dell the said cow and pay the charges of Court else exe.

138.   Certificate of land is granted to JOHN COLCLOUGH for 200 acres of land
       for the transportation of 4 persons into this Colony Vizt ROBERT JONES,
GEORGE GRIFFITH, HENRY LANE & NICHOLAS RAWLINS Certificate of land is granted
to SAML. HAYWARD for 350 acres of land for the transportation of 7 persons into
this Colony Vizt JOSEPH HAYWARD, SARAH HAYWARD, ROWLAND PHILLIPS, THOMAS BAKER,
JOHN HENEN, MARY WELLS, REBECAI NETHEW.

139.   The Court doth order that JOHN WILLIAMS have 1500 lb Tobo out of next
       levy for the keeping a ferry at Machotick.

140.   The Court doth order two ferrys be kept the one at Potomack Creek and
       the other at Acquia and that MASON MASON See to have it affected.

141.   The Court doth order that the Little house agst the Courthouse be fitted
       for a prison.

142.   The Court doth order that X̣ͨ LUND be Constable for the present year to
       Colo. ASHTONS Plantation.

Page 21.   Court held 6th June 1665.

143.   Certificate of Land is granted XTOPHER LUND for 100 acres for the trans-
       portation of 2 persons into this Colony Vizt HENRY PATE, ELIZABETH PATE.

144.   Certificate of land is granted to HENRY WALLER for 700 acres of land for
       the transportation of 14 persons into this Colony Vizt MATHEW FFEARSON,
ANTHONY ROYLEY, ALICE FFIGG, JOHN WELLS, JANE FFISH, JOHN HIBBITT, ANNE SHEP-
PARD, JOHN CANSEN, JOHN PREBIT, ANTHONY STANTON, LURR BULLY, HENRY PAURE,
WILLIAM PLUMPER.

145.   Whereas BURR HARRISON did arrest DAVID ANDERSON to this Court and had
       noe cause of accon the Court doth order the Said Harrison be nonsuited
and pay the said Anderson 50 lb Tobacco the 10th 8ber next with Charges of
Court else exe.

   Then the Court is adjourned to the Last Wednesday in August.

Page 21 (contd)

146. At a Court held for county of Stafford the 30th August 1665

      Present   Colo. John Dodman   Mr. Richd. Heabeard
                 Capt. John Alexander   Mr. Richd. Ffossaker   Justices
                 Mr. Hugh Donding   Mr. Edward Sanders

147. Whereas it doth appear to this Court that the Widow Beeze formerly sold
      a cow to PHILIP CARPENTER & hath not yet delivered it the Court doth
order the Widow Beeze forthwith deliver a good cow to the said Philip Carpenter or his assigns & that she pay charges of Court else exe.

148. Whereas it doth appear to this Court that a Heifer in dispute between
      Captain ALEXANDER and ROBERT BUTTERFIELD is more properly the mark Robert
Butterfeile the Court doth

Page 22. Court held 30th August 1665

order that Robert Butterfield enjoy and possess the said Cow untill a better
claim then the sd Butterfield appear & that Captain Alexander sell the sd cow
to the sd Butterfield & pay the charges of Court else exe.

149. Whereas RICHARD WELLS did arrest Mrs. FFRA: WILLIAMS administratrix of
      Mr. ROBERT WILLIAMS Deceased on an Accompt & whereas there is an attach-
ment of Mr. Williams in ballance of the same from the said attachment ballance
each other and that Mrs. Williams from an Order recover'd agst the sd Wells
pay the charges by Colo. WARNER for the death of a Negro & that the sd Wells
pay the charges of Court.

150. Whereas it doth appear to this Court that JOHN MATHEWS hath violently
      taken from the Widow Beeze two cows with two calves & marked the calves
of his own mark to her great Damages the Court doth order that the said Mathews
forthwith redeliver the said cows with her calves & that he pay for his unjust
detention to the Widow Beeze 350 lb Tobacco and Cask & that he pay the charges
of Court else exe.

151. Whereas JOHN MATHEWS did arrest DA: ANDERSON to this Court & had noe
      cause of accon the Court doth order that the said Mathews be nonsuited
and pay to Manfen 50 lb Tobo with charges of Court else exe.

152. The Court doth order a reference & that WM. HEABEARD sweare the witness
      and send a man to DANIEL SISSON to see if he own the wedges.

153. Whereas ELIZ. LANE Husband of WILLIAM LANE (sic) who hath absented him-
      self did petition to have possession

Page 23 Court held 30th August 1665

of her Husbands Estate giving in Security to pay all debts made and contracted
before his Departure the Court doth order that the hand according to Peticon.
JOHN WITHERS enter'd Security this day for ye Widow Lane.

154. HENRY GALLION the servant of Mr. ROBERT TOWNSEND was this day brought to
      Court to be adjudged of his age & how long he should serve the Court
adjudged him to be 15 years of age ordr him to serve his said Master according
to Act of Assembly.

155. Mrs. WILLIAMS craved a reference till the next Court at Mr. BOWLEY.

156. Whereas JOHN MATHEWS ordinary keeper did peticon this Court that all
      ordinary debts already contracted & to be contracted might be on execu-
tion the Court doth order that he have according to Petition.

                                                              146 - 156

Page 23 (contd)   Court held 30th August 1665

157.   Whereas it doth appear to this Court that Mr. ROBT. WMS. deceased did on
       the 17th of May last confess a Judgment to Mr. WM. STORK for 400 lb To-
bacco & cask in the presence of Colo. JOHN DODMAN the Court doth order that
the Judgment renewed agst Mrs. FFRA: WILLIAMS administx of the Estate of Mr.
Robt. Williams deceased & that she pay the same the 10th 9ber next else exe.

158.   Whereas it doth appear to this Court that JOHN PALMER who hath absented
       himself to owe to ANTHONY BRIDGES for charges in this Court 400 lb Tobacco
the Court doth order that the said Bridges have attachment against the Estate
of the said Palmer for soe much & that he pay the charges of Court.

159.   Whereas JOHN EDWARDS had his Boate pressed by Colo. JOHN DODMAN then high
       sheriff on the Counties Service & was lost the Court doth order that
Colo. John Dodman pay to the said Edmonds 1600 lb Tobacco & Cask with costs of
Sute else exe. on the 10th 9ber next. Mr. JOHN LORD atty of JOSEPH EDMONDS.
(Names as in record)

Page 24   Court held 30th August 1665

160.   Whereas it doth appear to this Court that Mr. VINCENT YOUNG did make
       satisfaction to Mr. FFRA: HALES of the Order of Court passed against the
sd Young at the Sute of the sd Hales the 6th of June last he having tendered
goods to the said Hales as by the Depositions doth appear the Court adjudge
Mr. Hales to receave them & that the tender was lawful.
       Collo. DODMAN, Capt. ALEXANDER disenting for the said Order.
       Capt. ASTON Atty for Mr. Young. Capt. BRENT atty for Mr. Young & Mr.
    Lord.
Mr. Ffra: Hales doth appeale to the 6th day of the next General Court to be
held before the Right Honble Governor & the Honble the Councill to be held
at James Citty.

161.   JOHN ROLT acknowledged Judgment to Mr. YOUNG as administra. of STEPHEN
       NORMAN deceased for 224 lb Tobo & Cask before Mr. DONDING & Mr. SANDERS
Justices. John Rolt made oath before Mr. Donding & Mr. Sanders that the ring
in dispute betwixt Mr. Young & doth not belong to the Estate of Stephen Norman
deceased.

162.   Whereas it doth appear to this Court that Mr. JOHN SAMWAIDS stands in-
       debted to Mr. HUGH DONDING 1620 lb Tobo & Cask the Court doth order the
said Samwaids put in security to the said Donding for the paymt of this sd
Debt the 10th 8ber next with charges of Court else exe.

163.   FRANCIS JOURDAN was this day accepted by the Court Security for JOHN
       SAMWAIDS for the paymt of 1610 lb Tobo & cask the 10th 8ber to Mr. HUGH
DONDING.

164.   Mr. VINCENT YOUNG & Mr. JAMES PRICE declared that having viewed

Page 25   Court held 30th August 1665

the crop of JOHN PALMER who hath absented himself doe adjudge the same worth
500 lb Tobacco & cask.

165.   Whereas it doth appear to this Court that ROBT. WMS. died at the house
       of THOMAS ROWLAND and was a great troble to him the Court doth order that
Mrs. FFRA: WILLIAMS adminisx of the Estate of Robt. Williams deced doe on the
10th 8ber pay unto Thomas Rowland or assigns 200 lb Tobacco wth charges of
Court else exe.

Page 25   Court held 30th August 1665

166. Whereas WM. LAMBE did arrest JOHN CHILES to this Court & had noe cause
      of accon the Court doth order that each bare their own charges. Capt.
ASHTON Atty of William Lambe. JOHN SAMWAIDS Atty of John Chiles.

167. Whereas it doth appear to this Court that JOS: EDMONDS did arrest RICHARD
      PEARCE to this Court and had noe cause of accon the Court doth order the
said Edmonds be nonsuited & pay to Richd. Pearce 50 lb Tobo with costs of Sute
to the said Edmonds with costs of Sute the 10th 8ber else execution. Capt.
ASHTON Atty of Richard Pearce.

168. Whereas it doth appear to this Court that Mr. ROBT. MASSEY did arrest
      JOSEPH EDMONDS and had noe cause of accon the Court doth order the sd
Massey be nonsuited & pay the said Edmonds 50 lb Tobo with charges of Court
the 10th 8ber else exe.

169. Whereas it doth appear to this Court that WILLIAM LICENCE did forwarne
      CHA: WOOD that he should goe to his land & that the sd Wood hath abused
the said Licence in several particulars which was put to a jury

Page 26   Court held 30th August 1665

It is the verdict of the Jury that Charles Wood pay 100 lb Tobo to the sd
Licence for breaching the Kings Peace & pay the charges of Court the 10th 8ber
else exe.

Mr. William Greene	Mr. Hen: Pictoe	Ffra. Jourdan
Mr. Arch. Combs	Robert Butterfield	Hen. Walker
Jos. Edmonds	Wm. Thomas	Mr. Massey
Mr. Sanders	Phill Carpenter	John Mathews

   The Court doth order that William Licence pay to THOMAS ROWLAND 60 lb Tobacco
for 2 days att on the Court.
      Ditto ELIZABETH ROWLAND
      Ditto WILLIAM WALLER, do JOHN ANIS peticon

   It is the Verdict of the Jury that Charles Wood pay to Thomas Rowland 10
groats for sheading of blood & 100 lb Tobacco for breaking the Kings Peace
and pay the charges of Court the 10th 8ber else exe.

Mr. William Greene	Mr. Hen: Pictoe	Ffra. Jourdan	
Mr. Arch. Combs	Robert Butterfield	Hen. Walker	Jurors
Jos. Edmonds	Wm. Thomas	Mr. Massey	
Mr. Sanders	Phill Carpenter	John Mathews	

   The Court doth order that the verdict of the Jury be enter'd for Judgment
& that Charles Wood pay all the charges of Court the 10th 8ber next else exe.
Whereas it doth appear to the Court that Charles Wood did arrest Wm. Licence
and had no cause of accon the Court doth order that the said Wood be nonsuited
& pay the sd Licence 50 lb Tobacco with costs of Suit the 10th 8ber next else
exe.

170. A reference is granted Capt. BRENT against JOHN EDMONDS to the next Court.

Page 27   Court held 30th August 1665

171. Whereas it is made appear to this Court that WILLIAM LANE stands indebted
      to ANTHONY BRIDGES for charges in this Court 450 lb Tobacco the Court
doth order that ELIZABETH LANE the wife of the said Lane pay to the said Bridges
the said some of 450 lb Tobacco with charges of Court ye 10th 8ber else Execution.

Page 27 (contd)   Court held 30th August 1665

172.   Whereas it doth appear to this Court that JOHN PALMER doth stand indebted
       to JOHN SAMWAID 205 lb Tobo the Court doth order the said Samwaid have
an attachment against soe much of the Estate of the sd Palmer he have absented
himself & the same order to JOHN MATHEWS ordinary keeper.

173.   Whereas it doth appear to this Court that JOHN PALMER stands indebted to
       FFRA: JOURDON the Court doth order the said Jourdon an attachment against
the Estate of the sd Palmer for soe much as he shall make appear.

174.   The Court doth order that JOHN ROLT be guardian of MOSES LAMBE Mr. HALES
       having this day enter'd his security.

175.   The Court doth order that Mr. HALES forthwith knock ye Doggson the head
       that drownded Abraham or else abide the Judgmt of the Court.
The Court doth order that Mr. RICHD. HEABEARD take the oaths of GEORGE HALES
about it.

   The Court is adjourned to the second Wednesday in Novr
   The Orphants Court the second Tuesday ditto

Page 28

176.   At a Court held for county of Stafford the 9th 10ber 1665
                          Present
       Colo. John Dodman   Mr. Richd. Heaberd
       Colo. Henry Meese   Mr. Richd. Ffossaker
       Capt. Jno. Alexander   Mr. Robt. Osburne
       Mr. Hugh Donding
   Mr. HENRY MEESE was this day sworne Left. Collo. of this County of Stafford and this day to be the oath of a Justice of the Peace.

177.   JOHN MATHEWS acknowledged six hundred acres of land to WM. BOURNE &
       RICHD. BOURNE the sons of his now wife in equal halves and from him his
heirs or assigns to them there heirs or assigns forever lyeing at the head of
Potomack Creek on the North West side of the runn and did this day before the
Court acknowledge the same.

178.   The Court doth order Mr. RICHD. FFOSSAKER have attachment against the
       Estate of WM. PALMER for what he shall justly make appear & that the
said Palmer pay the charges of Court & the Court doth order that Capt. JOHN
ALEXANDER have attachment against the Estate of JOHN PALMER for what he shall
justly make appear and that the said Palmer pay the charges of Court.

179.   Whereas it doth appear to this Court against Mr. JAMES CLIFTON for arrest
       Capt. GILES BRENT to this Court & had no cause to complain the Court doth
order that the said Mr. James Clifton be nonsuited & forthwith pay unto Capt.
Giles Brent 50 lb Tobo & by ye sd Clifton pay the charges of Court else exe.

Page 29   Court held for County the 9th 10ber 1665

180.   Whereas it doth appear to this Court that ROBERT WILLIAMS deceased did
       owe unto ROBERT RICHARDS 771 lb Tobacco and Cask the Court doth therefore
order that Mrs. FRANCES WILLIAMS administratrix of the Estate of Mr. Robert
Williams deceased forthwith pay unto the said Robert Richards the said sum of
771 lb Tobacco and Cask else Execution. Mr. JNO. WASHINGTON did this day
apeare the Attorney of Robert Richards.

Page 29 (contd) Court held 9th 10ber 1665

181. Whereas it doth appear to this Court that Mr. ROBT. WILLIAMS deceased
      did owe unto Mr. THOMAS BOWLER 2437 lb Tobacco & cask the Court doth
order that Mrs. FRANCES WILLIAMS administratrix of Mr. Robert Williams deceased
forthwith pay unto Left. Colo. HENRY MEESE Attorney of Mr. Thomas Bowler the
said some of 2437 lb Tobacco & cask else Execution and the Court doth further
order that Left. Colo. Henry Meese shall hereby discharge Mrs. Frances Williams
& her heirs or assigns from all Bills bonds special ties Judgments and Execu-
tions whatsoever from the beginning of the world to this day this said Judgment
of 2437 lb Tobacco & cask only excepted.

182. Whereas Colo. GERRERD FFOWKE did petition this Court for administration
      on the Estate of WILLIAM CORDWELL deceased as greatest credits the Court
doth therefore order that the said William Cordwell and that the next Court he
bring in an

Page 30. Court held 9th 10ber 1665

inventory of the said Estate. The Court doth order that Mr. ROGER PERFITT,
JOHN MASEY & THOMAS ATTKISON to be appraisers of the Estate of the said Cordwell deceased.

183. JOHN ROWLY acknowledged satisfaction of a Bill against HENRY JAQUES for
      1000 lb Tobacco and cask which Bill is lost.

184. Whereas it doth appear to this Court that Capt. GILES BRENT did arrest
      JOSEPH EDMONDS and had noe cause of action the Court doth therefore order
that the said Capt. Giles Brent be nonsuited and pay the said Edmonds fifty
pounds of Tobacco & that the said Brent pay the charges of Court forthwith
else exe.

185. Whereas THOMAS DERRICK did arrest Mrs. FRANCES WILLIAMS to this Court
      and had noe cause of action the Court doth order that the said Thomas
Derrick be nonsuited & pay to the said Mrs. Williams fifty pounds of Tobacco
and that the said Thomas Derrick pay the charges of Court forthwith else Execution.

186. Whereas it doth appear to this Court that Mr. ROBERT WILLIAMS did owe
      to Mr. JOHN WASHINGTON as the Collector of the Right Honble Sir WM.
BERKELY £7..9s for the two shillings per hhd the Court doth therefore order
with the concent of Mrs. FRANCES WILLIAMS administratrix of the Estate of Mr.
Robert Williams deceased that she forthwith pay unto the said Major JAMES
WASHINGTON (sic) as Collector etc. the Sterl. sums of £7..9s..0p in money in
Tobacco & cask at one penny per ct else execution.

187. Whereas Mrs. FRANCES WILLIAMS did petition this Court as administratirx
      of Mr. ROBERT WILLIAMS deceased for

Page 31. Court held 9th 10ber 1665

charges about the said Mr. Williams funeral entertainment at the Private Court
the Court doth order that she have & possess the Estate of the said Robert
Williams deceased 9000 lb of Tobacco & cask.

188. To the Right Worshipful his Maties Justices of the Peace of the County
      of Stafford the humble petition of BURR HARRISON sheweth that DAVID
ANDERSON hath at divers & severall Courts unjustly molested & troubled ye poore
petitioner about a sett of Wedges borrowed of Mr. SISSON by the said Andersons
order in the time the petitioner was the said Andersons overseer which Wedges

Page 31 (contd)   Court held 9th 10ber 1665

the said Anderson pretended was conveyed away by the poor petitioner to his great scandall but have been all this while in the possession of the said Anderson as the Petition can made appear. The premises considered the poore petitioner craveth repiveation as your worships shall think fitt for this his unjust molestation & refamation from the said Anderson And he shall ever pray. The Court doth order that the Verdict of the Jury be entered for a Judgment and that Mr. DAVID ANDERSON forthwith pay unto BURR HARRISON for damages 400 pounds Tobacco and cask and that the said Anderson pay the charges of Court. The Court doth order the sd David Anderson pay to JAMES HERLONY 100 pounds Tobacco for his attendance on this Court and other atendances.

Page 32 Court held 9th 10ber 1665

189.   Whereas the Widow BOWLES did arrest JOHN MATHEWS to this Court and had noe cause of action the Court doth order that the said Bowles be non-suited and pay to the said Mathews 50 pounds of Tobacco forthwith and charges of Court else Execution.

190.   Whereas JOHN MATHEWS did arrest JOHN MECHEM to this Court and had noe cause of action the Court doth order the said Mathews be nonsuited and forthwith pay unto sd Mechem 50 lb Tobacco with charges of Court else Execution.

191.   Whereas MAJOR GILSON did arrest Mr. VINCENT YOUNG to this Court on an action of defamation the said Young having produced his auther the said Court doth adjudge the said Gilson to have no cause of action and that he be nonsuited and forthwith pay unto the said Young 50 pounds of Tobacco with charges of Court else Execution.

192.   Whereas GEORGE JENKINS and ANNE HARWOOD were presented to this Court by Mr. VINCENT YOUNG the then churchwarden for fornication the Court doth therefore fine the sd George Jenkins and Anne Harwood according to Act of Assembly 500 pounds Tobacco each to be paid forthwith else Execution and charges. Capt. JOHN ALEXANDER did this day in Court become Security for George Jenkins for the paymt of said fine of 500 lb Tobacco forthwith. JOHN COLCLOUGH did this day become Security for Anne Harwood for paymt of 500 lb Tobacco forth-with.

Page 33. Court held 9th 10ber 1665

193.   Mr. HUGH DONDING was this day Sworne churchwarden.

194.   The Court doth order that WILLIAM FLORRENCE pay 205 lb of Tobacco to Cheatike for the firing of his gun.

195.   Whereas Mr. VINCENT YOUNG had a servant named RICHARD COLLINGS who un-lawfully absented himself from his Masters service by running away in the time of the crop and that the said hath proved an unsufferable damadge the Court doth therefore order that the said servant Richard Collings serve his said Master after expiration of his time by Indenture one whole year and that Mr. Young shall pay the charges of Court.

196.   JOHN SAMWAYS did this day appear the atturney of DAVID THOMAS Whereas David Thomas did this day prove his just service of Seaven years to his Mistres Mrs. FRANCES WILLIAMS and by her the said Mrs. Frances Williams the Court doth order that the said servant David Thomas be from this day free and that Mrs. Frances Williams forthwith pay unto the said David Thomas his Corne and cloaths according to the custom of the countrey else execution.

Page 33 (contd) Court held 9th 10ber 1665

197. Whereas Mrs. FRANCES WILLIAMS made complaint unto this Court of a maid
      servant that had a bastard child & did petition the Court for satisfac-
tion for the same according to Act of Assembly the Court doth order that GRACE
FFAIRWELL the said servant who was justly complayned upon serve her said Mrs.
Frances Williams two years according to Act of Assembly after the time of her
service expired and that the said Mrs. Wms. pay charges of Court else exe.

198. Mr. JOHN WELLS & Mr. HENRY PICTOE this day enter into Security with Mr.
      VINCENT YOUNG for the performance of a will made by STEPHEN NORMAN.

199. THOMS. HUMPHREYS & HENRY WALKER Security for ELIZABETH MAPHE for the
      performance of a will.

Page 34 Court held 9th 10ber 1665

200. Whereas ALEGALE TUMONS hath bin given to Mr. JOHN WHETSTONE who is a
      pretended guardian of ye children of NATHANIEL JONES deceased the Estate
being properly in and appertaining to the County of Stafford to which County
Court the sd Whetstone having not appeared the Court doth therefore order that
Capt. JOHN ALEXANDER by virtue of an order of this Court take into his sd
possession all and singular the Estate rights and Priviledges of Nathaniel
Jones deceased & least the property of the sd Estate be alter'd & he seize all
and singular the Estate of Mr. John Whetstone until he hath given a just accompt.

201. Whereas Mr. FRANCIS HALES who proved a will of JOHN GILES deceased hath
      bin often demanded for security for performance of sd will the Court
doth therefore order Major GEORGE MASON high sheriff seize all & singular the
Estate of the sd Ffrancis Hales until the sd Hales put in Security as afsd &
that the said Hales pay ye order of Court.

202. The Court doth order that the Widow Boes being all ( ) concerning her
      child to this next Court & ye shall then bring sufficient security for
the performance of the deed of Gift.

203. Whereas CHR. LUND did subpeney to this Court HENRY WALKER and ROBERT
      COULSON the Court doth order that the said Lund forthwith pay unto the
sd Walker & Coulson for their attendance on this Court 60 lb Tobacco each else
Execution.

204. Certificate of land is granted unto ROBERT MASSEY for 500 acres of land
      for the transportation of ten persons into this Colony of Virginia Vizt
ROBERT MASSEY, THOMAS MASSEY, EDWARD FFISHER, LUCY HEABERD, PRISILLA PORTER,
WM. TIPSON, EDWARD WOOLRIDGE, HUMPHR. BOONE and WM. CROSS, HENRY BUTTERFIELD.

205. SAML. HAYWARD sworne Clerk of this County Court.

206. Whereas it doth appear to this Court that there is due from the Estate
      of Colo. VALENTINE PEYTON 700 lb Tobacco to the Parish of Potomack now
in the County of Stafford the said Court doth order that there be an attachment

Page 35 Court held 9th 10ber 1665

against the Estate of the said Peyton in the hands of Major MASON.

207. Whereas it doth appear to this Court that there is due from the Estate
      of Colo. ROBERT WILLIAMS deced 500 lb Tobacco to the Parish of Potomack
now in county of Stafford the said Court doth order that Mrs. FFRANCIS WILLIAMS
administratrix of the sd Robert Williams be arrested to the next Court ye sute
of this County.

Page 35 (contd)   Court held 9th 10ber 1665

208. Whereas it doth appear to this Court that WILLIAM GREENE hath received
      of this County the last year 60 lb Tobo for the making of Rayles & stock
& hath only made a pair of stocks it is therefore ordered that he repay into
the Sheriffs hands three hundred and twenty pounds of Tobacco & cask which is
to be paid into the hands of Capt. JOHN ALEXANDER for the use of this County.

209. It is ordered that Capt. JOHN ALEXANDER take care to agree with a Work-
      man to build a Courthouse for use of this County.

  The Court is adjourned untill ye second Wednesday in January
  The Orphans Court the second Thursday ditto
  The Court is adjourned to the second Wednesday in Ffeb. 1665

210. At a Court held for County of Stafford this 14th & 15th February 1665
                              Present
          Colo. John Dodman   Mr. Richd. Heaberd
          Lt. Colo. Henry Meese   Mr. Richd. Ffossaker   Justices
Page   Capt. John Alexander   Mr. Robt. Osburne
36   Mr. Hugh Donding

211. Whereas it appears to this Court that WM. CORDWELL deced stood indebted
      to Colo. PETER ASHTON assigne of HEN. PARNHAM in the sum of 400 lb To-
bacco and Caske the Court doth therefore order that Colo. GEORGE FFOOKE admr
of the Estate of the sd Wm. Cordwell forthwith pay unto the sd THOMAS BUNBURY
atty of Colo. Ashton the sume of 400 lb Tobo & Cask forthwith else exe.

212. Whereas Major MASON did arrest WM. THOMAS to this Court at the suit of
      WM. RUST for 900 lb Tobo & Cask and that the sd Thomas did not appear
the Court doth therefore order that the sd Mason bring the sd Thomas to the
next Court to answer the suit of the sd Rust or else pay ye said Debt.

213. Whereas it doth appear by Evidence & VINCT YOUNGS one acknowledgment
      that the sd Young hath unjustly detained a hogshead of Tobacco belonging
to THOMAS BAREFOOTE wch he bought of NICO. PUTT the Court doth therefore order
that the sd Vinct Young forthwith deliver the sd hogshead of Tobacco to the sd
Barefoot with costs of suit except 50 lb Tobacco to the sd Barefoot which he
makes appear to be due else exe. Mr. Young appeales to the Govr. & Councill
on the 6th day of Court Capt. ALEXANDER security for Thomas Barefoot, Mr. WM.
STORK security for Vinct Young. Mr. JNO. SAMWAIDS did appear atturney for Mr.
Young.

214. Whereas THOMAS DERRICK had an attachment against OWEN JONES who absented
      himself out of this County for 500 lb Tobacco & Cask and that the said
Derrick did make his debt justly appear the court doth therefore order that
the said Derrick have & possess so much of the Estate of the sd Owen Jones as
shall be sufficient satisfaction for his sd Debt with costs of suit.

Page 37 Court held 14th & 15th February 1665

215. Whereas RICHARD PEARCE did make oath that JOS: EDMONDS stood indebted to
      him 1693 lb Tobacco and caske the Court doth therefore order that the
said Edmunds forthwith pay the said sume of 1693 lb Tobacco & Caske to the said
Pearce with costs of suit alias Execu.

216. Whereas it doth appear etc that JOHN GILES deced stood indebted to
      EDWARD HUGHES 700 lb Tobacco & caske the Court doth therefore order that
FRANCIS HALES admr of Estate of the sd Giles pay unto Hughs the sd sume of 700
lb Tobacco and caske forthwith else exe.

Page 37 (contd)   Court held 14th & 15th February 1665

217.   Whereas it doth appear to this Court that WM. CORDWELL deced had a pat-
       tent for a certain tract of land from Capt. JOHN ALEXANDER the Court
doth order that Colo. GERD. FOOKE admr. of the sd Cordwells pay to the said
Capt. Alexander 200 lb Tobacco & Caske forthwith else Execution.

218.   Whereas it doth appear to this Court that WILLIAM CORDWELL deced stands
       indebted to EDMUND NANFEN 900 lb Tobacco & Caske and 4 barrells of corn
the Court doth order Colo. Gerd. Fowke admr pay the said Edward Manfen 900
lb Tobacco & Caske else Execution.

219.   Whereas by an order from the County Court of Westmoreland it appears
       that Mr. ROBERT WILLIAMS deced did oblige himself to the Parish of Poto-
mack 500 lb Tobacco for the fine of GEORGE GLASS his servant for committing of
fornication the Court doth order that Mrs. FFRANCES WMS. admx of the Estate
of the said Robert Williams forthwith pay the said sum of 500 lb Tobacco unto
Capt. JOHN ALEXANDER for the use of the county alias exe.

220.   Whereas JO: EDMUNDS did transport THOMAS GILL out of this County and
       that Capt. BRENT did make oath that the said Gill stood Indebted to him
298 with cask the Court doth therefore order that the said Jos: Edmunds pay
unto Capt.

Page 38   Court held 14th & 15th February 1665

Brent the said 298 lb Tobacco and cask with costs of suit forthwith alias
Execution.

221.   Whereas JOHN ROLT did arrest JAMES LAMB to this Court and did not appear
       to prosecute his action the Court doth therefore order that the said
John Rolt be nonsuited and pay unto the said James Lamb 50 pounds Tobacco
with costs of suit forthwith alias Execution.

222.   Mr. JOHN SAMWAYS did appear attorney of JOS: EDMUNDS.

223.   Whereas Mrs. FRANCES WILLIAMS did petition this Court against MARY PYLES
       her servant for having a bastard child in time of her service which the
said servant hath confessed the Court doth therefore order that the sd Mary
Pyles serve her said mistress Mrs. Ffra. Williams after the expiration of her
time by Indenture or Custom two years according to Act of Assembly and that
Mrs. Williams pay the charges of Court alias Execution.

224.   Mr. JOHN STONE did appear atty of Mr. FOSSAKER. Capt. JOHN ASHTON attor-
       ney of ELIZA. LANE.   JOHN SAMWAYS atty of JOHN WITHERS & RALPH ELKIN.

225.   Whereas Mr. ROBERT OSBORNE did make it appear to this Court that RALPH
       ELKIN stands indebted to him 784 pounds Tobacco and cask the Court doth
therefore order that the said Ralph Elkin pay the said sume to the said Osborne
within 10 days with costs of suit alias exe.

226.   Mr. FFRA: HALES as administrator of the Estate of JOHN GILES deceased
       did this day acknowledge Judgment to Mr. JOHN WHETSTONE for 400 lb Tobo
& cask forthwith

227.   Whereas Mr. HOWSON did arrest Mr. PEARCE to this Court and did not enter
       his petition according to law a nonsuit etc.

Page 39   Court held 14th & 15th February 1665

228. Whereas JOS. EDMUNDS did arrest Capt. Brent to this Court & had noe cause of action nonsute etc.

229. Whereas there is an order passed against Majr. MASON for the nonappearance of WILLIAM THOMAS at the suit of WM. RUST for 900 lb Tobacco & cask the Court for the security of the said Sheriff doe order that he have attachment against the Estate of the said Thomas for the sd 900 lb Tobacco with charges.

230. Capt. ASHTON and Mr. BRIDGES atty for JOHN WILLIAMS.   JOHN SAMWAYS atty for JOHN MILLS. Whereas John Mills did put in an information to this Court against JOHN WILLIAMS for the unlawful killing of a hogg the Court doth adjudge the said Mills to have no cause of action and doe therefore order that the said John Mills be nonsuited and pay unto the said John Williams 50 lb Tobacco with costs of suit forthwith alias Execution.   John Mills doth appeale to the Governor & Councill on the 6th day of the General Court held at James City.   CHRISTO. LUND & PHILIP CARPENTER security for John Williams.   JOHN MATHEWS & JNO. KEECH SEcurity for John Mills.

231. Whereas it doth appear to this Court that OWEN JONES did convert a Bill of EDWARD HUGHES of 986 lb of Tobacco to his own use the said Bill belonging to Mrs. FFRA: WILLIAMS the Court doth therefore order he return the said Bill to the said Mrs. Williams to returne the Tobacco on said Bill if Owen Jones makes it appear hereafter that he legally received this Bill of Mr. ROBT. WILLIAMS deceased for his own use and they further order that the sd Jones pay the sd Mrs. Ffra. Williams 1495 lb Tobacco which was a debt upon the cook rased out by the sd Jones & 1252 lb Tobacco due to the sd Mrs. Ffra: Williams by Bill with costs of suit forthwith alias Execution.

232. Whereas it doth appear to this Court that Mr. ROBERT WILLIAMS deceased stood indebted to Capt. JOHN ALEXANDER 268 lb Tobacco & cask the Court doth order that Mrs. FFRA: WILLIAMS admx of the Estate of the sd Robt. Williams forthwith pay the sd debt alias exe.

Page 40   Court held 14th & 15th February 1665

233. Whereas Mr. ROBERT NURSE hath taken care to procure & bring the Acts of Assembly for this County the Court doth therefore order that the sd Mr. Nurse have paid unto him or his assigns 300 lb Tobacco out of the next levy.

234. THOMAS DERRICK is ordered 60 lb Tobacco from Mrs. WILLIAMS for his attendance.

235. Whereas PEARCE did arrest JOS. EDMUNDS to this Court and had noe cause for action the Court doth therefore order that the said Pearce be nonsuited etc.

236. The Court doth order that JAMES LAMB have of THOMAS BAREFOOT 60 lb of Tobacco for his attendance at Court forthwith alias Execution.

237. The Court doth order JOHN MILLS pay unto JOHN JAMES and SAMUEL SPOONER 60 pounds Tobacco apeace for their attendance on the Court forthwith alias exe.

238. Reference is granted Mrs. FFRA: WILLIAMS & PEARCE the Court doth order that Mr. ROBERT MASSEY pay JOHN BLAGGRAVE 120 lb Tobacco for 4 days attendance on this Court forthwith alias Execution.

239. Reference is granted Mr. HOWSON and JAMES TENANT.

228 - 239

Page 40 (contd)   Court held 14th & 15th February 1665

240.   Whereas the sudden death of Mr. ROBERT WILLIAMS did for the better dis-
        patch in sea affaires ocation the calling of a private Court the Court
doth order that Mrs. FFRA. WILLIAMS admx of the Estate of the sd Robert Williams pay unto Major GEORGE MASON high Sheriff 800 lb Tobacco with cask forthwith alias Execution.

241.   Whereas Mr. FOSSAKER had an attachment against the Estate of WILLIAM
        PALMER who absented himself out of this

Page 41 Court held 14th & 15th February 1665

County for so much as he should justly make appear the Court doth therefore
order that the said Fossaker have and possess so much of the Estate of the sd
Palmer as shall be sufficient satisfaction for 520 lb Tobacco thereof due to
him by Bill & 60 as Atturney of HENRY BEERE.

242.   The Court doth order that Capt. JOHN ALEXANDER against any person possess
        and enjoys so much of the Estate of JOHN PALMER who absented himself out
of this County as makes him full satisfaction for his Debt with costs of suit.

243.   The Court doth order Mrs. FFRA: WILLIAMS pay to EDWARD HUGHES 60 lb To-
        bacco for 2 days attendance on the Court.

244.   Whereas Capt. JOHN ALEXANDER did attach a cow belonging to the Estate of
        JOHN PALMER which cow FFRA. JORDEN hath made appear to be his the Court
doth therefore order that the sd Ffra. Jorden pocess the sd cow without trouble
or molestation of any person whatsoever.

245.   EDWARD HUMSTED as Atty for Mr. HOWSIN did this day acknowledge Judgment
        before Mr. HUGH DONDING and Mr. ROBERT OSBURNE unto Capt. PETER JENNINGS
for 68£ Sterling with costs of suit and damages according to the laws of England and to make payment in Tobacco according to Act forthwith.

246.   Mr. VINCT YOUNG as administrator of STEPHEN NORMAN did this day before
        Mr. DONDING and Mr. OSBURNE acknowledge Judgment to Lt. Colo. JOHN
WASHINGTON for 531 pounds of Tobacco etc. Mr. Vinct Young as administrator of
Stephen Norman did this day before Colo. DODMAN & Lt. Colo. MEESE acknowledge
Judgment to Mr. WM. STORK for 400 lb of Tobacco and caske forthwith.

247.   Whereas it doth appear to this Court that Mr. ROBERT WILLIAMS deceased
        stands indebted to JOHN MATHEWS ordinary keeper 698 lb Tobacco and cask
the Court doth therefore order that Mrs. FFRA. WILLIAMS admx of the Estate of
the sd Robt. Williams forthwith pay unto the said Mathews the said 698 lb of
Tobacco and cask etc.

Page 42 Court held 14th & 15th February 1665

248.   The Court doth order that Lt. Colo. MEESE have 1600 lb Tobacco out of
        the next leavey for keeping the ferry until the 20th 9ber next.

249.   The Court doth order that Mr. FFOSSAKER take care to provide that a ferry
        be kept at Acquia and that he allow not above 2600 pounds of Tobacco
for the same and the year to be accompld to the 20th 9ber next Ffeb ye 25th.

250.   Whereas EVEN MORGAN hath made it appear that there is due to him from
        the Estate of JOHN GILES deceased three Barrels Corne & aparill according
to the Custom of the Countrey the Court doth therefore order Mr. FFRA; HALES
admr of the Estate of the said Giles forthwith pay unto the sd Morgen the
corne & aparill alias Exe.

Page 42 (contd)   Court held 14th & 15th February 1665

251.   Whereas Mr. ARUNDELL hath bin at expense for a certain child of WM.
       CORDWELLS deced the Court doth order that Colo. GERRARD FOOKE adminis-
trator of the Estate of the sd Corwell pay unto the sd Arundell 300 pounds Tobacco & cask forthwith alias exe.

252.   The Court doth order that Mr. HEABERD an orphan of WILLIAM CORDWELL deced
       named WILLIAM CORDWELL until she attains to the years of 21 the sd MARY
being two years old next May (names as in record).

253.   The Court doth order that JOHN WHETSTONE give security for his guardian-
       ship of the orphans of NATHL. JONES deceased Capt. JOHN ALEXANDER and
Mr. Heaberd did this day offer themselves to be security wth Mr. JOHN WHET-
STONE for the said orphans. The Court doth order that Mr. John Whetstone
pay 1000 lb Tobo according to the will of Nathaniel Jones deceased wch Tobacco
be paid into the hands of Capt. Alexander.

254.   Whereas Colo. GERRARD FOOKE has not put in security to this Court for
       the Widow Bell deced according to law and complaint hath bin made if ye
child is abused the Court doth therefore order that the said Colo. Fooke be
summoned to the next Court and with him bring ye child and provide sufficient
security for the Deced Estate.

Page 43   Court held 14th & 15th February 1665

255.   The Court doth order that Mrs. FFRA: WILLIAMS Deliver all the Estate of
       JOHN GILES deced upon oath into the hands of GEORGE CAMPIN and that the
next Court she bring an Inventory of the sd Estate and good security according
to Law. The Court doth order that Mr. HUGH DONDING and JOHN WILLIAMS be appraisers of the Estate.

       The Court is adjourned to the Second Wednesday in April
       The Orphans Court to the Second Thursday ditto

256.   At a Court held for the County of Stafford 11th April 1666
                                Present

           Colo. John Dodman   Mr. Richd. Heaberd
           Lt. Colo. Hen: Meese   Mr. Richd. Fossaker   Justices
           Capt. John Alexander   Mr. Robt. Osborne
           Mr. Hugh Donding

257.   Whereas Mr. RUST did arrest WM. THOMAS to this Court and had no cause
       of accon the Court doth order that the said Rust be nonsuited and pay
unto the said Thomas 50 pounds of Tobo with costs of suit the 10th 8ber next
else Exe. with charges.

258.   Whereas FFRA. GRAY did arrest GEORGE CAMPIN to this Court and had noe
       cause of accon the Court doth order that the said Gray be nonsuited and
pay 50 pounds of Tobacco 10th 8ber next else exe.

259.   Whereas it doth appear to this Court that JOS. EDMUNDS sold a cow to
       ROBERT HOWSON and appointed a time for the speedy delivery of the same
and that the said Howson hath paid him 400 lb Tobacco in part the Court doth
order that the sd Edmunds deliver unto the sd Mr. Howson the sd cow forthwith
and it is

Page 44   Court held 11th April 1666

further ordered that Mr. Howson pay unto Jos. Edmund 100 pounds of Tobacco
being the full payment for the cow and ye Edmunds pay the costs of suit.

251 - 259

Page 44 (contd)   Court held 11th April 1666

260. Whereas DAVID ANDERSON did petition this Court DANL. KILLAHORNE for taking
      away his Boate the Court doth order that the Estate of the said Killahorne
be secured untill the next Court.

261. It is ordered that JOHN WILLIAMS continue keeping of ferry & be allowed
      1500 pounds of Tobo out of the next leavey.

262. Whereas JAMES CLIFTON did arrest THOMAS ATTKINSON to this Court and had
      noe cause of accon It is ordered that the said Clifton be nonsuited and
pay unto the sd Attkinson 50 pounds of Tobacco with costs 10th 8ber next else
exe. The Court doth order that the land in controversey between Mr. Clifton
and Thomas Attkinson & now in the possession of the sd Attkinson be by Capt.
JOHN ALEXANDER surveighor for this county surveighed according to the Lease by
which the said land is held.

263. Whereas JAMES CLIFTON hath Deteyned a Rapier and Pistoll from ROWLAND
      THORNBROUGH Late Servt of the sd Clifton the Court doth order that the
said Clifton pay unto the said Thornbrough 200 pounds of Tobacco & caske the
10th 8ber next. And whereas there is due to the sd Thornbrough aparell according to the custom of this county It is further ordered that the said Clifton pay him his cloathing when the year to be procured and that Mr. Clifton
pay the costs of suit alias exe.

264. Whereas by order from the Genl Court held at James City

Page 45 Court held 11th April 1666

the 28th March last This Court is to consider the charges which JOHN WILLIAMS
hath ben at in his suit with JOHN MILLS and to order the said Williams redress
the Court doth order that the said John Mills pay unto the said John Williams
1500 pounds of Tobacco & cask with costs of suit. John Mills did this day in
Court acknowledge himself sorry for his scandalizing of John Williams and en-
deavouring to take away his good name.

265. Whereas WILLIAM CORDELL deced stood indebted to THOMAS GRIGG 400 lb To-
      bacco & caske the Court doth order that Colo. GERRARD FOOKE admr of the
Estate of the sd Cordwell pay the sd sume to the sd Grigg the 10th Oct next
alias exe.

266. The Court doth order that the Clerk receive of Capt. ALEXANDER 1000 lb
      Tobacco for the use of the County & that it remain in hands till further
from the Court.

267. It is the Request of the Court that Mr. MEESE & Mr. RICHARD HEABERD
      agree with one to make a horse bridge over Paspitanzy Creeke.

268. The Court doth order that JOHN SAMWAYS pay into the Clerks hands 500
      lb of Tobacco to the use of the County he having proffered himself se-
curity to the Court for the fine of GEORGE GLASS for committing fornication
and it is further ordered that George Glass provide for the maintenance of the
bastard child which he begat of GRACE FFAREWELL servant of Mrs. FRANCES WIL-
LIAMS forthwith the exe.

269. Mr. JOHN SAMWAYS Attur. for THOMAS ATKINSON.

270. JOHN SAMWAIES Atturney for RICHARD GRANGER did this day acknowledge the
      sale of 500 acres of land to COLO. PETER AUSTIN and did oblige himself
to bring the date of patent for the said land.

Page 45 (contd)   Court held 11th April 1666

271. Whereas WILLIAM HORTON did arrest OWEN JONES to this Court and did not
      appear to prosecute the action the Court doth order that the said Horton
be nonsuited and pay unto the said Jones 50 pounds of Tobo the 10th October
next else exe.

272. This Court doth request the Court of Westmoreland in behalf of JOHN
      WILLIAMS to doe them the sivell favour to augment 300 lb Tobacco apeace
more than was formerly allowed.

Page 46   Court held 11th April 1666

273. Whereas Mr. EDWARD SANDERS, MICHL. HILL & GAD CHRISMAS were subpoened to
      this Court by THOMAS ATKINSON the Court doth order that the said Atkinson
pay unto the said Sanders, Hill & Chrismas 40 po; Tobacco a peace for their
coming to attendance on the Court the 20th October else exe.

274. The Pecke formerly taken from Capt. THOMSON the Indian was this day
      brought into Court & apraysed by Mr. JOHN HEABERD and THOMAS GRIGG per
the appoynment who valued the said Pecke at 1700 pds of Tobacco & cask. The
Court doth order that Lt. Colo. HENRY MEESE pay unto Colo. JOHN DODMAN 400 lb
Tobacco and cask out of the said Pecke. It is ordered that Colo. Meese pay
Major MASON 800 lb Tobo & cask out of the said Pecke. Mr. JOHN HEABERD &
THOMAS MEREDITH are ordered to have the rest between them being 500 lb Tobacco
& cask.

275. Reference is granted with the concent of ROBT. HALL between & Colo. Nico.
      SPENCER.

276. Capn. JOHN ALEXANDER was this day sworne High sheriff of this County.
      JOHN CLERK under sheriff likewise was sworne.

      The Court adjourned till the 2d Wednesday in June.
      The Court adjourned to the last Wednesday in June 1666

      At a Court held for County of Stafford 27th June 1666
      Present   Colo. John Dodman   Mr. Richd. Heabeard
                 Lt. Colo. Hen: Meese   Majr. Geo: Mason   Justices

Page 47   Court held 27th June 1666

277. Whereas CHRISTR. LUND stands bound with ANDRW. WATSON for the Estate of
      MARY MAPHE Daughter & Orphant of ROBT. MAPHE Deced the Court doth order
that within one month the sd Watson secure the said Lund from any danger that
he may sustain by ocation of this sd Bond and pay charges.

278. Whereas HENRY WALKER & ANDREW WATSON stands joyntly bound to THOMAS
      BAREFOOTT in 2850 lb Tobacco & cask in consideration of a servant named
JOHN BOULTON & in regard Andw. Watson hath the said servant wholy to his own
use It is therefore ordered that the sd Watson secure the said Walker from the
sd Debt & ye Henry Walker pay costs of Sute.

279. Whereas Mr. FOSSAKER has an attachment against the Estate of THOMAS WADLE
      who unjustly absented himself out of this County for 522 lb Tobacco &
cask that he hath made the said Debt appear The Court doth therefore order that
the sd Mr. Fossaker have & pocess so much of the Estate of the sd Wadle to
attach as shall make him full satisfaction for his said Debt with charges of
Court & that THOMAS ATKINSON & JOHN MASSEY be appraisers.

Page 47 (contd)   Court held 27th June 1666

280.   Mr. WM. PRICE did appear Atty for EDMD. KELLY. Mr. ANTHO. BRIDGES Attur.
       for Mrs. FFRA. WILLIAMS. Whereas the wife of Edmund Kelly was by me
Ffrances Williams imployed to deliver a servant woman of here then in Travell
& did perform the same the Court doth order that the said Mrs. Ffrances Wil-
liams pay unto the sd Kelly 200 lb Tobo and cask with costs of Sute the 28th
October next alias Execution. The Court doth order that Edmund Kelly pay unto
Mr. JOHN SAMWAYES & JOHN PEARCE 4 pounds Tobacco for the attendance on the
Court at his Suit.

Page 48   Court held 27th June 1666

281.   Whereas EDMUND KELLY did arrest Mrs. FFRANCES WILLIAMS to this Court and
       had noe cause of action the Court do order that the sd Kelly be nonsuited
and pay unto the said Mrs. Williams 50 lb Tobacco with charges of Court the
10th Oct next alias exe.

282.   Whereas JOSEPH LUCAS did arrest HENRY WALKER to this Court and had noe
       cause of action the Court doth order that the said Lucas be nonsuited
and pay unto the said Walker 50 pounds of Tobacco and charges of Court the
10th Oct next alias exe.

283.   Whereas WILLIAM THOMAS did take his oath that the cow in controversey
       between him and JOHN WILLIAMS was his own cow the Court doth therefore
order that the said Thomas have and possess the said cow and that John Williams
pay the costs of suit alias exe.

284.   Whereas the Relict and Widow of DAVID COLLINGS did prove the will of
       her said Husband Deceased the Court doth order that JOHN MARTIN, WILLIAM
HARRIS and WILLIAM WITHERS be appraysers.

285.   Whereas JOHN JAMES did arrest Mr. ROBERT TOWNSEND to this Court and had
       noe cause of action the Court doth order that the said James be nonsuited
and pay to the said Mr. Townsend 50 lb Tobacco with charges of Court the 10th
Octr next else exe. The Court doth order that John James pay unto THOMAS
DERRICK 60 pounds of Tobacco for 2 days attendance etc.

Page 49   Court held 27th June 1666

286.   The Court doth order that JOSEPH LUCAS pay unto JOHN BOULTON and SAMUEL
       SPOONER 40 lb Tobacco apeace for attendance etc.

287.   Mr. WM. PRICE Attry of THOS. ATKINSON. Whereas Mr. JAMES CLIFTON did
       arrest Thomas Atkinson to this Court and had noe cause of action the
Court doth order that the said Clifton be nonsuited and pay unto the said
Atkinson 50 lb Tobacco with charges of Court the 10th Octr next alias Execution.

288.   The Court doth order that WILLIAM THOMAS pay unto JAMES LAMB, JOHN
       MATHEWS and RICHARD COLLINGS 60 lb Tobo apeace for their attendance on
this Court.

289.   Whereas Mr. ROBERT PICKERNELL hath proved his just service of 4 years by
       Indenture the Court doth order that he be from this day free and that
Mr. ROBERT TOWNSEND his said Master pay him his Corn and Cloaths with charges
of Court else Exe.

290.   Whereas WILLIAM PARSON hath proved his service of 5 years by two Evi-
       dences the Court doth order that JOHN MATHEWS his late Master pay unto
him the sd Parsons his Corn and Cloaths with charges of Court else Exe. The

Page 49 (contd)   Court held 27th June 1666

Court doth order that WILLIAM PARSONS pay unto GEO. GLASS and the Purtugalls
40 lb Tobacco apeace for there attendance on the Court.

291. Whereas Mr. ROBERT WILLIAMS deceased having Drawne a Bill of Exchange on
      Mrs. FFRANCES WILLIAMS or Mr. ROBERT TOWNSEND of London for account of
the Right Honble Sir WILLIAM BARKLEY for £3..7.6 Sterling for the payment of
the duties of 218d per hhd which Bill is returned protested the Court doth
therefore order that Mrs.

Page 50   Court held 27th June 1666

Ffrances Williams admx of the Estate of the sd Robert Williams pay unto Lt.
Colo. JOHN WASHINGTON Collector for the Duties aforsd the sd sume of £3..7.6
Sterling according to law.

292. Mr. WILLIAM PRICE did this day appear the atturney of Mr. JOHN BRICTON
      and JOSEPH LUCAS.

293. Whereas it doth appear to this Court that Mr. ROBERT WILLIAMS deceased
      stands indebted unto Mr. ROBERT TOWNSEND 148£ Sterling the Court doth
order therefore that Mrs. FFRANCES WILLIAMS admx of the Estate of Robert Williams pay unto the sd Mr. Townsend the said sum of One hundred and forty eight
pounds sterling the 10th Oct next alias Execution.

294. The Court doth order that out of the family of Mr. ROBERT TOWNSEND and
      Mrs. FRANCES WILLIAMS an able man and arms be pressed and one out of the
house of Mr. ANDREW GILSON and one out of the house of Colo. ASHTON and one
from OLIVER BALFSES being from the present strengthening of some weake frontiere plantations untill further order and to repair to the house of Lt. Colo.
MEESE forthwith.

      The Court is adjourned till the last Wednesday in August

295. At a Court held for the County of Staf the 29th Augt 1666
                          Colo. John Dodman
      Present Lt. Colo. Henry Meese   Mr. Heaberd
               Majr. Geo: Mason   Mr. Osburne   Justices

296. Whereas Mr. HENRY HUDSON hath made oath of the transportation of 40 per-
      sons into the Colony ye Certificate is therefore granted to the sd Hud-
son for 2000 acres of land

Jno. Robinson	Thad. Kelly	Wm. Fyer	Ellin Collings
Wm. Kingt	Den. Cragh	John Bell	Thos. Crafford
Jno. Edwards	Jno. Caddell	John Wallis	Edwd. Ffallin
Nich. Chapman	Wm. Arkill	Thos. Key	Dennis Magrough
Jno. Robinson	John Collings	Wm. Avice	Edmd Power
Wm. Edwards	Robert Ffoster	Jon. Ffoster	Robt Brunston
Nich. Humphries	Alice Lee	An Hart	Robt Shelton
Morris Ffitzgd	Richd Lee	Jas. Allen	Wm. Martin
Ann Chapman	Tho. Gregery	Ricd. Griggs	Edwd Bragger
Ann Martin	Ann Arkill	Thos. Griffin	John Richards

Page 51   Court held 29th August 1666

297. The Court doth order that Lt. Colo. Meese pay unto THOMAS WILLMOTT 60
      lb Tobo subp. at his suit.

291 - 297

Page 51 (contd)   Court held 29th August 1666

298. Whereas PHILIP CARPENTER did arrest JANE BOEZ to this Court and had noe
      cause of action the Court doth therefore order that the sd Philip Carpen-
ter be nonsuited and pay to the sd Jane Boez 50 lb Tobacco the 10th Octr next
else Exe.

299. Whereas ROGER POOLE did acknowledge judgment to GEORGE CAMPIN for 1854
      lb Tobacco and cask and three Barrills of Corne the Court doth order that
the said Poole pay the sd Debt the 28th October next else Execution with costs
of Suit.

300. Mr. JOHN SAMWAIES did arrest Mr. ANTHONY BRIDGES to this Court and had
      noe cause of action the Court doth order therefore that the sd Samwaies
be nonsuited and pay to the said Bridges 50 lb Tobacco with charges of Court
the 28th October next else exe. Whereas it doth appear to this Court that Mr.
John Samwaies stands indebted to Mr. Anthony Bridges Admr of WILLIAM BAKER 374
lb Tobacco and caske the Court doth order that the said Samwaies give the said
Bridges good security for the payment of the sd Debt the 10th Octr next with
costs of suit. EDWARD ROGERS did this day in Court become security for the
payment of 374 lb Tobacco and cask to Mr. Bridges in the behalf of John Samwaies with costs ye 10th Octr Else Exe.

301. The Court doth order that Mr. FFRA. GRAY have an attachmt against the
      Estate of JOHN BOOTH being 3 barrils corne in the hands of GEORGE CAMPIN
and that he make his Debt apear the next Court.

302. Whereas Mrs. FFRA. WILLIAMS did arrest EDMD. KELLY and his wife to this
      Court and had noe cause of action the Court doth therefore order that
the sd Mrs. Fras. Williams be nonsuited and pay unto the sd Edmund Kelly 50
lb Tobacco the 10th Oct next else Execution.

303. The Court doth order that Mr. DAVID ANDERSON have attachmt against the
      Estate of DANL. KILLAHONE in the hands of Majr. MASON for that the said
Killahone did illegally take away the Boate of the said Anderson. Mr. David
Anderson did this day acknowledge Judgment to the Court for their security
in granting an attachment against the Estate of Danl. Killahone. Mr. WILLIAM
PRICE did this day appeare the atturney of Edmund Kelly.

304. Whereas Mr. DAVID ANDERSON did produce in Court a bond of JAMES SUMPTNERS
      for five pounds sterling and that Mr. ANTHONY BRIDGES and Mr. ROBERT
TOWNSEND did become security for the sd Sumptners who did not personally appear
the Court doth

Page 52   Court held 29th August 1666

order that in case the said Sumptner doth not appear the next Court Mr.
Bridges and Mr. Townsend shall be liable to pay the Debt provided Mr. Anderson
made the said Debt appear to be due.

305. Whereas a difference doth depend in this Court between ALEXANDER SYNNETT
      and OLIVER BALFE the Court doth order that it be Referred to next Court.

306. Whereas Mrs. FRANCES WILLIAMS did bring an acct of the Estate of Mr.
      ROBERT WILLIAMS her late Husband Deced and hath satisfyed the creditors
to the full value of the said Estate the Court doth order therefore that the
said Mrs. Williams have a Quietus est and that she be cleared from the payment
of any other debts belonging to the said Mr. Williams deceased.

Page 52 (contd)   Court held 29th August 1666

307.   Whereas Mrs. FRANCES WILLIAMS hath made complaint to this Court that a
       woman servant of hers GRACE FAREWELL hath had a bastard child which the
sd Grace Farewell did confess the Court doth therefore order that the sd Grace
Farewell serve her said Ms. Mrs. Ffra: Williams two years according to Act of
Assembly after the expiration of her former service.

308.   Whereas Mr. FRANCIS HALES hath willfully neglected to bring an Inventory
       of the Estate of JOHN HILES deced according to Law and that the said
Hales hath altered ye property of the sd Estate and converted the same to his
own use the Court doth therefore order that the Sheriff forthwith seize all
and singular the Estate of the said Francis Hales in this County untill he
shall answer his contempt and that he pay the charges.

309.   The Court doth order that ROGER PERFITT and Mr. EDMD NANFEN appraise the
       horse of DANL. KILLAHONE for which Mr. David Anderson hath an attachment.

310.   The Court doth order that the soldiers which were pressed in this county
       forthwith disbanded.

311.   The Court doth order that JOSEPH LUCAS pay unto ANDREW WATSON 120 pounds
       of Tobacco for three subpeneas at his suit.

312.   The Court doth order that Colo. JOHN DODMAN Inventory the Estate of Mr.
       HENRY PICTOE deced and secure the same in Behalf of the Court untill
further order and that the Sheriff give the sd Colo. Dodman possession of the
Estate.

313.   Whereas LUCY ABDOLORUM aged about 70 years did peticon this Court that
       she might be exempted from the payment of leaveys the Court taking it
into

Page 53   Court held 29th August 1666

consideration have ordered that the sd Lucy Abdolorum have according to her
petition and that from this day she be exempted from the same.

314.   Whereas it doth appear to this Court that JOSEPH EDMUNDS hath transported
       THOMAS GILL out of this County and that the said Gill stood indebted by
Bill jointly and severally with JOHN SMYTH to Mrs. MARGARET BRENT 2000 lb Tobacco and cask in consideration of a tract of land which Capt. Brent atturney
of Mrs. Margaret Brent did acknowledge the Court doth order that the sd Edmunds
pay unto the sd Mrs. Margaret Brent the sume of 1000 lb Tobacco and cask the
10th Octr next according to Act of Assembly with costs of suit alias Execution.
Mr. WM. PRICE did apeare attry of Jos. Edmunds.

315.   Whereas Mrs. FFRANCES WILLIAMS hath Imployed Mr. JOHN SAMWAIES and did
       promise him satisfaction for his Labour the Court doth order that the
said Mrs. Williams pay unto the said Mr. Samwaies 300 lb Tobacco and cask with
costs of suit the 10th October next als exe.

316.   The Court doth order that JOS. EDMUNDS have thirty lashes for his pill-
       fering.

317.   The Court doth order that no Faraigners shall plead in this Court.

318.   JAMES PRICE was this day sworne Constable for the lower parts of this
       County.

       The Court is adjourned to the 2d Wednesday in October

307 - 318

Page 53 (contd) Court held 10th October 1666

319. At a Court held for the County of Stafford Oct 10th 1666
        Present   Colo. John Dodman   Mr. Hugh Donding
                  Lt. Colo. Henry Meese   Mr. Rich. Heaberd   Justices
                  Major Geo: Mason   Mr. Robert Osborne

320. Whereas Mr. JOHN STONE did appear Atturney of Colo. CATLETT & Mr. ANDREW
        GILLSON to prove the Will of HENRY PICTOE deced the Court doth order that
noe probate be granted untill one or both appear to give security to the Court
and if they or either of them doe not appear at the next Court held for this
County then Colo. JOHN DODMAN to proceede according to a former order of this
Court.

321. Mr. ROBERT NURSE did appear Atturney of FRANCIS GRAY the Court doth order
        that JANE BOEZ pay unto ROBERT MOSLEY 40 lb Tobo for his attendance on the
Court. Mr. Robert Nurse did appear the Atturney of Mr. DAVID ANDERSON.

Page 54 Court held 10th October 1666

322. Whereas it doth appear to this Court that JAMES SUMNER of London Heaber-
        dasher stands indebted to DAVID ANDERSON the sum of five pounds Sterling
as by two Bonds or writings may appear & for as much as Order passed against
Mr. ANTHONY BRIDGES and Mr. ROBERT TOWNSEND security for the said Sumner the
last Court for payment of the said Debt if they produce not the Body of the
said Sumner this Court the Court taking the same into consideration doth order
and it is accordingly ordered that if the said mony be not paid between this
and the 20th of Aprill next or one of the said Bonds be returned satisfied
then Judgmt to be confirm'd against the said Bridges and Townsend with damages
and charges of this Court else Execution but in case the said Order be satisfied within a twelve month after the Judgment takes force then the said Anderson to reimburse the said money to the said Mr. Bridges and Mr. Townsend or
their order else Execution. Mr. Bridges apeales to the 6th day of the next
General Court.

323. Whereas ALEXANDER SYNNETT did arrest OLIVER BALFE to this Court and did
        not appear to prosecute his action the Court doth order that the said
Synnett be nonsuited and pay to the said Balfe 50 lb Tobacco & charges of Court
forthwith else execution.

324. Whereas JOSEPH EDMUNDS did arrest PHILIP CARPENTER to this Court and had
        noe cause of action the Court doth order that the said Edmunds be non-
suited & pay to the said Carpenter 50 lb Tobacco with all costs & charges he
hath ben at concerning the sute forthwith else execution.

325. Whereas Colo. PETER ASHTON did petition this Court for a division of a
        certain tract of land containing 2000 acres taken up by Colo. GERD. FOOKE
Mr. WILLIAM HORTON, THOMAS GRIGG and RICHARD GRANGER and now in the possession
of (sic) the Court doth order therefore that the surveyor lay out all their
lands severally be the 22d of November next and that JAMES PRICE & WILLIAM
GREEN, THOMAS HUMPHREYS

Page 55 Court held 10th October 1666

and ANDREW WATSON be assistants in the said Division.

326. Whereas JOSEPH EDMUNDS did arest JANE BOEZ to this Court for a Heafer
        and Calfe the Court doth adjudge according to the Evidences that the
said Edmunds hath received the Heifer And do further order that the said Boez
forthwith pay to the said Edmunds the Calfe with costs of sute else Execution.

Page 55 (contd)   Court held 10th October 1666

327. JOHN SAMWAIES did appear Atturney for JOHN HATTON and PHILIP CARPENTER.
      Mr. ANTHO. BRIDGES Atturney for JOSEPH EDMUNDS. Whereas GRACE HATTON
the wife of John Hatton did serve Mr. DAVID ANDERSON Two months and ten days
the Court doth order that the said Anderson pay to the sd Hatton 200 lb Tobo
and cask in full satisfaction for the said terme forthwith with costs of suit
else execution.

328. Whereas Mr. THOMAS BUNBURY did bring an Indenture to this Court for a
      servant of Colo. ASHTONS named JOHN WHITCRAFT wch Indenture now Defeased
the Court doth adjudge that the sd Whitcraft was to serve foure years by the
sd Indenture.

329. JOHN SAMWAIES Atturney for Mr. FRANCIS GRAY.

330. Whereas WILLIAM THOMAS hath made sufficient proofe of the transportation
      of 28 persons into this Colony Certificate is therefore granted to the
said Thomas for 900 acres of land Viz.

Thomas Greene	James Forner	Bridgett Bron
William Floyd	Saml. Jones	Nicho. White
John Staves	Mary Johnson	Nathl. Bride
William Stoell	Thos. Ffletcher	George Hanes
Jane Abbe	Timothy Stacey	Mary Merse
Mary Filer	William Knitt	Beth Inkson

(Compiler's Note: Only 18 names shown. With 50 acres per headright, the
figure of 28 persons would be incorrect in the entry.)

331. Whereas there hath ben former orders for the clearing the Highways the
      Court taking it into consideration doe order that the Highways be cleared
through the County according to Act and that if there be any dificalty in
chusing the said ways that then the surveyors goe to the next Justice and fol-
low his instructions and if the surveyors neglect the clearing and marking the
sd Roads by the next Court then to be fined according to Act to the sd Road
be from pastenare to the filly at Potomack Creek & from thence to the Ferry at
Acquia & from then to Chopwamsick Cr. The Court doth order that JOHN MATHEWS
and WILLIAM HARRIS be surveighors from Paspetanze to Potomack Creek & Mr.
EDWARD SANDERS   and WM. WITHERS from thence to Aquia and Mr. ROBERT

Page 56   Court held 10th October 1666

MOSLEY and Mr. WILLIAM BEACH to Chopmowamsick. The Court doth order that JOHN
AXTON take the Neighbourhood & make a Bridge at Wipsenassensen Creeke by the
next Court.

      Then the Court adjourned to last Wednesday in November

332. At a Court held for county of Stafford the 28th 9ber 1666
      Present Colo. John Dodman   Mr. Richd. Fossaker
               Lt. Colo. Henry Meese Major Geo. Mason   Justices
               Mr. Hugh Donding   Mr. Robert Osburne

333. Whereas NICHOLAS BALLBROOKE did arest HUM. BALY to this Court and had
      noe cause of action the Court doth order the said Ballbrooke be nonsuited
and pay to the said Baly fifty pounds of Tobacco with charges of Court forthwith als exe. Mr. JOHN SAMWAIES did appear Attur of Hum. Baly.

Page 56 (contd)   Court held 28th 9ber 1666

334. Whereas by former order of this Court the Estate of Mr. FRANCIS HALES
      was seized untill he should bring the Inventory of the Estate of JOHN
HILES deced which he hath this Court performed the Court doth order that the
sd seizure be now voyd & that he be released.

335. Whereas Difference doth depend in this Court between GEORGE BLAKE &
      WILLIAM BEACH the Court doth order it be referred to the next Court.

336. Capt. BRENT Atturney for Mr. MOSLEY. Whereas it doth appear to this
      Court that Mr. JOSEPH WILLIAMS hath transported THOMAS GILL out of this
County and that the said Gill stands indebted to Mr. ROBERT MOSLEY 1000 lb Tobacco and cask due by condition & 359 pd accompt on Oath the Court doth therefore order that the sd JOSEPH EDMUNDS pay the said Robert Mosley the said sume
of 1359 lb Tobacco & cask forthwith with costs of suit else exe. (Names as in
record.)

337. Whereas JOSEPH EDMUNDS was subpened to this Court at the suit of GEORGE
      BALFE & did not appear to give his Evidence the Court doth order that
the sd Edmunds pay for default 350 lb Tobacco according to ye Act of Assembly
forthwith als exe.

Page 57   Court held 28th 9ber 1666

Whereas Joseph Edmunds was subpened to this Court at the suit of GEORGE BLAKE
& did not appear to give his evidence the Court doth order that the sd Edmunds
pay for default 350 lb Tobacco according to ye Act of Assembly forthwith als
exe. JOHN SAMWAIES Attry of Geo. Blake.

338. The Court doth order that Mr. ROBERT MOSLEY pay unto JANE BOEZ 80 lb of
      Tobacco for attendance on the Court with charges of Court forthwith
else exe.

339. To the Worshipful the Justices of the Peace for the County of Stafford
      The petition of ROBERT OSBURNE sheweth that your Petitioners horse
ranging to Pasbetanzy NICOLAS BRULY did acknowledge to Mr. BUNBURY that he had
taken up the said Horse and putt him in his Tobacco house and since has owned
to the Petitioner that he sent his servant WILLIAM FLORENCE with the said
horse to your Petitioners house and your Petitioner on the 15th Instant going
to Looke his horse mett with the sd William Florence and questioned him concerning his horse. He replyed he knew not where he was but thought he should
pay for him and the said Florence hath reported to others that he supposed the
sd Horse was dead all which your Petitioner shall make appear. The premises
considered he humbly prayes the order of this worshipful Court for restoration
of his sd loss with Damages & cost of suit etc. We find by the depositions of
THOS. NETHAWAY & MARY ELKING that the Horse was in possession of Nico. Bruly.

Mr. Wm. Horton	Thos: Humphreys	Richd. Wells	
John Heabeard	Robt. Butterfield	Jno. James	
Thos. Derrick	Wm. Williamson	James Price	Jury
John Blagrove	Wm. Thomas	Thos. Grigg	

The Court doth order that the Verdict of the Jury be ordered for a Judgment
And that if the said Bruly deliver not the said Horse in two months then to pay
to the sd WILLIAM OSBURNE (sic) 2000 lb Tobacco and cask with costs of suit
else exe. and it is further ordered that if Nico. Bruly pay for the sd Horse
according to the sd order then the sd Brully to enjoy the sd horse to his own
proper use. JOHN SAMWAIES Attry of Nicholas Bruly. John Samwaies atturney
of William Florence. It is ordered that the Jury have 72 lb Tobacco.

Page 58   Court held 28th 9ber 1666

340.   Whereas it doth appear to this Court that HENRY BACKWELL recd a kettle
        of Majr. GEO: MASON the Court doth order that Lt. Colo. JNO. WASHINGTON
attorney of the sd Backwell pay to the said Major George Mason 400 lb Tobacco
and cask with costs of suit forthwith else execution. And it is further ordered that if the said Lt. Colo. John Washington makes it appear by the last
of April next that the said Kittle was cast away then the said Major Mason to
reimburst the said sume to the said Washington else execution.

341.   Whereas JOSEPH EDMUNDS did arest JANE BOEZ to this Court & did not appear
        to prosecute his action the Court doth order that the said Edmunds be
nonsuited and pay to the said Jane Boez 50 lb Tobacco with charges of suit
forthwith else execution.

342.   The Court doth order that NICHOLAS BRULY pay unto JOHN JAMES 60 lb Tobacco
        for attendance on the Court with charges.

343.   Whereas NICO. RUSSELL did arest JOHN KEECH to this Court & did not ap-
        pear to prosecute his action the Court doth order that the said Russell
be nonsuited & pay to the said Keech 50 lb Tobacco with charges of Court forthwith else execution. Whereas Nicho. Russell did arest HENRY JAQUES to this
Court & did not appear to prosecute his action the Court doth order that the
said Russell be nonsuited & pay to the said Jaques 50 lb Tobacco with charges
of Court forthwith else execution.

344.   The Court doth order that the probate of a will be granted unto COLO.
        JOHN CATLETT and MAJOR ANDREW GILSON Executors of the Estate of Mr.
HENRY PICTOE deced and that JOHN WILLIAMS, VINCENT YOUNG, ROBERT BUTTERFIELD
and ROBERT STREETE be appraysers of the sd Estate.

Page 59   Court held 28th 9ber 1666

345.   The Court doth order that JOHN JAMES pay unto RICHARD WELLS and THOMAS
        DERRICK 60 lb Tobacco apeace for there attendance on the Court with
charges forthwith else execution.

346.   Whereas the Right Honble Govr. hath given to this County & Westmoreland
        a Bond of Colo. GERRARD FOOKE for 25000 pounds of Tobacco the Court doth
order and it is accordingly ordered that Capt. JOHN ALEXANDER High Sheriff be
hereby impowered to receive & make payment of the said Tobacco according to
the apoynment of the Court hereafter nominated else execution.

	Ł	TOBO
To Westmoreland County	DR	8380
To Major Mason		2000
To Samuel Rosier		0400
To Thomas Grigg		0400
To Robert Collingwood		0400
To William Withers		0400
To Thomas Grigg		0450
To Mr. John Heabeard		0450
To Dr. Robert Hall		6000
To Capt. John Alexander		0810
To John Mathews Ordy. Keeper		2720
To Capt. John Alexander to receive for the use of the County		2600
	Tobo	25000 *

(* amount as shown in record totals 25010)

340 - 346

Page 59 (contd)   Court held 28th 9ber 1666

347. Whereas JOHN JAMES did arest Mr. ROBERT TOWNSEND to this Court & had noe
       cause of action the Court doth therefore order the said John James be
nonsuited & pay to the sd Mr. Townsend 50 lb Tobacco with charges of court
forthwith else execution.

Page 60   Court held 28th 9ber 1666

348. The Court doth order that a supersedas be granted to Major ANDREW GILSON
       to stopp proceedings against him concerning a former order of this Court
to Mr. ANTHONY BRIDGES for 1300 lb Tobacco and cask.

349. Whereas Mr. ROBERT TOWNSEND being Impanneled on a Jury and sworn foreman
       thereof to attend the Court did illegally absent himself the Court doth
therefore order that the said Mr. ROBERT MOSLEY (sic) be fined and pay unto
Capt. JOHN ALEXANDER High Sheriff 300 lb Tobacco for the use of the County
forthwith else exe.

350. The Court doth order CHRISTOPHER LUND being of the Jury illegally absen-
       ting himself be fined and accordinly pay Capt. JOHN ALEXANDER High
Sheriff 150 lb Tobacco for the use of the County forthwith else exe.

351. The Court doth order that Major ANDREW GILSON pay unto MATHEW BUROT 120
       lb Tobacco for three times coming to Court to prove the will of Mr. HENRY
PICTOE deced with charges of Court forthwith else exe.

352. Colo. JOHN DODMAN did this day proffer himself security for Mr. FFRA.
       HALES concerning the Estate of JOHN HILES deced.

353. Whereas JOHN WITHERS did bring an Inventory of the Estate of DAVID COL-
       LINGS deced to this Court Major GEORGE MASON did proffer himself security
for the said Withers concerning the sd Estate. Whereas John Withers did formerly stand security for ELIZABETH LANE the Court doth order he be discharged
from the same.

Page 61. Court held 28th 9ber 1666

354. The Court doth order that Mr. DAVID ANDERSON doe immediately perform the
       order of Westmoreland Court concerning RICHARD STURMAN sonne of JOHN
STURMAN else within 20 days to deliver the said orphants to the Sheriff of
Westmoreland or his order.

355. To the worshipful Justices etc The humble petition of EDMD NANFEN sheweth
       that MICHAEL PICKERNELL hath unjustly killed a shoat of your Petitioners
which he shall make appear. Wherefore he craves order of this Worshipful
Court against the said Pickernell for such redress as the Law hath provided
with costs of suit. We find by the testimony of Major MASON & MICH. HILL the
Defendant killed a shoate of Mr. Nanfens. The Court doth order that the Verdict of the Jury be entered for a Judgment and that Mich. Pickernell have 30
lashes & pay costs of suit forthwith else exe. Ordered that the Jury have
72 lb Tobacco.

356. Whereas BURR HARRIS (sic) did arest THOMAS CHABERITE to this Court & did
       not appear to prosecute action the Court doth order that the said Harris
be nonsuited and pay to the said Chakawrite 50 lb Tobacco with charges of Court
forthwith else exe.

357. The Court doth order that the fferrys remain as they formerly were ex-
       cept 300 lb Tobacco for the fferry at Machotock.

Page 61 (contd)   Court held 28th 9ber 1666

358.   Certificate of land granted to JOHN KEECH for 1000 acres of land for the transportation of 20 persons into the Colony Vizt.

Thomas Burton	Wm. Sallaway	Hen: Tostin	Robt Sandys
Mary Story	Elizabeth Sandys	Jno. Wilton	Robt Harding
Edwd Burr	Wm Burr	Susan Todd	Jas. Hatton
John Sorrell	Thos: Ratting	Jane Blond	Tho. Yapp
Henry Gostell	Hum: Tallwood	Josp. Sorrell	( )

359.   Certificate is granted to Mr. HOWSON for 1000 acres of Land by and for the transportation of 20 persons into this Colony Vizt.

James Tennent	Tho: Bell	John Willson	Waltr. Wharton
Thos. Hankins	John Clerk	Ann Thomson	Wm. Tayloe
Step: Jackson	Tho: Price	Chr. Hickes	Ann Ballance
John Margillory	Thos. Smith	James Tomson	Ann Harvey
Fras. Tomson	John Smith	Robt Price	Mary Palmer

Then the Court adjourned to the first Wednesday in Ffeby.

Page 62   At a Court held for county of Stafford the 11th Ffeby 1666

360.   Presenct Colo. John Dodman   Mr. Hugh Donding
                 Lt. Colo. Hen: Meese   Mr. Richd. Heabeard   Justices
                 Majr. Geo: Mason   Mr. Robt Osborne

361.   The Court doth order that EDMUND HUGHES and GEORGE CAMPIN to close prison and secured by irons.

362.   Whereas it doth appear to this Court that JAMES LAMB hath assigned and made over his Estate to JOHN ROLTE in case he should fail of his obligation which by the same at large doth appear and according to proofe of the said Rolt have and pocess the whole Estate of the said Lamb and that he put in security for the Payments of all debts that shall be made appear against the Estate within a year.   JOHN MATHEWS did enter security for John Rolt.

363.   Whereas it doth appear to this Court that JAMES LAMB stands indebted to JONAS REVETT 425 pounds of Tobacco and cask per Bill the Court doth order that JOHN ROLT Processor of the said Estate pay unto the said Revett the said Debt forthwith with charges of Court else execution.

Page 63   Court held 11th Ffeby 1666

Mr. ANTHONY BRIDGES Atty of John Rolt.

364.   Whereas it doth appear to this Court that JOHN MATHEWS alias MATHEWS (sic) did make over his Estate to JOHN ROLT in case he should faile of his obligation which the said Rolt did make appear the said Estate being likewise made over to the said Rolt as by his Bill have the procession of the said Estate and he pay all debts that shall appear against the same so performance of this order.   John Mathews did enter Security for John Rolt.   The Court doth order that OLIVER BALFE and ROBERT STREETE be appraysers of the Estate of John Mathews.

365.   Whereas JOHN GILES did attach the Estate of JOHN MATHEWS and declared against him by petition but did not appear to prosecute the Court doth order that the sd Giles be nonsuited and pay unto JOHN ROLT processor of the said Estate 50 lb Tobacco with charges of Court forthwith else Execution.

Page 63 (contd)   Court held 11th Ffeby 1666

366.   The Court doth order that the fine against JOSEPH EDMUNDS the last Court
       be remitted he having proved same.

367.   Whereas it doth appear to this Court that JOHN MATHEWS alias MATOONE
       stands indebted to Mr. HUGH DONDING a cow & five hundred pounds of Tobacco
and cask per Bill the Court doth order JOHN ROLT processor of the sd Estate
pay unto the said Mr. Donding the said Debt with charges of Court forthwith
else Execution.

Page 64   Court held 11th Ffeby 1666

368.   Whereas it doth appear to this Court that JAMES LAMB stands indebted to
       Mr. HUGH DONDING 460 pounds Tobacco and cask the Court doth order that
JOHN ROLT processor of said Estate pay the said Mr. Donding the sd Debt with
charges of Court forthwith else Execution.

369.   Whereas Mr. ANDREW GILSON did obtain an order the last Court for a super-
       sedeas to stop proceedings against him for a former order which Mr. ANTHONY
BRIDGES obtained for 2300 pounds of Tobacco and cask the Court doth order that
the said supersedeas be voyd and that proceedings lay open to the said Mr.
ANTHO. BRIDGES against the said Gilson with charges of Court else Execution.

370.   Whereas it doth appear to this Court that Mr. HENRY PICTOE deced stood
       indebted to THOMAS DERRICK assign of JAMES LINDSAY 400 lb Tobo and cask
per Bill the Court doth order that Collo. JOHN CATLETT and Major ANDREW GILSON
Executrs. of the said Pictoe forthwith pay the said Dirrick the sd sume of 400
pounds of Tobo and cask else execution.

371.   Whereas DANIEL GAINES hath proved his just service of four years by In-
       denture the Court doth therefore order that he be from this day free and
that Mr. ANDREW GILSON his late Master pay unto him Ten pounds Sterling

Page 65 'Court held 11th Ffeby 1666

according to the said Indenture with costs of suit forthwith else execution.

372.   Whereas Mr. HENRY PICTOE deced stood indebted to JOHN BLAGROVE by Bill
       bearing date the 8th of 10br 1665 three cows between the age of three
and eight years old great with calfe or calves by their sides which were to
be delivered the Aprill following which debt remaining umpaid the Court doth
order that Colo. JOHN CATLETT and Mr. ANDREW GILSON Executrs of the said Pictoe
forthwith deliver the said cows with their calves which they had the last year
according to the said Bill else execution.

373.   Whereas it doth appear to this Court that JOSEPH EDMUNDS stands indebted
       to JANE BOEZ 800 pounds of Tobacco and cask by Bill the Court doth order
that the sd Edmunds forthwith pay to the sd Boez the sd Debt with charges of
Court else Execution and it is further ordered that they give discharges to
each other from the Beginning of the world to this Present day else Execution.

374.   Mr. VINCT YOUNG admr of STEPHEN NORMAN did this day confess Judgment to
       Mr. FRANCIS HALES administrator of JOHN GILES for 316 pounds of Tobacco
and cask before Colo. JOHN DODMAN and Lt. Colo. HENRY MEESE to be paid forthwith else exe.

375.   Whereas a former order passed against ANTHONY BRIDGES and Mr. ROBERT
       TOWNSEND of JAMES SUMPTNER for the payment of five pounds Sterling to
Mr. DAVID ANDERSON the Court taking the same into consideration have ordered
that in case David Anderson take out Execution of the said Debt that he give

Page 65 (contd)   Court held 11th Ffeby 1666

security for the reimbursement of the sd money in case it be afterwards proved to be paid else exe.

376.   Whereas it doth appear to this Court that THOMAS MOSS stands indebted to ROBERT STREET 1200 pounds of Tobo and cask by Bill the Court doth order that the sd Moss doth pay unto the said Streete the said 1200 pounds of Tobacco and cask with costs of suit forthwith else execution. Mr. ANTHONY BRIDGES did appear Atturney of Thomas Moss.

Page 66   Court held 11th Ffeby 1666

The Court doth order that Robert Streete pay unto Capt. ASHTON 300 lb Tobacco for attendance on the Court with charges forthwith else execution. The Court doth order that Robert Streete pay unto THOMAS SHARP 60 lb Tobacco for attendance on the Court with charges forthwith else execution. Whereas Thomas Moss did arrest Robert Streete to this Court and had no cause of action the Court doth order that Thomas Moss be nonsuited and pay the said Streete 50 pounds of Tobacco with charges of Court forthwith else execution.

377.   Whereas JOHN WILLIAMS did put in his information to this Court against JOHN MATHEWS alias MATOONE for unlawfully killing a hogg belonging to the sd Williams he having proved the same by two depositions the Court doth order that the said Williams have Judgment against the Estate of the said Mathews for 2000 pounds of Tobacco according to Act with charges of Court forthwith else Execution. Whereas it doth appear to this Court that John Mathews alias Matoone stands indebted to John Williams 300 pounds of Tobacco and a barril of Indian Corn the Court doth order that the said Williams have Judgment against the Estate of the said Mathews for the said Debt with charges of Court forthwith else exe.

Page 67   Court held 11th Ffeby 1666

378.   Whereas Mr. VINCT YOUNG amde oath that JOHN MATHEWS stands indebted to him 400 pounds of Tobacco and half a barrell of Corn as by the account on record may appear the Court doth therefore order that JOHN ROLT processor of the Estate of the said Mathews pay to the sd Vinct Young the sd Debt with charges of Court forthwith else exe.

379.   The Court doth order that WILLIAM CORDWELL an Orphant be and remain in the tuition of JOHN FISHER till he come to the age of one and twenty years.

380.   Whereas Mr. ANTHONY BRIDGES hath Evidences that when he was Clerke there was a Bill of JOHN HILES deced wherein he stood indebted to THOMAS SHARPE a case of brandy the Court doth therefore order that Mr. FRANCIS HALES admr of the said Giles (sic) forthwith pay unto the sd Sharpe the sd case of brandy unless it appear to be paid before else execution.

381.   Whereas it doth appear to this Court that JAMES CLIFTON hath abused the Honourable Govr. and uttered scandalous speeches against the Court it is therefore ordered that the said Clifton be forthwith committed to prison untill he shall give good security according to Law to answer for his contempt and misbehaviour and that all persons whom the Sheriff or his Deputies shall require are hereby commanded to assist him and it is further ordered that if the said Clifton shall appear to the next Court and make his humble acknowledgment in regard to his

376 - 381

Page 68   Court held 11th Ffeby 1666

presumption and offence committed against the Honourable Govr. and the Court
and Colo. JOHN DODMAN to give good security for his future behaviour and good
abaring then to be released.

382.   Whereas VINCT YOUNG hath made oath that he hath paid the full quantity
        of Tobacco out of the Estate of STEPHEN NORMAN deced as by the Inventory
it was appraysed sixty six pounds of Tobacco excepted the Court doth order that
a Quietus Est be granted to the said Young.

383.   Whereas it doth appear to this Court that GERRARD MASTERS stands indebted
        to HENRY GILBERT Four hundred pounds of Tobacco and cask by Bill the
Court doth order that the said Masters forthwith pay to the said Gilbert the
said Debt with costs of suit else execution.

384.   Whereas etc. DAVID ANDERSON stands indebted to JOSEPH EDMUNDS 1020
        pounds of Tobacco & cask per Bill the Court orders that the said Ander-
son pay to the said Edmunds the said sume of 1020 pounds of Tobacco and cask
with charges of Court in forty days else execution.

385.   Whereas it doth appear to this Court that GEORGE BLAKE stands indebted
        to JOSEPH EDMUNDS 2996 lb Tobacco and cask by Bill the Court doth order
that the said Blake forthwith pay the said Edmunds one half of the said Debt
and give security for the payment of the other half in the year 1668 which if
the said Blake neglect or refuse to doe then execution issue for the whole sum
and that Blake pay costs of suit.

386.   Whereas etc ROBERT HALL stands indebted to JOSEPH EDMUNDS 4503 pounds
        of Tobacco and cask by Bill

Page 69   Court held 11th Ffeby 1666

the Court doth order that the said Hall forthwith pay to the said Edmunds one
half of the sd Debt and give security for the payment of the other half in the
year 1668 which if the said Hall neglect or refuse to do then execution issue
for the whole sum and that Hall pay costs of suit.

387.   Whereas etc. WILLIAM BEACH stands indebted to JOSEPH EDMUNDS 3261 pounds
        of Tobacco and cask per two bills the sd MOSLEY having legally discounted
in Court 1622 pounds of Tobacco and cask It is therefore ordered that the sd
Mr. Mosley pay unto the sd Edmunds 1650 pounds of Tobacco and cask with charges
of Court. One half to be paid in the year 68 with good security for the payment
thereof which if the said Mosley neglect or refuse to doe the execution to
issue for the wole sume.

388.   Whereas it doth appear to this Court that WILLIAM FISHER Mariner stands
        indebted to Capt. GILES BRENT 3122 pounds of Tobacco & cask as also two
men servants as by obligation under his hand & seale may appear the Court doth
order that the sd Fisher forthwith pay to the sd Capt. Brent the sd 3122 pounds
of Tobacco & cask and the two men servants according to the sd obligation else
Execution with costs of suit.

389.   Whereas it doth appear to this Court that THOMAS GILL stood joyntly &
        severally indebted with JOHN SMITH unto Mrs. MARGARET BRENT the sume of
1000 pounds of Tobacco & cask by Bill the Court doth order that JOSEPH EDMUNDS
who transported the sd Gill out of this County pay unto Mrs. Margaret Brent
the sd debt with costs of suit forthwith else execution.

390. Certificate of land is granted to Capt. GILES BRENT for 300 acres by and
      for the transportation of six persons into this Colony Vizt.

Page 70   Court held 11th Ffeby 1666

Edward Davis	Edmund Lambert	John Meredith
Thomas Hardy	Elizabeth Fido	Diana Beard

391. Whereas JANE BOEZ did arest ROBERT HALL to this Court & had noe cause of
      action the Court doth order that the sd Boez be nonsuited and pay to the
sd Hall 50 pounds of Tobacco with charges of Court forthwith else Execution.

392. Cerfficate of land is granted Mr. WILLIAM HEABEARD for 350 acres by and
      for the transportation of seven Persons into this Colony Vizt.

Thos. Wasson	John Vincent	Anne Gerrat
Denis Reue	Jaha Clark	Rich. Muns
Amb. Baxter		

393. Whereas JANE TAYLOR did petition this Court that JOHN MATHEWS having
      gotten her with child and absenting himself out of this County she was
likely to become a great misery and that she might have what was left of his
Estate after his Debts were paid for the maintenance of the child the Court
doth order that she have according to her petition.

394. Reference is granted in the case depending between Mr. ANTHO. BRIDGES &
      JOHN SAMWAIES.

395. Whereas JOSEPH EDMUNDS hath paid several sumes of Tobacco for the trans-
      portation of THOMAS GILL out of this County the Court doth therefore order
that the sd Edmunds have Judgment against the said Gill or his Estate for what
damages he shall make appear.

396. Whereas it was omitted at Laying of the Leavey to allow the Sheriff
      sallery for 26000 and odd pounds of Tobacco it is ordered he pay himself
out of the 2600 (sic) pounds of Tobacco remaining in his hands.

Page 71   Court held 11th Ffeby 1666

397. The Court doth order the persons hereafter nominated be of the Vestry
      and they meete on the 14 Instant at the Courthouse.

Capt. John Alexander	Mr. Jno. Heabeard	Wm. Greene
Mr. Richard Fossaker	Mr. Wm. Heaberd	Thos. Humphrey
Mr. Richd. Heabeard	Mr. Vinct Young	Thos. Grigg

   The Court doth order that Mr. ROBERT OSBORNE and JOHN WITHERS be churchwardens and sworne the next Court.

      The Court is adjourned till the first Wednesday in Aprill.

398. At a Court held for the County of Stafford the 3d April 1667
                            Colo. John Dodman

Prst. Lt. Colo. Henry Meese	Mr. Richd. Fossaker	
Mr. Richd. Heabeard	Mr. Robert Osborne	Justices

399. Whereas it doth appear to this Court that Mr. ROBERT OSBORNE is and
      stands indebted to ROBERT PICKERNELL his freedom apparell the Court doth
order that the said Mr. TOWNSEND (sic) forthwith pay the sd Mr. Pickernell a
cloath or Kearsey sute of cloaths with a capp shirt shoes stockings & pay
charges of Court else Execution.

Page 71 (contd)   Court held 3d April 1667

400.   The Court doth order ROBERT PICKERNELL pay unto THOMAS PRICE, THOMAS
       SPEEDY, JOHN WHITCRAFT and CHRISTOPHER LUND 40 pounds of Tobacco apeace
for attendance in the Court being supd at his suit forthwith else Execution.

401.   The Court doth order that NICO. RUSSEL pay to JOHN KEECH 40 lb Tobo for
       attendance in the Court else exe.

Page 72   Court held 3d April 1667

402.   Whereas it doth appear to this Court that DAVID ANDERSON stands indebted
       to Capt. JOHN LEE 2000 pounds of Tobacco & cask by Bill dated the 4th of
July 1664 and due the 20th October following the Court doth order that the said
Anderson forthwith pay to the said Lee or his assigns the said sume of 2000
pounds of Tobacco and cask with forebearance and costs of suit else Execution.

403.   Whereas it doth appear to this Court that GEORGE CAMPIN stands indebted
       to Capt. JOHN ALEXANDER 1225 pounds of Tobacco & cask by Bill for which
Debt the said Alexander had an attachment against the Estate of the said Campin
and accordingly executed on cattle belonging to the said Campin so attached
for the sd Debt with charges of Court else Execution.

404.   Whereas it doth appear to this Court that DAVID ANDERSON stands indebted
       to Lt. Colo. JOHN WASHINGTON 2624 pounds of Tobacco & cask by Bill as
also several goods as appears by account on record the Court doth therefore
order that the said Anderson forthwith pay to the said John Washington the sume
of 2624 pounds of Tobacco & cask and the said goods in Kind with charges of
Court else execution.   Wherea Lt. Colo. John Washington did acknowledge that
he stood indebted to David Anderson 87 Foote of Glass and 7 iron casemts deyed
and one water barr hookes and tacke the Court doth therefore order that the
said Colo. Washington pay to the said Anderson the said 87 Foote of Glass and
the sd casemts forthwith else execution.

Page 73   Court held 3d April 1667

405.   The Court doth order that FRANCIS HALES have attachment against the Es-
       tate of GEORGE CAMPIN for 2000 pounds of Tobacco and cask & that he make
his Debt appear the next Court.

406.   The Court doth order that a reference be granted in a case depending
       between the WIDOW COLLINGS and GEORGE BLAKE.

407.   Whereas a former order of this Court passed against GEORGE BLAKE for the
       payment of 1996 pounds of Tobacco and cask due to JOSEPH EDMUNDS by Bill
one half thereof forthwith and the other half the 20th October 1668 the said
Edmunds having petitioned the Court that in regard the cessation is now voyd
and confeantly the Acts for the payments of half Debts That he might have Present payment the Court taking the same into consideration have ordered that
the said Blake pay the said Edmunds the said 1996 pounds of Tobacco and cask
forthwith with charges of Court else exe.

408.   Whereas a former order of this Court passed against ROBERT HALL for the
       payment of 4472 pounds of Tobacco and cask due to JOSEPH EDMUNDS by Bill
one half thereof forthwith and the other half in the year 1668 the sd Edmunds
having petitioned the Court that in regard the cessation is now voyd and consequently the Act for Payment of half Debts that he might have present payment
of his Tobacco the Court taking the same into consideration have ordered that
the said BEECH (sic) pay unto the said Edmunds the full debt of 4472 pounds of
Tobacco and cask with charges of Court forthwith else exe.

Page 73 (contd)   Court held 3d April 1667

409.   Whereas a former order of this Court passed against ROBERT MOSLEY for
       the payment of 1650 pounds of Tobacco and cask to JOSEPH EDMUNDS one half
thereof forthwith else exe.

Page 74   Court held 3d April 1667

410.   Whereas it doth appear to this Court that THOMAS KELLISON stands indebted
       to JOSEPH EDMUNDS 1200 pounds of Tobacco and cask per Bill the Court
doth therefore order that the said Kellison forthwith give good security to the
sd Edmunds for the payment of the said Debt with forebearance & charges of
Court else execution the 10th October next.

411.   Whereas WILLIAM HORTON did arest R. MOSLEY to this Court and had noe cause
       of action the Court doth therefore order that the said Horton be non-
suited and pay to the said Mosley 50 pounds of Tobacco with charges of Court
the 10th October next else Execution.

412.   Whereas FRANCIS JORDON did petition the Court that JOS: EDMUNDS who is a
       pilfering person might give security or depart the county the Court
taking the same into consideration have ordered that the said Edmunds forthwith
give good security for his good and honoust behaviour else depart the County
and that Jos: Edmunds pay charges of Court else Execution.

413.   The Court doth order that OLIVER JONES pay unto JOHN ANCRAM and MILES
       RAINFORD 40 pounds of Tobacco apeace for their attendance on the Court
else exe.

414.   Whereas it doth appear to this Court by Evidence that JOHN COLCLOUGH
       did buy a certain parcell of Corn by the Sump of OLIVER JONES for which
corn the said Colclough stands indebted to the sd Jones 750 pds of Tobacco and
cask the Court doth therefore order that the said Colclough forthwith pay
unto the sd Jones the sd 750 pounds of Tobacco and cask with costs of suit else
execution.

Page 75   Court held 3d April 1667

415.   The Court doth order that Capt. JOHN ALEXANDER high sheriff bring JOHN
       ROLT to the next Court to answer in an action at the Suit of Mrs. FRAN-
CES WILLIAMS else pay the Debt.

416.   Whereas it doth appear to this Court that GILES ANDREWS who hath absented
       himself out of this County stands indebted to JOHN CLERK 331 pounds of
Tobacco and cask have Judgment against Estate of said Andrews formerly attached
for the said debt with charges of Court else execution.

417.   The Court doth order that THOMAS ASILAVANT pay to MARY SIMONS 80 pounds
       of Tobacco being subpd at his suit with charges of Court the 10th Octr
next else exe.

418.   Whereas the Court is informed that there is a defect in the apraysing
       the Estate of Mr. HENRY PICTOE deced and that there hath been noe Inven-
tory brought into this Court It is therefore ordered that Colo. JOHN CATLETT
and Mr. ANDREW GILSON Executors of the Estate bring an Inventory thereof to
the next Court and that the Sheriff summon the said Executors to perform the
same and that the said Executors pay the order of Court.

419.   Whereas THOMAS BAREFOOTE did arest Mr. ROBERT OSBORNE to this Court and
       had noe cause of action the Court doth order that the said Barefoote be
nonsuited and pay to the said Mr. Osborne 50 pounds of Tobacco and charges of
Court the 10th Octr next else exe.

409 - 419

Page 75 (contd)   Court held 3d April 1667

420. The Court taking into consideration the great loss which Mr. RICHARD
     FOSSAKER hath lately sustained doe hereby request the Honourable Governer
that he would be pleased to confirm the sheriffs place upon him for the year
ensueing.

Page 76   Court held 3d April 1667

421. Whereas Mr. DAVID ANDERSON did petition this Court that forasmuch as he
     had kept ROBT. STURMAN an Orphant for the term of ten years or there-
abouts and hath ben at great charge in maintaining the said Orphant the Court
taking the same into consideration have ordered that Mr. RICHARD STURMAN of
Westmoreland County forthwith pay to the said Anderson 3000 pounds of Tobacco
and cask in satisfaction for the sd charge or less the Orphant to remain in
the custody of the said Anderson.

422. The Court doth order that the Minister preach in three particular places
     in the County Vizt at the southwest side of Aquia and at the Courthouse
and at Chotanck at a house belonging to Mr. ROBERT TOWNSEND to officiate every
sabath Day in one of these places successively untill further order.

423. Whereas Mrs. MARY PARFITT hath sufficiently prov'd the Will of ROGER
     PARFITT her late Husband deced the Court doth order that a probate of
the said Will be granted unto her.

424. The case depending between Mr. BRIDGES and JOHN SAMWAIES is again re-
     ferred to the next Court.

     The Court adjourned to the 12th of June next

425. At a Court held for Stafford County the 12th of June 1667

     Presence Colo. John Dodman   Mr. Richd. Heaberd
              Lt. Colo. Hen: Meese   Mr. Richd. Fossaker   Justices
              Majr. George Mason

Page 77   Court held 12th June 1667

426. Whereas by a former order of this Court Judgment was to be confirmed
     against Mr. ANTHONY BRIDGES & Mr. ROBERT TOWNSEND security of JAMES
SUMPNER for the payment of five pounds Sterling with damages and charges of
this Court unto Mr. DAVID ANDERSON in case the said money was not paid by the
20th of April or one of the Bonds by which the sd money is due returned satisfied neither of which being proved by the said Sumpner nor security the Court
doth therefore order that the said Antho. Bridges and Robert Townsend or either
of them pay unto the said David Anderson or his assigns the said sume of five
pounds sterling with damages according to Act & charges of Court forthwith
else exe.

427. Whereas JOHN EDMUNDS servant of Mr. VINCENT YOUNG did unlawfully run
     away from his sd Master and absent himself from the 12th of August till
the 14th of March and took with him ANDREW CANNOE a new fishing line and a
Hatchett and that the sd Young hath ben at great charges as by Certificate on
record may appear the Court doth therefore order that the said Edmunds serve
the said Mr. Vincent Young or his assigns the terme of twenty months after the
Expiration of his time by custom or his Indenture in satisfaction of the sd
charges else Execution.

Page 77 (contd)   Court held 12th June 1667

428.   Whereas it doth appear to this Court that Lt. Colo. HEN: MEESE did draw
       Bills of Exchange on Mr. JOHN BENBOE of London Merchant for thirty two
pounds sterling which said Bills have date the 22d of February 1664 & Payable
to DANIEL HUTTON & his assigns accordingly assigned to Colo. VOLLINTINE PAYTON
which Bills were not Excepted by the said Benbow or his Executors but returned
protested into this Colony of Virginia the Court taking the same into consideration have ordered that the said Lt. Colo. Henry Meese pay unto Mr. JOHN
APPLETON who married the Relict of the said Colo. Vallte Peyton

Page 78   Court held 12th June 1667

the sume of thirty two pounds sterling with damages according to Act & costs
of suit forthwith else Execution the said Benbow being dead nonsolvent as by
the protest did appear JOHN MARIUS being Public Notary.

429.   Whereas it doth appear to this Court by Evidence that RICHARD PEARCE
       stands indebted to DAVID ANDERSON Eight hundred pounds of Tobacco and
cask the Court doth order that the said Anderson have Judgment against the
Estate of the said Pearce for the payment of the said Debt 10th October next
else Execution.

430.   Whereas GEORGE BLAKE did arest RABECKAH COLLINS to this Court and did not
       appear to prosecute his action the Court doth therefore order that the
said Blake be nonsuited and pay the said Collins fifty pounds of Tobacco with
charges of Court the 10th Octr else exe.

431.   Whereas it doth appear to this Court that CHARLES RANGER stands indebted
       to FRANCIS ROWSON 400 pounds of Tobacco and cask by Bill the Court doth
therefore order that the said RAGAN (sic) pay the same else exe.

432.   Whereas Capt. JOHN ALEXANDER did arest THOMAS BAREFOOTT to this Court &
       had noe cause of action the Court doth order that the said Capt. Alexan-
der be nonsuited and pay to the sd Barefoot 50 pounds of Tobacco with charges
of Court the 10th October next else execution.

433.   The Court doth order that WILLIAM GREENE, ROBERT BUTTERFIELD view the
       work of THOMAS BAREFOOTT done at Capt. Alexanders and bring report to
next Court.

Page 79   Court held 12th June 1667

434.   Whereas DANIEL JAMES stands bound to JOHN ROLT to dwell with him as by
       the Obligation on Record more at large appears which obligation the said
James hath not performed the Court doth therefore order that the sd James give
good security to the sd John Rolt for the payment of 400 Tobo & cask with costs
of suit the 10th Octr next else execution.

435.   The Court doth order that a probate of a Will be granted to JANE BRULY
       Relict & Extrx of NICHO. BRULY deced she having sufficient proved the
Will of her said Husband.

436.   The Court doth order that there be a Pillery forthwith & Mr. RIC'D
       HEABEARD is requested to agree with one to make it and also to repair the
stocks.

437.   Mr. RICHD. FOSSAKER was this day Sworne high sheriff for this County.
       JOHN CLERK sworne undersheriff. Lt. Colo. HENRY MEESE & Mr. RICHD. HEA-
BEARD became security for Mr. Richd. Fossaker for the true performance of his
said office.

428 - 437

Page 79 (contd) Court held 12th June 1667

438. The Court doth order ye Vestry be as follows

Colo. John Dodman	Mr. Richd. Heabeard	John Wiser
Lt. Colo. Hen: Meese	Mr. Robt. Townsend	Thomas Grigg
Majr. Geo: Mason	Mr. Wm. Heabeard	Vincent Young
Capt. Jno. Alexander	Mr. Wm. Greene	David Anderson

The Court is adjourned to the 7th Augt next 1667

439. At a Court held for the County of Stafford the 7th August 1667
                        Colo. John Dodman

Present Lt. Colo. Hen: Meese   Capt. John Alexander
        Majr. Geo: Mason   Mr. Richd. Heabeard   Justices

440. Whereas MARY BAULSON was arested to this Court for severall Debts due
      from her Husband who is now absent out of this County THOMAS HATHAWAY
Attorney of the said Mary did in Court promise to pay the Debts of JOHN BAUL-
SON her said Husband to the value of his Estate being justly made appear
Thomas Hathaway attorney of Mary Baulton wife of John Baulton acknowledged
Judgment to ANDREW WATSON for twelve hundred and thirty five pounds of Tobacco
and cask with charges of Court the having made his Debt justly appear.

Page 80 Court held 7th August 1667

The said Tobacco to be paid the 10th day October next else execution. Thomas
Hathaway attorney of Mary Baulton did acknowledge Judgment to Capt. JOHN
ALEXANDER for one hundred and twenty pounds of Tobacco and cask with charges
of Court to be paid the 10th September next else execution. Thomas Hathaway
attorney of Mary Baulton did acknowledge Judgment to ROBERT RICHARDS' for
Four hundred ninety six pounds of Tobacco and cask with charges of Court he
having made his Debt justly appear the sd Tobacco to be paid the 10th Octr next
else execution.

441. Whereas JOHN JAMES did in behalf of himself and SAMUEL SPOONER petition
      this Court that the share of JOHN BAULTONS crop might be appraised the
Court doth order that JESPER BENNETT and JAMES PRICE appraise the same as well
as the rest of his Estate and it is further ordered that the wife of the said
Baulton have four barrels of corn delivered to her out of her said Husbands
as else a small feather bed and the furniture belonging to it to her only use
else execution. Whereas John James did arest Mary Baulton to this Court & had
noe cause of action the Court doth order that the sd John James be nonsuited
& pay to the sd Mary Baulton fifty pounds of Tobacco & charges of Court the
10th Octr next else execution.

442. The Court doth order that JOHN WISTEN who married the relict of Mr. HUGH
      DONDING deced have administration on the said Estate a pretending Will
being produced and by the Court judged noe Will there being no execution nominated. Mr. HEABEARD decents from this order. The Court doth order that Capt.
JOHN ALEXANDER, JOHN WILLIAMS, OLIVER BALFE and VINCT YOUNG be appraisers of
the said Estate and that Mr. John Wiston bring the Inventory to the next Court.
Mr. WILLIAM HEABEARD & Mr. DAVID ANDERSON became security to Mr. John Wiston
on the Estate of the sd Mr. Hugh Donding deced.

Page 81 Court held 7th August 1667

Capt. JOHN ASHTON did appear the Attorney for Mr. John Wiston. Mr. ANTHONY
BRIDGES Attorney of Mr. ROBERT BUTTERFIELD.

Page 81 (contd)   Court held 7th August 1667

443. Whereas Mr. RICHARD FOSSAKER did arest THOMAS BAREFOOT at the suit of
      the County who did not appear nor baile for him the Court doth therefore
order that if the said Mr. Fossaker bring not the body of the said Barefoot
to the next Court that then order pass against him for damages as shall be made
appear against the said Barefoot and that he pay the order of Court else Execution.

444. SYMN. THOMAS Attorney of HENRY JAQUES. Whereas JOHN CLERK had no cause
      of action against Henry Jaques the Court doth therefore order that the
said John Clerk be nonsuited and pay to the said Henry Jaques fifty pounds of
Tobacco and charges of Court the 10th Octr next else execution.

445. Whereas NICO. BROOKS had no cause of action against JAQUES the Court doth
      therefore order that the said Brookes be nonsuited and pay to the said
Henry Jaques fifty pounds of Tobacco & charges of Court the 10th 8ber next
else execution.

446. Whereas Capt. GILES BRENT had no cause of action against HENRY JAQUES
      the said Capt. Brent be nonsuited and pay the said Henry Jaques 50 pounds
of Tobacco & charges of Court the 10th October next Else Execution not appeare.

447. Whereas JOHN FARBIN did arest ROBERT BUTTERFIELD to this Court and had
      no cause of action the Court doth order that the said Farbin be nonsuited
and pay the said Butterfield or his assigns 50 pounds of Tobacco and charges
of Court the 10th 8ber next Else execution.

448. Whereas ROBERT SAMSON did arest JOSEPH EDMUNDS to this Court and did not
      appear to prosecute his action the Court doth order that the said Ed-
munds fifty pounds of Tobacco and charges of Court the 10th of October next
else Execution.

449. PAUL KATELEECH servant to Lt. Colo. HENRY MEESE was this day brought to
      Court to have his age judged & how long he should serve the Court doth
judge the said servant to be sixteen years of age and to serve according to
Act.

450. GEORGE EARLE servant to Mr. WILLIAM HEABEARD was this day brought to Court
      to have his age judged & how long he should serve

Page 82   Court held 7th August 1667

the Court doth judge the said George Earle to be fourteen years of age and to
serve his said Master according to Act.

451. HENRY CISSEN servant to THOMAS GRIGG was this day brought to Court to
      have his age judged & how long he should serve the Court doth judge the
said servant to be sixteen years of age and to serve according to Act.

452. Whereas Mr. DAVID ANDERSON did obtain an order of this Court for five
      pounds Sterling with damages and costs of suit against Mr. ANTHONY
BRIDGES and Mr. ROBERT TOWNSEND Security for JAMES SUMPNER the Court taking
the same into consideration doth therefore order that the said James Sumpner
forthwith pay unto the said Anthony Bridges and Robert Townsend the said sum
of five pounds Sterling with damages and all charges of Court suffered and
sustained in behalf of the said Sumpner else Execution.

453. Mr. ANTHONY BRIDGES attorney of Mr. WM. HEABEARD. Whereas GERERD MASTERS
      did arest Mr. William Heabeard to this Court and had no cause of action
the Court doth order that the said Masters be nonsuited and pay to the said

443 - 453

Page 82 (contd) Court held 7th August 1667

WILLIAM HEABEARD 50 pounds of Tobacco and charges of Court the 10th Octr next
else Execution.

> The Court adjourned to ye 16th 8ber next
> The Orphants Court to ye 17th ditto

454. At a Court held for Stafford County the 23d 8ber 1667
      Present   Colo. John Dodman

          Lt. Colo. Hen: Meese   Capt. John Alexander   Justices
          Majr. Geo: Mason   Mr. Richd. Heabeard

455. Whereas JOHN AXTON administrator of EDWARD CARRY deced faithfully satis-
      fied and paid all Debts due from the said deceased the Court doth there-
      fore order that the said John Axton have a Quietus est.

456. The Court doth order that Lt. Colo. HENRY MEESE & Majr. GEORGE MASON be
      commissioners concerning

Page 83 Court held 23d 8ber 1667

the fort to meete the Gentlemen of the Assotiation according to Act of Assembly.

457. JOHN ROLT did appear attorney of MARY MILLS. Whereas it doth appear to
      this Court that JOHN MILLS is and stands indebted to Colo. JOHN DODMAN
1000 pounds of Tobacco and cask the Court doth therefore order that the said
Colo. John Dodman have judgment of the said Debt with charges of Court else
execution. John Rolt attorney of Mary Mills did acknowledge judgment in behalf of the said Mary for the payment of 350 pounds of Tobacco to SAMUEL HAY-
WARD with charges of Court forthwith else execution. John Rolt did for and in
behalf and as attorney of Mary Mills acknowledge judgment to Lt. Colo. HENRY
MEESE for 503 pounds of Tobacco and cask with charges of Court to be paid
forthwith else exe. Whereas John Mills hath absented himself out of this County
and that his wife did petition this Court to have the possession of her Husbands
Estate the Court doth order that the said Mary Mills wife of the said John
Mills have according to petition in possessing the Estate of her Husband
aforesaid and give security for the payment of the Debts to the value of the
Estate. The Court doth order WILLIAM GREENE and THOMAS BAXTER view the work
of John Mills now at Mr. FRANCIS HALES plantation.

458. The Court doth order that WILLIAM GREENE concerning the entertainment of
      Indians be reversed and that Liberty be given to all Persons as in other
places according to Act of Assembly.

459. THOMS. HATHAWAY did this day appear the attorney of FRANCIS RAWSON:/:
      Whereas the Courts of Rapahanock and Westmoreland hath appointed to bound
the counties The Court doth appoynt and impower Capt. JOHN ALEXANDER and Mr.
RICHD. HEABEARD to meete with the Gentlemen appoynted by the said counties to
conclude concerning the bounds by this and the other counties.

460. JOHN REYNOLDS servant to Capt. JOHN ALEXANDER was by this Court judged
      to be seventeen years of age & ordered to serve according to

Page 84 Court held 23d 8ber 1667

Act of Assembly and the court doth further order that the former order in June
last concerning the said Reynolds be voyd in regard Judgment was given according
to Act of Assembly then repealed.

Page 84 (contd)   Court held 23d 8ber 1667

461. JOHN ROLT attorney of MARY MILLS did acknowledge Judgment to Capt. JOHN
      ALEXANDER for 351 pounds of Tobacco and cask with charges of Court forth-
with else Execution.

462. Whereas it doth appear to this Court that THOMAS BAREFOOT is and stands
      indebted to SAMUEL HAYWARD 195 pounds Tobacco as per the ballance of an
account on record plainly sheweth the Court doth therefore order that the said
Samuel Hayward have Judgment against the Estate of the said Barefoot for the
said Debt with charges of Court forthwith else execution Provided that no attorney appear which if they doe then this order to be void and the said Hayward
to prosecute the said attorney for the said Debt.

463. Whereas Colo. JOHN DODMAN did petition this Court that he might Imploy
      an Indian the Court doth order that he have according to his Petition
and that the said Colo Dodman proceed therein according to Act of Assembly
in that case provided.

464. Whereas Lt. Colo. HENRY MEESE did petition this Court that he might imploy
      an Indian the Court doth order that he have according to his Petition and
that the said Colo. Meese proceed therein according to Act of Assembly in that
case provided.

465. Whereas Mr. RICHARD HEABEARD did petition this Court that he might Imploy
      an Indian the Court doth order that he have according to his Petition
and that the said Mr. Heabeard proceed therein according to Act of Assembly
in that case provided.

Page 85 Court held 23d 8ber 1667

466. Whereas it doth appear to this Court that CHARLES RANGER who hath absented
      himself out of this County is and stands indebted to SAMUEL HAYWARD 75
pounds of Tobacco for fees the Court doth therefore order that the said Samuel
Hayward have Judgment against the Estate of the said Charles Ranger being in
the possession of Mr. JAMES CLIFTON for the said sum of 75 pounds of Tobacco
with charges of Court forthwith else execution.

467. Capt. GILES BRENT Attorney of Mr. CLIFTON. Whereas Mr. JAMES CLIFTON
      hath made oath that CHARLES RANGER is and stands indebted to him 1447
pounds of Tobacco as by an account on record may in perticulers appear the said
Ranger being absent out of this County the Court doth therefore order that the
said Mr. James Clifton have Judgment against the Estate of the said Ranger
for the payment of the said Debt with charges of Court (which estate was attached by the said Mr. Clifton) forthwith else execution. JOHN MASSEY and JOHN
MATHER are ordered 60 pounds of Tobo apeace from Mr. Clifton for attendance
with charges of Court forthwith else execution. Whereas it doth appear to
this Court that Charles Ranger stands indebted to FRANCIS RAWSON 400 pounds of
Tobacco and cask by Bill the Court doth therefore order that the said Francis
Rawson have judgment against the Estate of the said Ranger for the said Debt
with charges of Court forthwith else execution.

468. Capt. JOHN ASHTON was by this Court appoynted to View the accounts of
      Capt JOHN ALEXANDER and Mr. ROBERT TOWNSEND and deliver the Ballance
thereof into the Court. Whereas it doth appear to this Court that Mr. Robert
Townsend is and stands indebted on the Ballance of an account unto Capt. John
Alexander 1009 pounds of Tobacco and cask the Court doth therefore order that
the said Mr. Townsend forthwith pay unto the said Capt. Alexander

461 - 468

Page 86   Court held 23d 8ber 1667

the said 1009 pounds of Tobacco and that upon the payment of the said Tobacco they give to each other full and lawfull discharges and pay their own charges of Court else execution.

469.   Whereas Mr. ROBERT TOWNSEND was the last year fined 300 pounds of Tobacco the Court doth order that in Regard they were then misinformed the said fine being now remitted and deducted out of the account of Capt. JOHN ALEXANDER who received the said fine forthwith else execution.

470.   Whereas JOHN COLE and WILLIAM BALL were supen'd by this Court by order of JOHN NEWTON the Court doth order that the said Newton pay unto them 60 pounds of Tobacco apeace for their attendance with charges of Court forthwith else exe.

471.   Whereas it doth appear to this Court that JOHN HALL stands indebted to Mr. ROBERT TOWNSEND 1262 pounds of Tobacco and cask the said Hall being absent out of this County the Court doth therefore order that the said Townsend have Judgment against the Estate of the said Hall for the sd sum of 1262 pounds of Tobacco and cask with charges of Court forthwith else execution.

472.   Capt. JOHN ASHTON attorney of JOHN MATHEWS.

473.   Whereas it doth appear to this Court by three depositions that JOHN NEW-TON did bring Indentures into this Country for four years and hath served Mr. HUGH DONDING deced the said term the Court doth therefore order that the said John Newton be from this day free and that Mr. JOHN WHISTON administrator of Mr. Hugh Donding Deced did not Inventory the whole Estate of

Page 87   Court held 23d 8ber 1667

said deceased the Court doth order that the residue thereof be Inventoryed and apraised and brought to the next Court Except cattle which shall be Inventoryed but not appraised but devided according to Law the said Mr. Donding not dying in debt.

474.   The Court doth order that for the year ensueing WILLIAM BEACH be Surveyor of the High Ways from the frontiere Westmoreland down to the head and ferry at Aquia and that Mr. MICHL. HILL and JOHN MASSEY be Surveyors of the High Ways from thence to the ferry and head of Potomack Creek and that they clear the Ways to the Ferry and only make the Ways to the heads of the Creeks where the most convenient Passage is and that Mr. WILLIAM HEABEARD for Derection in making the outward way and clearing the road from the said Ferry to the Courthouse to the Horse Bridge and take warrants from Capt. JOHN ALEXANDER for help therein and that CHRISTOPHER LUND be Surveyor from the Plantation of Mr. RICHARD HOPE to the ferry at Potomack.

475.   Whereas there is noe certain place in the upper presincts of this County for the reading of Deume Service the Court doth order that JOHN WITHERS Churchwarden for these presincts agree for a House to Read in at the most convenient place.

476.   EDWARD ROGERS did in Court oblige himself to begin to Build a bridge and to finish the same with what Expidition may be over Pasbitansy Creek according to the Agreement made with Mr. RICHARD HEABEARD And the Court doth hereby impower the said Rogers to take the timber to build the said Bridge off from the land of Mr. TRAVERSE and that he have sufficient help to bring the timber in place.

477.   Whereas sufficient notice hath ben given to ye Inhabitants

Page 88   Court held 23d 8ber 1667

of this County to bring in a list of Tithables of their Families to the
respective Justices and forasmuch as JONAS REVETT, JOHN GILES, JOHN WILLIAMS,
WOLSTD. NORWOOD, THOMAS MOSS, JOHN BUCKNER, THOMAS DUTTON, THOMAS SHARP, JOSP.
EDMUNDS. ROBERT STREET, JOHN BUTLER, DIXY WARD, RICHARD AYLIFFE, ROBERT HOWSON,
ROBERT KING, ROBERT POTTER, JOHN AXTON, WILLIAM NORTHALL and VINCENT YOUNG
did neglect to bring in their lists as aforesaid the Court taking into consideration the trouble and care JOHN CLERK hath had in taking the list and the great
damage that they and every one of them would have sustained if the Law had ben
fully executed doe hereby order and it is accordingly ordered that they and
every one of them forthwith pay the said John Clerk fifty pounds of Tobacco
with charges of Court to be Levyed by the High Sheriff and that upon default
of payment he make distress.

478.   Judgment granted against BAREFOOT for the counties work.

       The Court is adjourned till the 11th of December next

479.   At a Court held for Stafford County the 11th of December 1667
       Present   Colo. John Dodman

          Lt. Colo. Hen: Meese   Capt. John Alexander
          Majr. Geo. Mason   Mr. Richd. Heabeard   Justices

Page 89   Court held 11th December 1667

480.   The Court doth order that a Refferance be granted to JOHN ROLT in the
       case depending between him and Mrs. FRANCES WILLIAMS untill the next
Court.

481.   Whereas Capt. GILES BRENT did arest JOSEPH EDMUNDS to this Court in an
       action of the case and forasmuch as the attorney of the said Capt. Brent
did deny to take the Oath of Allegiance and Supremice being thereunto required
the Court doth therefore order that the said Capt. Giles Brent be nonsuited
and pay to the said Joseph Edmunds fifty pounds of Tobacco with charges of
Court forthwith else execution.

482.   Whereas Capt. PETER ASHTON, Capt. JOHN ALEXANDER, Mr. WILLIAM HORTON
       and ROBERT STREETE did petition this Court that having a parcel of land
bounded on the land of Mr. ROBERT HOWSON who claimeth more land then his Just
due whereby he deprives the persons aforesaid of part of their lands and also
obstructs the division of the same the Court taking the same into consideration
doe order that Mr. JAMES HAYLAND Survey the land of the said Howson according
to Petition of the parties aforesaid.

483.   The Court doth order that a Refference be granted in the cause depending
       between LEWIS MARKHAM and Mr. JOHN WHISTON.

484.   Whereas Lt. Colo. HENRY MEESE did arest GARARD MASTERS to this Court for
       1200 pounds of Tobacco and cask the said Masters to the intent that so
Just a Debt might be satisfied and paid did in Court promise on Demand to pay
the said Lt. Colo. Henry Meese the said sum of 1200 pounds of Tobacco and cask
which Tobacco is already Stript but not Packt for want of the said cask and
did further declare and acknowledge the Tobacco already stript as aforesd to
be and belonging to and as the Person all Estate of the said Colo.

Page 90   Court held 11th December 1667

Meese and to no other person whatsoever and further that he will pack the said
Tobacco for the said Colo. Meese.

478 - 484

Page 90 (contd) Court held 11th December 1667

485. The Court doth order that a Refference be granted untill the next Court
      in the cause depending between Capt. GILES BRENT and THOMAS HEALING.

486. Whereas it doth appear to this Court that WILLIAM BEACH stands indebted
      to JOSEPH EDMUNDS 1241 pounds of Tobacco and cask by Bill the Court doth
therefore order that the said Wm. Beach forthwith pay unto the said JOHN
EDMUNDS (sic) the said sum of 1241 pounds Tobacco and cask with costs of suit
else Execution.

487. Whereas it doth appear to this Court that WM. FISHER stands indebted to
      MORGAN JONES 5390 pounds of Tobacco and cask by Bill the Court doth
therefore order that the said William Fisher forthwith pay unto JOHN MATHEWS
Attorney of the said Morgan Jones the said sum of 5390 pounds of Tobacco and
cask with charges of Court else Execution.

488. Whereas it doth appear to this Court that JOHN HAYLE is and stands indebted
      to Capt. GILES BRENT 492 pounds of Tobacco and cask the Court doth there-
fore order that the said Hale forthwith pay unto the said Capt. Brent the sd
Debt with costs of suit else execution.

489. GERRARD MASTERS did this day in Court confess Judgment to JOSEPH EDMUNDS
      for 1117 pounds of Tobacco and Cask due by Bill to be paid forthwith else
execution.

490. Whereas it doth appear to this Court that CHARLES WOOD is and stands in-
      debted to JOSEPH EDMUNDS 609 pounds of Tobacco and cask

Page 91 Court held 11th December 1667

by Bill the Court doth therefore order that the said Charles Wood forthwith
pay to the said Edmunds the said Debt with costs of suit else Execution.

491. MICHAEL PICKERNELL did in Court acknowledge Judgment to Mr. JOHN SAMWAIES
      for 400 pounds of Tobacco and cask due by Bill to be paid forthwith with
charges of Court else Execution.

492. Whereas it doth appear to this Court that HUMPHREY BAILY is and stands
      indebted unto JOSEPH EDMUNDS 1725 pounds of Tobacco and cask by Bill the
Court doth therefore order that the said Baly forthwith pay to the said Debt
to the said Joseph Edmunds with charges of Court else execution. Whereas it
doth appear to this Court that HUMPHREY BAILY is and stands indebted to JOHN
CLERK 430 pounds of Tobacco and cask by Bill the Court doth therefore order
between JOHN KEECH and JOHN ROLT (sic).

493. Whereas it doth appear to this Court that JOHN ANCRAM is and stands in-
      debted to GEORGE BILLOPS 305 pounds of Tobacco and cask the Court doth
therefore order that the said Ancram pay unto JOHN COLCLOUGH Attorney of the
said Billops the said sum of 305 pounds of Tobacco and cask with costs of suit
forthwith else execution.

494. Whereas Mr. ROBERT TOWNSEND did present GEORGE GLASS for committing for-
      nication which the said Glass did confess the Court doth therefore order
that for his said offence he have forty nine lashes or fifty lashes.

Page 92 Court held 11th December 1667

495. The Court doth order that JOHN ANCRAM pay unto JOHN COURTNEY and JOHN
      JAMES 40 pounds Tobacco apeace for attendance on the Court with charges
forthwith else execution.

Page 92 (contd)   Court held 11th December 1667

496.   Whereas Capt. JOHN ALEXANDER did upon his Positice Oath formerly taken
       in Court obtained a Judgment against Mr. ROBERT TOWNSEND for Eighteen
hundred and eighty nine pounds of Tobacco and cask forthwith else execution.
Capt. John Alexander doth appeale to the sixth day of the next General Court
to be held at James City the Right Honble Governor and Honble Councill. Mr.
RICHARD HEABEARD became Security with Capt. Alexander for Prosecuting the appeale. Colo. JOHN DODMAN became Security with Mr. Townsend to answer the appeale. Mr. JAMES HAYLORD did appear Attorney of Capt. John Alexander. Whereas
Capt. John Alexander did the last Court bring in an account against Mr. Robert
Townsend the ballance whereof only remain upon record the Court doth therefore
order that the said Capt. Alexander deliver the account formerly brought in as
aforesaid into the Clerk who is hereby required carefully to record the same.

Page 93   Court held 11th December 1667

497.   Whereas ANDREW WATSON who married the Relict and Execution of ROBERT
       MAPHEE deced hath fully paid all debts due from the Estate of the sd
deced the Court doth order that he have his Quietus est and that all bonds concerning the same be conselled.

498.   Whereas ROBT. KING hath made sufficient proofe of the transportation of
       five persons into this Colony certification is therefore granted to the
said King for 205 acres of land: WILLIAM KING, ELIZA. KING, JOHN NIBBS, EDWD.
MILLS, ROBT. JONES.

499.   Certificate is granted to WILLIAM BEACH for 350 acres of land by and for
       the transportation of seven persons into this Colony (Vizt) RICD. HATLOFFT,
WM. BEACH, JOHN WINCHCOM, JONAS BROWN, GILES CLERK, WALTER HARVEY, WILLIAM
ALLEN.

       The Court adjourned till the last Wednesday in January next

500.   At a Court held for the County of Stafford the 29th of January 1667/8

       Present Colo. John Dodman   Majr. George Mason
              Lt. Colo. Hen: Meese   Mr. Robt. Townsend   Justices
              Mr. Richd. Heabeard   Mr. Robt. Howson

501.   Whereas JOSEPH EDMUNDS did the last Court obtain a Judgment against Mr.
       JAMES CLIFTON for the payment of Eight hundred pounds of Tobacco and cask
and forasmuch as it doth appear that the said debt is

Page 94   Court held 29th January 1667/8

not due till the year ensueing (Vizt) 1668 the Court taking the same into consideration doe order that the said Edmunds pay the former charges of Court and
that Mr. JAMES CLIFTON forthwith give good security to the said Edmunds for the
true payment of the said Debt when due as aforesaid with the present charges
of this Court else execution.

502.   JOHN ROLT did in Court acknowledge Judgment to Mrs. FRANCES WILLIAMS for
       600 pounds of Tobacco and cask to be paid forthwith with charges of Court
else execution.

503.   Whereas NICO. BRULY did attend and administer Phisick to Mr. HUGH DONDING
       deced the Court doth order that Mr. JOHN WHISTON administrator of the said
Donding Estate pay unto LEWIS MARKHAM who married the Relict of the said Bruly
200 pounds of Tobacco and cask forthwith else execution.

504. The Court doth order that Colo. JOHN DODMAN have Judgment against JOHN
        MATHEWS for 7714 pounds of Tobacco and cask being justly due by Bill to
be paid forthwith charges of Court else execution.

505. EDWARD HUMSTON attorney of ABRAM FLOOD.

506. Whereas it doth appear to this Court that WILLIAM BOURNE is and stands
        indebted unto ROBERT RICHARDS five barrells of Indian corne by Bill the
Court doth therefore order that the said Bourne forthwith bring & deliver the
said five barrells of Corn into the Loft of the sd Richards accordg to ye
specialty and pay charges of Court else execution.

    The Stafford County Order Book 27th May 1664/29th January 1667/8
    ends with the above entry. The material was taken from photostat
    copies and not the original book.

Page 1   At a Court held for Stafford County December the 11th 1689

507.   Present Coll. William Fitzhugh
            Capt. Geo. Mason, Mr. William Buckner, Mr. Edwd. Thomason,
        Mr. Mathew Thompson Justices

508.   RICHARD AYLIFF complaining sheweth that RICHD. HOOD late of this County
        stood indebted to him the sum Six hundred and ninety three pounds of
Tobacco ..

509.   MARTIN SCARLET complaining sheweth that JOHN BASFORD of this County stood
        indebted to him the sum of Sixteen hundred pounds of Tobacco in cask ..

510.   ROBERT BRENT complaining sheweth that RICHARD NIXON late of this County
        stood indebted to him Fifteen hundred and thirty five pounds of Tobacco ..

511.   Whereas SIMON STACEY made humble petition to this Court that ROBT.
        PENNEWALL of this County stood indebted to him sume of one thousand pounds
of Tobacco ..

Page 2   Court held 11th December 1689

512.   WM. BUNBURY the Attorney of EDWARD SMITH complaining sheweth that JOHN
        FOWKE late of this County stood indebted to him the sum of Four hundred
and fourteen pounds Tobacco in cask ..

513.   ROBT. STREET complaining sheweth that RICHARD CHAPMAN stands indebted to
        him the sum of four hundred pounds of Tobacco in cask ..

514.   Upon motion made to this Court by Capt. GEORGE BRENT with ack of directions
        from the Society of Surveyors concerning the land of Capt. WILLIAM DOWNHAM
& EDWARD WHEELER It is considered by this Court that the said Capt. Downham
Pattent is Independent of itself by reason of the last clause in the pattent
mentioned Vizt For the transportation of servants into this Colony according
to Law and that the aforsd Capt. Brent is ordered by this Court to proceed in
the Survey of Wilkensons pattent according to the directions of the Surveyors
afsd sent to this Court.

515.   Capt. GEORGE BRENT Atturney of JOHN RAYLEY complaineth against DAVID
        DARNELL .. indebted in the sum of four hundred pounds of Tobacco due by
Bill ..

Page 3   At a Court held for the County of Stafford Xbr 12th Anno 1689

516.   Present Colo. William Fitzhugh, Mr. Saml. Hayward, Capt. George
            Mason, Mr. Edward Thomason, Mr. John Withers, Mr. William Buckner,
            Mr. Matthew Thompson Justices

517.   WILLIAM BARTON son of NATHAN BARTON of this County late deced made peti-
        tion to this Court that FFRANCIS HAMMERSLEY detains and keeps from him
his two Brothers and one Sister Orphans of the said Nathan Barton deced under a
specious pretense that the said orphans was left to his care and Tuition from
their deced Father and seeing that the said ffrancis Hammersley is a Roman
Catholic he doubts that the said Orphans may be brought up by him in the
Roman religion he therefore prays that the said orphans may be delivered from
the said Fras. Hammersley into his care and tuition or that the said boys be

507 - 517

Page 3 (contd)   Court held Xbr 12th Anno 1689

bound out to some Trade according to Law in such cases hath provided concerning orphans And the Court having Throughly considered the premises doe accordingly order therefore tis ordered that NATHAN BARTON the oldest of the two boys orphans to Nathan Barton deceased shall remain in the custody of AUGUSTINE KNEATON until the next Court that he may then be by the Court bound out to the afsd Kneaton or some other good trade and that THOMAS the Younger son of Nathan Barton shall remain in the custody of Majr. ANDREW GILSON until the next Court to be bound out to him or some other Trade according to Law and that WILLIAM BARTON the Petr as afsd shall have the tuition of his Sister MARTHA the other orphan she being to be delivered from Mr. Fras. Hammersley as afsd William Barton paying the costs.

518.   DANIEL HANKEN came into Court and confessed Judgment unto JOSHUA DAVIS
       the attorney of JOHN MINOR for Four hundred pounds of Tobacco due to the
said John Minor by Bill under hand and seale ..

519.   JAMES WANSTLEY by SAMSON DARRELL his Attorney complaining sheweth that
       ye petr by Indenture out of England for the Form of four years next after
his arrival in this country by virtue whereof was sold and assigned unto MATHEW THOMPSON of this County which said Forme ye petr hath faithfully and honestly served and compleated without any Exceptions as he humbly conceives but forasmuch as your petrs said Master did some small time a month or thereabouts before the Expiration of your petrs first indented time did Strenously and Surprizingly make and contrive an Instrument of Writing or rather an article of one part as your petr since conceives by virtue whereof your Petrs said Master doth demand two years service more and whereas your Petr was by the rigid and awful command of his said Master Tempted and as he conceives decoyed into such Service and that as your Petr humbly conceives such Irregular proceedings and contracts between Masters and Servants to be fully against an Act of Assembly in such cases provided for which reason your petitioner humbly begs your worships charitable discharge against such fraudulent Service or that your worships will upon good security given by ye Petitioner may have equal pleading to answer the Suite that may be brought against him by his said Master And the Court having duly and throughly considered the Premises and after many arguments held on both sides the Court finding that the afsd Wanstley Indenture or Articles of Agreement made betwixt him and his

Page 4   Court held Xber 12th Anno 1689

said Master Matthew Thompson as afsd is firme and good in Law by being made in such forme as the Law directs Therefore its ordered that the said James Wanstley shall returne home to his afsd Master and shall serve out the time accordingly therein specified by the aforementioned Indenture.

520.   Upon complaint made to this Court by WILLIAM WILLIAMS that one JOHN HAR-
       PER doth unlawfully unjustly and without any the leave and Lycence of
him the said William Williams Inhabit and live upon his plantation having no right or just reasons to show for the same And the Court having throughly con sidered of the matter doe accordingly order therefore tis ordered ROBERT COLSON the Deputy Sheriff shall presently goe to the aforesaid Plantation of the aforesaid William Williams and remove the aforesaid John Harper from the aforementioned plantation without he can show any just and lawful reasons for his abiding there.

Page 4 (contd)   Court held Xber 12th Anno 1689

521.   THOS. WHICKERS and GEORGE PILLERS by Capt. GEORGE BRENT their attorney
        humbly sheweth that ye Petrs being in England their native country about
the 29th of September 1685 at the town of Topsham in the county of Devon and
minding to transport themselves into Virginia did then and there agree with
JOHN LYLE Transportation clothing and so forth did indent each respectively
with the said John Lyle to serve him or his assigns after the arrival in Virginia four years which said reciprocal Indentures were sealed and Executed before and attested by WILLIAM GLYDE Esqr. a Justice of the Peace of the Town of
Topsham and afterwards your Petrs came into Virginia in Capt. WALTER LYLES ship
and their Master John Lyle after their arrival which was the first day of December 1685 sold them to RICHARD AYLIFFE with whom they have duly served ever
since and showed their Indentures to divers people which they safely kept until
about 3 or 4 months since they were taken out of the room where they lodged by
some Sinister practise which the said Ayliffe refuseth to discharge your Petrs
or to pay them their corn and cloaths wherefore they have brought their humble
complaint to your worships and doe most humbly pray that their witnesses may be
sworne to prove their Indenture that they may be discharged from their service
and the said Ayliffe may be ordered to pay your Petrs their corn and clothes
together with such costs as they shall be out to the Clerke for the said Order
And now forasmuch as the said Thomas Whickers and George Pillers did in Court
prove by the oaths of two sufficient Evidences upon the holy Evangelist of
almighty God that they had each of them respectively lawful and authentick
Indentures for four years time as aforesaid Therefore tis ordered that the said
THOMAS WHICKERS and GEORGE PYLLER of and from Richard Ayliffe their Master
shall be free and that the said Richard Ayliffe shall pay each of them their
corn and clothes with all country dues respectively with all costs als Execution.

522.   EDWARD WATTS in propria persona came into Court and confessed Judgment
        unto JOHN WITHERS Attorney of ROBERT HEWET for Four hundred and fifty
pounds of Tobacco ..

Page 5   Court held Xber 12th Anno 1689

523.   JOHN ATTERTON came into Court and confessed Judgment unto JOSHUA DAVIS
        for Thirteen hundred and sixteen pounds of Tobacco ..

524.   MARY MASSEY the Widow and Executrix of Capt. ROBERT MASSEY deced complaining
        sheweth that Major ANDREW GILSON stands indebted to the Plt in the sum
of Fifteen thousand and ninety three pounds of Tobacco in cask due to her the
said Plt by Bill and account .. And the said Major Andrew Gilson the Deft came
here in Court and legally discounted the sum of Five thousand three hundred and
thirty one pounds of Tobacco out of the foresaid sum in the declaration prayed
for Therefore tis ordered that the said Major Andrew Gilson shall make present
payment of the sum of Nine thousand seven hundred and sixty two pounds of Tobacco in cask unto the said Mary Massey ..

525.   JOHN WILLIAMS complaineth against RICHARD GIBSON for that that is to say
        that he stands indebted to the Plt the sum of Four thousand six hundred
and two pounds of Toba .. which the Deft refuses to pay or come to account
altho often demanded and required fairly to come to account ..

526.   Capt. GEO. BRENT complaineth against JOHN WILLIAMS for that that is to
        say he stands indebted to the Plt in the sum of One thousand and seventy
pounds of Tobacco in cask ..

521 - 526

527.   GEORGE LUKE who married the widow and administratrix of Doctr. RALPH
       SMITH late of this County deced came into Court and confessed Judgment
unto JOHN NEWTON for Three hundred and seventy pounds of Tobacco due to him by
account ..

528.   JOHN JONES of Westmoreland County complaineth against GEORGE KING of this
       County for that he the said George King on or about the 16th of January
last past did take up and ride a horse of your Petrs without the licence leave
or consent of your Petr for his so doeing and the said horse hath soe abused
that he is not Serviceable to your Petr whereby he is damnified and hath damage
to the value of Four thousand pounds of Tobacco Wherefore he hath brought his
action against George King .. George King by RICHARD GIBSON his attorney came
into Court and pleaded to the declaration laid against him not guilty and for
Tryal puts himself upon the Country and the Plt likewise. Therefore tis ordered
that the Jury Enquire the Fact. Capt. WILLIAM DOWNING, AUGUSTINE KNEATON,
WILLIAM PERKINS, WILLIAM TODD, WILLM. HAMBLETON, WILLIAM SMITH, JAMES MONKE,
JOHN CARR, THOMAS MOSS, GEORGE LYLES, SIGISMUND MASSEY, PATRICK HUMES which
said Jurors Elected Tryed and Sworne doe say upon their Oaths we find for the
Defendant noe cause of action. Therefore tis ordered Judgment be entered on
the Verdict of the Jury that the said John Jones shall be nonsuited and shall
pay unto the said George King fifty pounds of Tobacco with all costs als Exe-
cution. Ordered George King pay the Jury 72 pounds Tobacco. Ordered that
George King shall make present payment unto JOHN BREWTON, WILLIAM COCKE and
JOHN JACKSON Eighty pounds of Tobacco apeace for their attendance in Court
Two daies ..

529.   EDWARD FORD made humble petition that he being ordered to give bond for
       his good behaviour he performed the same and having as he humbly hopes
civilly and peaceably behaved himself towards their Majesties and all their
Subjects he humbly prays to have his bond delivered up and cancelled .. tis
ordered by this Court that the said Edward Ford from his bond and security
given for his good behaviour shall be free and that the said bond be delivered
up and cancelled he paying this costs als Execution.

530.   JOHN HALEY humbly complaining sheweth and your daily orator that some
       time in October last your Orator coming to the house of JOSEPH EYRES in
this County and there after some discourses the said Eyres did offer to Employ
him to maul Rayles and other work and did make many fine promises and protes-
tations honestly to satisfie your Orator which fair and feigned words did the
more Enduce your Orator to believe him and so to enter upon the said worke as
also to do any other matter the said Eyres did desire him after which upon further faire words the said Eyres did offer to Seate

your Orator upon a plantation and build him a house and give him a good authentick lease with warranty for which your Orator was to give him a mare Now so
it is that the said Eyres intend wholly to deceive your Orator having not really
any such plantation to let after he had taken your Orators mare from him which
now he withholds and keeps and did use your Orator very unworthily threatning
to have him whipt out of the parish not allowing him one farthing for his worke
and also detains the said mare and your Orator being by the Strict rules of the
Common Law debarred of any satisfaction in the premises humbly desires relief
in this Equitable Court of Chancery according to the merits of his case as in
your worships wise Judgment shall seeme most agreeable to Equity and good con-

Page 7 (contd)   Court held Xber 12th Anno 1689

science and the said JOSEPH EYRES by GERRARD LOWTHER his Attorney comes in
Court —nd craves respite until the next Court for to bring in his answer to
this Bill of JOHN HALEY in chancery against him which unto him is granted.

531.   RICHARD GIBSON complaining sheweth that ANTHONY BATTALIA did binde and
        oblige himself to the Plt to fall maul and cut of one thousand Rayles be-
tween the 9th of May 1687 and the last of October last past for the Plts use
which if he failed to doe he would pay your Petr Five hundred pounds Tobacco
and for which he hath given his warrant of attorney to confess a Judgment in
this Court now soe it is the said Battalia hath not performed his said Bargaine
to the Plts great damage Wherefore he craves Judgment for the said Five hundred
pounds of Tobacco against the said Battalia with costs and the said Anthony
Battalia came here in Court in propria persona and legally proved that he had
felld mauld and cut Seven hundred Rayles of the afsd One thousand in the declaration prayed for so that there appears to be due to the afsd Richard Gibson
the Plt only three hundred rayles out of the afsd sume Therefore tis ordered
that the said Anthony Battalia shall presently go and maul for the aforesaid
Richard Gibson the Plt Three hundred good sound and strong rails according to
his former agreement and each party to pay costs als execution.

532.   Ordered that JOHN PEAKE SENIOR shall make payment of One hundred and
        twenty pounds of Tobacco unto JOSEPH HINSON and THOMAS CHAPMAN for their
attendance in Court three days in a Sute depending between him and DANIEL
MERRIT with costs alias execution.

533.   GEORGE LUKE who married the widow and admx of Doct. RALPH SMITH late of
        this County deced came into Court and confessed Judgment to JOHN WYTHERS
for the sum of Two pounds nine shillings sterling .. Luke to pay being the ballance of all accounts between them ..

534.   Ordered by this Court that DANIEL JEFCOAT of this County shall presently
        pay One thousand pounds of Tobacco for the upper parish of this County
for his fine according to Act of Assembly for his committing Fornication with
SUSANNA SWAN and having one child by her and that the said Susanna Swan be
taken by the Sheriff or her Secty to be brought to the next Court it to save
the parish harmless alias execution.

535.   Ordered that the Sheriff bring the body of RICHARD MILDMAY unto the next
        Court to answer the complaint of JONATHAN WHITALL or else be lyable ac-
cording to Act of Assembly and pay costs.

Page 8   Court held Xber 12th Anno 1689

Attachment according to Act of Assembly is granted the Sheriff against the Estate of Richard Mildmay for his nonappearance at this Sute of Jonathan Whitall
with costs.

536.   Ordered that the Sheriff bring the body of JOHN DAVIES unto the next
        Court to answer the complaint of AUGUSTINE KNEATON or else be Lydble
according to Act of Assembly and pay costs.   Attachment according to Act of
Assembly is granted to the Sheriff against the Estate of John~Davis for his
nonappearance at the suit of Augustine Kneaton with costs.

537.   SYMON THOMAS made humble petition to this Court that he hath been a long
        liver in this County which is very well known by some of your worships
and now is not able to doe that Labour which he was wont to doe by reason of
his age Therefore prays that he may be discharged from paying any further levys
or publick duties in this County And the Court throughly considering the pre-

Page 8 (contd)   Court held Xber 12th Anno 1689

mises and taking it unto their charitable and favourable consideration did
accordingly order Therefore tis ordered that the said Simon Thomas shall be
freely and fully discharged from paying any further Levys or publick duties he
paying this costs.

538.   RALPH ELKIN made humble petition to this Court that he hath been a long
       time liver in this County and is now sick and weake and past his Labour
Wherefore he humbly prays that he may be discharged from paying any further
levys or publick duties in this County And the Court throughly considering the
premises and taking it unto their charitable and favourable consideration did
accordingly order Therefore tis ordered that the said Ralph Elkin shall be
freely and fully discharged from paying any further Levys or publick duties he
paying this costs.

539.   JOHN PEAKE SENR. humbly complaining sheweth that your Petr had Judgment
       against THOMAS SHAW of this County for Three thousand and three hundred
pounds of Tobacco and caske which Judgment was date the 9th of February anno
1687/8 at which time the said Shaw did by many fair and large specious pretenses
insinuate to this Worshipful Court the hard measure he had by that Judgment
being only security for another man and so prayed for a Cossat Execution till
March Court following in which time he did not doubt to bring the principal
Vizt. MARTIN BEACH mentioned in the said order to pay the Debt to your Petr
and for which he became bound which false pretensions which was on purpose to
deceive your Petr and to abuse this Worshipful Court favour unto him in stop
of that Execution as shall be fully made appear for the Interim between the
date of the said Judgment and the Cossat Execution he the said Shaw did not
only absent himself and run away out of this County amingly to Evade payment
of the said Debt but did Immediately Endeavor to convey his Estate away alsoe
unto the County of Rappahannock near adjacent to Potomack Creek where the said
Shaw at the time of the said Judgment then lived to effect which designe and
to defraud your Petr as afsd one DANIEL MERRIOTT a dweller in Rappa County in
combination with the said Shaw did at several times and in the night drive and
carry away into the county of Rappa and out of the Jurisdiction of this Court
all the said Shaws Estate Vizt. 3 cows 2 cow calfes and a heifer of three years
old & other things belonging to the said Shaw by means whereof your Petr is
defrauded

Page 9   Court held Xber 12th anno 1689

of his said Debt and hath therefore brought his action against the said Merriott
for unlawful carrying away the said cattle and the rest of the Estate aforesaid
and prays for Judgment for his aforesaid Debt of Three thousand three hundred
pounds of Tobacco and caske with damages sustained for want of the said cattle
at least one thousand pounds of Tobacco with costs of Suit And the said Daniel
Merriott comes into Court and defends the force and injury and put in plea ..
not guilty in manner and form aforesaid And now forsomuch as it does appear to
this Court by the Oaths of 2 Lawful and sufficient men .. did depose in Court
that the said Merriott had the said cattle of the aforesaid Shaw in his possession in Rappahannock County as aforesaid Therefore tis ordered that the said
John Peake the Plt shall have Judgment against the said Daniel Merriott for the
aforesaid 3 cows 2 calves and a heifer of 3 years old with all costs.

540.   Ordered that the Sheriff do make choice of and summon Twenty four able
       men of his Bayliwick to be of the grand jury of this County and every of
them soe summoned as aforesaid shall make their personal appearance at the

538 - 540

Page 9 (contd)   Court held Xber 12th anno 1689

Court the next Court to be held in March for this County then and there to take
their Oaths accordingly that thereupon the grand jury for the time being may be
discharged and that the said grand jury be then and there present with their
presentments.

541. DAVID DARNELL made humble petition to this Court that he being bound in
        bonde with security for his good behaviour towards their Majesties and
all their Liege Subjects and he hath as he hopes civilly and peaceably behaved
himself .. may have his bond delivered up .. and whereas MATTHEW THOMPSON one
of their Majesties Justices of this County did here in Court maintain and justifie that the said David Darnell is a man of a wicked Lewd life and conversa-
tion and one that doth not a bear himself towards their Majesties and Liege
Subjects Therefore tis ordered that David Darnell continue bounde in bonde
with good & honest security for his good behaviour until he bring good proof
and honest reasons of his civil behaviour unto this Court ..

542. Capt. GEORGE BRENT did appear in Court the Atturney of JOHN RAYLEY.
        DAVID DARNELL of MATHEW THOMPSON ats of JAMES WINSTANLEY for THOMAS
WHICKERS and GEORGE PILLARS. RICHARD AYLIFF for JOHN JONES. GEORGE KING for
RICHARD RICHIE ats GIBSON for WILLIAM BOWRNE ats Mr. Gibson for AUGUST KNEATON
JOHN DAVIS for JOHN PEAKE SENR.

543. Mr. GERRARD LOWTHER did appear in this Court the Atturney of BURR HARRI-
        SON ats ROBERT BRENT for CHARLES BALDRIDGE in the three actions ats WM.
LOXHAM. Mr. RICHARD GIBSON did appear in this Court the Atturney of DAVID
DARNELL ats JOHN RAYLEY of Mr. MATHEW THOMPSON ats JAMES WINSTANLEY of GEORGE
KING ats JOHN JONES of JOHN JEANES ats Capt. BRENT of JOHN PEAKE DANIEL MERRIOTT.
Mr. ROBERT BRENT did appear in this Court atty of FRANCIS HAMMERSLEY abt
NATHAN BARTONS orphans of JONATHAN WHITALL and RICHARD MILDMAY. SAMPSON DARRELL
did appear in this Court the Atturney of JAMES WINSTANLEY Mr. MATHEW THOMPSON.

Page 10   Court held Xber 12th anno 1689

        The Court is adjourned till the 2d Wednesday in February next God save
        their Majesties.

544. Ordered by this Court that the sum of 40 pounds of Tobacco be paid by
        every respective Tithable in this County for the paying and defraying
of the publick charge of the county being the publick county levy for this present year and that Capt. MALACHY PEALE High Sheriff of this County shall levy
and collect the same and that he pay it to the several persons or claimers in
this County to whom it is proportioned by this Court.

545. At a Court held for the County of Stafford March the 10th 1689/90

        Present Collo. William Fitzhugh, Capt. George Mason, Mr. Samuel
        Hayward, Mr. William Buckner Justices

546. JEFFREY WOOD complaining sheweth that RALPH SPEED late of this county
        standed Indebted unto the Plt the sum of twelve hundred and eight pounds
of tobacco due to him by Bill ..

547. Whereas WILLIAM BUNBURY made humble suit to this Court that he had faith-
        fully served in the office and place of a Constable for the upper parts
of the lower parish of this County one whole year and did there pray EDWARD
PLATT might be chosen in his Room and place Therefore tis ordered that the said
Edward Platt shall serve in the room and stead of the said William Bunbury in
the office of Constable .. until March Court next ensueing and that Collo.

WILLIAM FITZHUGH swear him accordingly.

548. Whereas WILLIAM RUSTALL made humble suit to this Court that he had faith-
      fully served in the office and place of a Constable for the Precinct of
Pasbitanzy in this County one whole year and did therefore pray that DAVID
ANDERSON might be chosen in his Room and place Therefore tis ordered that the
said David Anderson shall serve in the room and stead of the said William Rus-
tall in the office of a Constable .. until March Court next ensueing and that
Capt. GEORGE MASON swear him accordingly.

549. Whereas SYMON STACEY made humble suit to this Court that he had faith-
      fully served in the office and place of a Constable for the Precinct of
Potomack Creek in this County one whole year and did therefore pray that JOHN
HIGGISON might be chose in his Room and place Therefore tis ordered that the
said John Higgison shall serve in the

Page 11   Court held 10th March 1689/90

room and place of the afsd Symon Stacey in the office of a Constable .. until
March Court next ensueing and that Capt. GEORGE MASON swear him accordingly.

550. Whereas JEFFREY WOOD made humble suit to this Court that he had faith-
      fully served in the office and place of a Constable for the precinct
of Chopawamsick in this County one whole year and did therefore pray that
MATTHEW GOSSE might be chosen in his Room and place Therefore tis ordered that
the said Matthew Gosse shall serve in the room and place of the afsd Jeffrey
Wood in the office of a Constable .. until March Court next ensueing and that
MATTHEW THOMPSON swear him accordingly.

551. Whereas WILLIAM BALTHROP made humble suit to this Court that he had faith-
      fully served in the office and place of a Constable for the precinct of
the lower Parish Vizt of St. Pauls in this County one whole year and did therefore pray that THOMAS ELLIS might be chosen in his Room and place Therefore tis
ordered that the said Thomas Ellis shall serve in the room and place of the
afsd William Balthrop in the office of a Constable .. until March Court next
ensueing and that WILLIAM BUCKNER swear him accordingly.

552. Whereas AUGUSTINE KNEATON did arrest JOHN DAVIS to this Court and did not
      appear to prosecute said action against him .. Kneaton pay John Davis 50
pounds of Tobacco ..

553.   Mr. JOHN WITHERS Present
      JOHN WAUGH Clerke complaining sheweth that WILLIAM FARRIER late of this
County stood indebted to the Plt in the sum of Four hundred pounds of Tobacco
.. attachment served upon corne in the hands of WILLIAM BALTHROP ..

554. ELIZA. MINTHORNE the Widow and relict of RICHARD MINTHORNE late of this
      County deced made humble suit to this Court that her husband dyed intestate
and made no will did therefore humbly pray that she might have Letters of
administration granted her of her deced Husbands estate she being ready to give
security to the Court to perform what the Law does in such cases direct touching
the said Estate and the Court having accordingly considered the premises do
order therefore tis ordered that the said Eliza. Minthorne shall have administration granted her of her Husbands Estate she giving security to the Court ..
and Capt. GEORGE MASON became security with her to perform what the law requires
.. Ordered that JONATHAN MOTHERSHED, CHARLES ROSE and WM. BETTY shall on the
25th of this Instant appraise the Estate of Richd. Minthorne late of this county
and that Mr. MATHEW THOMPSON swear them accordingly.

Page 12   Court held 10th March 1689/90

555.   Ordered that EDWARD WATTS shall make present payment of Two hundred pounds
       of Tobacco to JOHN SMITH and ANN his wife and WILLIAM SPINCE (?) per piece
for five days attendance at Court in a suit between him and CHRISTOPHER HERRINGE
with costs alias Execution.

556.   Whereas SUSANNAH MANNINGTON Servant unto JOHN COLCLOUGH was summoned to
       this Court for having had a bastard child in the time of her service
Therefore tis ordered that the aforesaid Susannah Mannington shall serve John
Colclough her afsd Master Two years and a half after her time by Custom or Indenture is expired according to Act of Assembly. Forasmuch as John Colclough
did in open Court assume the payment of the fine of Susannah Mannington for committing fornication unto the Lower Parish of this County Therefore tis ordered
that the said John Colclough shall pay the sum of two hundred pounds of Tobacco
in cask unto the Lower Parish of this County at October next alias Execution.

557.   Whereas Capt. GEORGE BRENT did arrest JOHN JEANES to this Court and did
       not appear to prosecute his action against him ..

558.   RICHARD GIBSON complaineth against THOMAS OWSLEY for that that is to say
       that he stands indebted to him the Plt the sum of Two hundred and twenty five
pounds of Tobacco due to him by account ..

559.   GERRARD LOWTHER complaining sheweth that JOHN SIMSON late of this County
       deced at the time of his death stood indebted unto your Plt by Bill and
account for attorneys fees the sum of Six hundred pounds of Tobacco in cask
for which your Plt hath brought his action against JOHN WYTHERS the admr of
the Estate of John Simson ..

560.   WILLIAM MINTORNE complaining sheweth that JOHN SIMSON late of this county
       deced stood indebted to the Plt at the time of his death the sum Eight
hundred and eighty eight pounds of Tobacco due him by Bill bearing date 26th
March Anno 1687 for which he hath brought his action against JOHN WYTHERS as
admr of the Estate of John Simson ..

Page 13   Court held 10th March 1689/90

561.   Coll. WM. FITZHUGH complaining sheweth that JOHN SIMSON late of this
       County deced stood indebted to the Plt at the time of his death the sum
Six hundred and seventy nine pounds of Tobacco due him by bill for which he
hath brought his action against JOHN WYTHERS as admr of the Estate of John
Simson ..

562.   SIMON ROBINS complaining sheweth that JOHN SIMSON late of this county
       deced stood indebted to the Plt at the time of his death the sum Eight
hundred pounds of Tobacco due per bill under his hand and seale dated the 12th
day of October Anno Dom 1687 for which he hath brought his action against JOHN
WYTHERS as admr of the Estate of John Simson ..

563.   Whereas NICO. OLIVER made humble petition to this Court that he had
       justly and faithfully served THOMAS ODENELL his Master according to his
Indenture which he is here ready to averr and prove to this Worshipful Court
it notwithstanding the said Thomas Odenell doth unjustly detain and keep from
your Petr one new shirt and new hat being part of his freedom cloathes as that
he doth alsoe detain and keep from him your Petr his freedom corne contrary
to all Law Equity and good conscience .. Thomas Odenell to pay the sum of Five
hundred pounds of Tobacco for his freedom corne ..

Page 13 (contd)   Court held 10th March 1689/90

564.   PETER BAKER made humble petition to this Court that JOHN COLLUME late of
       Plymouth England deced died intestate and in your Petrs debt the sum of
five pounds five shillings and two pence ..

Page 14   Court held 10th March 1689/90

and now forasmuch as there did appeare by Capt. GEORGE BRENT in this Court a
debt of Colo. SPENCER of greater sum and quality then this of the aforesaid
Baker against the Estate of Colume as aforesaid and that the said George Brent
had no power to prosecute or administer upon the said Estate Therefore tis
ordered that this petition shall be reposited to the next Court to be better
informed concerning it.

565.   ROBERT BRENT made humble petition to this Court that whereas he had on
       the Twentieth day of July Anno Dom 1689 contracted and made an agreement
with one JOHN HALL as appears per a writing or Indenture signed and sealed by
the hand of the said Hall unto your Petitioner Robert Brent to and for the
space of five years as relation being had unto the said Indenture will more
fully appear in which time the said Hall hath several times absented himself
out of your petitioners service to his great losse and detriment .. pray for
an order the said John Hall to remain and serve out his time with your Petr
all to the tenor of the aforecited Indenture and to order him to serve ye Petr
for his soe absenting himself out of his service acdording to Act of Assembly
.. wherein it was fully proved that he had a just and Lawful right to the said
John Hall during the time abovementioned .. Therefore tis ordered that the said
John Hall servant to Robert Brent shall returne home to his said Master and
shall serve out his full time which is full four years and four months ..

566.   AUGUSTINE KNEATON complaining against NICO. WANSFORD in a plea of Debt
       .. in sum of Five thousand eight hundred and twenty nine pounds of To-
bacco and caske .. Nico. Wansford did not appear in this Court to answer the
plea therefore Augustine Kneaton did appear in this Court by Capt. GEORGE BRENT
his attorney and prayed for Judgment against MALACHI PEALE high sheriff of
this County for his afsd Debt according to Act of Assembly with costs And the
said Malachi Peale high sheriff came into Court and by RICHD. GIBSON his atturney comes and defends the force and injury and for plea saith that the Plts
declaration and the matter therein contayned is not sufficient in Law for the
Plt to have or maintain his action against him .. and of and from this suit
prays to be dismissed with costs ..

Page 15   Court held 10th March 1689/90

action dismissed and Augustine Kneaton pay costs And the said Capt. George Brent
atturney for Kneaton not being content with the Judgment of Court appeals to
the fifth day of the General Court to be heard before his Excellency and the
Honourable Council of State at James City.   ROBERT BRENT became security with
Augustine Kneaton and George Brent his atturney to prosecute the appeale.   And
Capt. GEORGE MASON became security with MALACHI PEALE high sheriff to answer
the appeale.

567.   RICHD. GIBSON complains against RICHARD RICHEE in a plea of debt .. in
       sum of Fourteen hundred and sixty pds of Tobacco due by Bill .. Richard
Richee discounted sum .. out of THOMAS MARLEY Estate which account not being
at present allowed by the Court the aforesaid Richard Richee who married the
admx of the aforesaid Thomas Marley pleading in Court that he had paid as farr
as assets ..

Page 15 (contd)   Court held 10th March 1689/90

568. Whereas RICHARD BANKES an Orphan made humble suit to this Court against
      RICHARD GIBSON that he the said Richard Gibson his Master did beat misuse
and unlawfully use him .. prays discharge him from his Service from the said
Gibson .. the Court .. that the said Gibson was to learn him to read and write
either by himself at home or at school abroad and no progress being made therein
Therefore tis ordered by this Court that Richard Gibson shall immediately take
effectual care for the cureing of Richard Bankes scald head and for putting him
to school .. and that he bring him to next court to see what progress he makes
therein and that Richard Bankes Orphan shall serve the said Gibson until he
comes to the full age of twenty one years ..

569. Whereas JONATHAN MOTTERSHED made humble suit that he hath faithfully
      served in the office of Constable for the upper precincts of this County
one whole year and did therefore pray that he might be discharged of his said
office and that GILES VANDECASTAIL might be chosen in his Room and stead Therefore tis ordered that the said Giles Vandecastail serve in the Room and place
of the afsd

Page 16   Court held 10th March 1689/90

JNO. MOTTERSHED for the upper precincts of this county until March Court ensueing and that Mr. MATHEW THOMPSON swear him accordingly.

570. Whereas GEORGE LUKE made humble suit to this Court that he had upon the
      Fourteenth of October last past made and contracted an agreement with
ANDREW and JOHN BOWRNE late of Plym. Devon in England to serve him for the full
terme of four years from this (blank) of April next ensueing from the date of
these presents for and in consideration of paying their passage with their
Mother and one child more being the sum of Five thousand pounds of Tobacco in
cask which said agreement and contract was made by and between the said George
Luke and Andrew Bowrne and John Bowrne the day and year above written before
Mr. SAMUEL HAYWARD .. and drawn authentically by JAMES HEARSE deputy clerk of
the peace for this County .. and forasmuch as the said Andrew and John Bowrne
did then at the time of drawing their said Indenture clandestinely steal and
carry away that part which did belong to their said Master George Luke which
he is ready to aver and prove .. prays that an order for the said Andrew and
John Bowrne to serve according to the time profixed .. and whereas Andrew Bowrne
having absented himself out of ye petrs service for the space of sixteen days
may be judged to serve me according to Act of Assembly .. ordered Andrew and
John Bowrne serve George Luke from the Fourteenth October 1689 unto the (blank)
day of April which shall happen to be in the year 1693 .. and Andrew Bowrne
shall serve his master the space of Thirty two days after the Expiration of
his Indenture for his fugitively absenting himself ..

571. Ordered by this Court that JOHN SIMSON shall immediately pay unto ELIZA-
      BETH NICKSON late widow of RICHARD HOLMES of this County one Barrel of
Indian Corn and that he bring it home to her house either by himself or servant and pay the costs ..

572. WILLIAM YOUNG complaineth against ANDREW BOWRNE, ROBERT STANLEY and
      ELIZABETH DESBOROUGH in a plea of trespass that whereas by the one hund-
red twenty fifth Act of Assembly it was enacted and provided that whosoever
shall steal or unlawfully kill any hogs which is not their owne and the said
fact being proved by sufficient Evidence he or they so offending shall pay to
the owner of the said hog one thousand pounds of Tobacco and one thousand

Page 16 (contd)   Court held 10th March 1689/90

pounds to the informer and in case of inability to pay and satisfie to serve
according to Act and now so it is that Andrew Bowrne, Robert Stanley and Elizabeth Desborough all three servants of Mr. GEORGE LUKE did on or about the 23d
day of January last past and within the jurisdiction of this Court kill and unlawfully carry away one of ELIZABETH YOUNGS hogs Widow and relict of VINCENT
YOUNG late of this county deced and your Petrs Mother for which said fact they
was all three brought before Mr. SAMUEL HAYWARD a member of this Worshipful
Court and by him bound over to answer the same before your Worships ..

Page 17   Court held 10th March 1689/90

pray for Judgment according to Act of Assembly .. (accused) pleaded not guilty
and for Tryal puts himself upon the country and the Plt likewise Therefore tis
ordered that the Jury Enquire the fact BURR HARRISON, JONATHAN WITTALL, SIMON
STACEY, RICHARD WILLIAMS, DAVID DARNELL, DAVID STRAWHAN, XPO. BUTLER, WM.
HAMBLETON, WILLIAM BOWRNE, STEPHEN SEBASTIAN, WILLIAM TODD, JOSEPH EYRES which
said Jurors doe say upon their oaths we find for the Defendants not guilty in
manner and form afsd Therefore it is ordered that the Judgment shall be entered on the verdict of the Jury and the said Andrew Bowrne, Robert Stanley
and Elizabeth Desborough of and from this action shall be dismissed and that
William Younge the Plt shall pay costs .. Ordered that William Young shall pay
the Jury Seventy two pounds of Tobacco with costs.

573. Ordered that the Sheriff bring the body of ABRAM AMIS to the next Court
      to answer the complaint of Capt. GEORGE MASON or else be lyable according
to Act of Assembly & pay costs. Attachment according to Act of Assembly is
granted the Sheriff against the Estate of Abram Amis for his nonappearance at
the suit of Capt. Geo. Mason with costs JOHN WEST secty.

574. Ordered that the Sheriff bring the body of JOHN WADDAN to the next Court
      to answer the complaint of ROBERT BRENT or else be lyable according to
Act of Assembly & pay costs. Attachment according to Act of Assembly granted
to the sheriff against the Estate of John Waddan for his nonappearance at the
suit of Robert Brent with costs.

575. Ordered that the Sheriff bring the body of WILLIAM PAGE to the next Court
      to answer the complaint of ANTHONY WILLIAMS ..

576. Ordered that the Sheriff bring the body of HENRY THOMPSON to the next
      Court to answer the complaint of RICHARD MARTIN ..

577. Ordered that the Sheriff bring the body of THOMAS CHAPMAN to the next
      Court to answer the complaint of CHRISTOPHER HERRING ..

578. Ordered that the Sheriff bring the body of JOHN ATTERTON to the next
      Court to answer the complaint of Coll. WM. FITZHUGH ..

Page 18. Court held 10th March 1689/90

579. Ordered that the Sheriff bring the body of JOHN BEACH to the next Court
      to answer the complaint of THOMAS DERRICK JUNR. ..

580. Ordered that the Sheriff bring the body of HENRY THOMPSON to next Court
      to answer the complaint of GEORGE SHEPARD ..

581. Ordered that the Sheriff bring the body of JOHN GUNNAWAY to the next
      Court to answer the complaint of PATRICK MICKLEROY or else be lyable
according to Act of Assembly and pay costs. Attachment according to Act of

Page 18 (contd)   Court held 10th March 1689/90

Assembly is granted the Sheriff against the Estate of MATTHEW SEAS Security for the said John Gunnaway ..

582.   Ordered that the Sheriff bring the body of JOHN BUCKLEY to the next
       Court to answer the complaint of FRANCIS HAMMERSLEY or else be lyable according to Act of Assembly and pay costs. Attachment according to Act of Assembly is granted the Sheriff against the Estate of RICHARD MARTYN Security for the said John Buckley ..

583.   Ordered that the Sheriff bring the body of JOHN HODGEN to the next Court
       to answer the complaint of JOHN WITHERS or else be lyable according to Act of Assembly and pay costs. Attachement according to Act of Assembly is granted the Sheriff against the Estate of ELIZABETH KING Widow security for the said JOHN HODGEN ..

584.   Ordered that the Sheriff bring the body of RICHARD MILDMAY to the next
       Court to answer the complaint of JONATHAN WHITTALL ..

585.   Ordered that the Sheriff bring the body of JOHN DAVIS to the next Court
       to answer the complaint of AUGUSTINE KNEATON ..

Page 19   Court held 10th March 1689/90

586.   Ordered by this Court that the Sheriff summon Mrs. FRANCES MASON the
       widow and relict of Collo. GEORGE MASON late of this County deceased to answer the complaint of SAMPSON DARRELL who intermarried with MARGARET the only surviving child of Capt. JOHN NORGRAVE deced ..

587.   Ordered that THOMAS MARLEY Orphan of THOMAS MARLEY late of this County
       deced be brought to the next Court to set forth and justifie his complaint against RICHD. RICHEE his Master and that the said Richard Richee be here at the next Court to answer the aforesaid Thomas Marley his servant and they likewise bring the Indenture made between them to the Court.

588.   JOHN SIMSON complaining sheweth that JOHN BASFORD late of this county
       stands indebted to the Plt the sum of Fifteen hundred and ten pounds of Tobacco due him by Account .. attachment was lawfully served in the hands of WILLIAM ENOE, GEORGE ENOE and JOHN CARR upon the Estate of JOHN BASFORD ..

589.   Whereas JAMES WILD made humble petition to this Court he had justly and
       faithfully served SAMPSON DARRELL his Master according to his Indenture which he is here ready to aver and prove notwithstanding the said Sampson Darrell his Master doth unjustly and unlawfully detain and keep from him his corn and freedom cloathes .. Court ordered Sampson Darrell pay three barrels of Indian corn unto James Wild and the remaining part of his cloaths which is a coat and breeches when ships come into this country or else the value in Tobacco ..

590.   JOHN MINNIFEE complaining sheweth that JOHN HARRISON late of this County
       stands indebted to the Plt the sum of Three hundred and thirty pounds of Tobacco in cask by account .. attachment served into the hands of HENRY MEREST upon the Estate of John Harrison .. and now forasmuch as the said John Minnifee the Plt did by his Oath upon the holy Evangelist to his account here in Court Exhibited against the said John Harrison justly made appear his afsd debt to be due Therefore tis ordered that the said John Minnifee shall have Judgment ..

Page 19 (contd)   Court held 10th March 1689/90

591. WILLIAM LOXHAM complains against CHARLES BALDRIDGE in a plea of Debt
      for that Charles Baldridge did at several times and severall

Page 20   Court held 10th March 1689/90

place loose to the Plt Two thousand Eight hundred and twenty five pounds of
Tobacco and cask at a game on the card called Whiske wherefore he hath brought
his action .. Court finding the said Debt was wholly and altogether won at
the aforesaid game or play Therefore tis ordered that Charles Baldridge shall
make present payment of the sum of Eight hundred pounds of Tobacco it being
adjusted by this Court to be the full ballance of all acompts between them ..

592. RICHARD GIBSON made humble suit to this Court the Petr hath a woman ser-
      vant named MARY MASON who hath runaway at several times to the number of
ninety days and the trouble charges and damages after her amounts to the sum
of Fourteen hundred and fifty pounds of Tobacco and cask for which runaway time
your Petitioner hath taken Certificate from Mr. MATHEW THOMPSON according to
Law .. ordered Mary Mason serve her Master one year and a half after the expiration of her time ..

593. ROBERT BRENT did appear in this Court atturney of GILBERT CLARKE of
      Maryland and did assume to pay what damages might accrew unto STEPHEN
SMITH in an action depending in this Court between the said Smith the Defendant and Gilbert Clarke Plt.

594. At a Court held for County of Stafford March 13th 1689/90

          Present Collo. William Fitzhugh
              Mr. Samuel Hayward   Capt. George Mason
              Mr. Edward Thomason   Mr. John Withers   Justices
              Mr. William Buckner   Mr. Matt. Thompson

595. ROBERT BRENT complaineth against JOHN PORE in a plea of Debt for that
      the said John Pore stands indebted to the Plt the sum of One thousand
Seven hundred and thirty pounds of Tobacco and cask for which he hath brought
his action .. and John Pore by RICHARD GIBSON his atturney comes and for plea
saith that the said declaration and matter therein contained is not sufficient
in Law for the Plt to have or maintain his action ..

Page 21   Court held 13th March 1689/90

all which being duly considered by the Court accordingly order Therefore tis
ordered that the said John Pore the Deft of and from this action be dismissed
and that Robert Brent the Plt shall pay costs.

596. Ordered by the Court that the Sheriff summon THOMAS NEROS to the next
      Court to answer the complaint of THOMAS KNIGHT son and orphan of GEORGE
KNIGHT late of this county deced and that Thomas Knight shall come to the
Court to prosecute his complaint.

597. Whereas ROBERT BRENT did arrest BURR HARRISON to this Court and there
      did not appear on the cause of action ..

598. Whereas JOHN MOORE the admr of EDWARD SANDS late of this county deced
      made humble suit to this Court that he hath fully administered on the
Estate of Edward Sands and that he might have a Quietus granted unto him ..
whereas John Moore by his atturney GERRARD LOWTHER came into Court .. appeared
he hath paid more than assets .. ordered John Moore shall have a Quietus
granted ..

Page 21 (contd)   Court held 13th March 1689/90

599.   JOSHUA DAVIS did appear in this Court the atturney of MICHAEL WELLINGTON
          the Atturney of ANNE CHEWINGE who is Extx. of THOMAS CHEWINGE late deced
and hath exhibited a probate of the afsd Thomas Chewinges will granted to the
said Anne Chewinge whereby her power is approved by this Court to be lawful
and authenticke.

600.   GERRARD LOWTHER the Attorney of HUGH FRENCH made humble suit to this
          Court that RICE HOOE stood indebted to the aforesaid French the sum of
four hundred pounds of Tobacco due per bill which bill being left the said
Rice Hooe refuses to pay the same Wherefore your Petr craves Judgment against
the said Rice Hooe for his said debt with costs of suit And the said Rice Hooe
came into Court and confessed Judgment to the said Bill and Exhibited to this
Court an account against the said Bill which being fully proved in Court by
his Oath upon the Holy Evangelist to his aforesaid account Therefore tis ordered that the said Rice Hooe of and from the aforesaid Bill shall be freely
and fully discharged and Hugh French pay costs als Execution.

601.   MATHEW THOMPSON complains against ROBERT BRENT in a plea of debt for
          that the said Robert Brent stands indebted to the Plt the sum of Two
thousand six hundred and fifty three pounds of Tobacco due by Bill and Account
here in Court ready produced for which he hath brought his Action against the
said Brent the defendant and prays Judgment with costs of suite And the Aforesaid Robert Brent came into Court and legally discounted the sum .. therefore
tis ordered that Robert Brent

p. 22   Court held 13th March 1689/90

shall make present payment ..

602.   RICHD. GIBSON complaining sheweth that NATHAN OARES at the time of his
       · death stood indebted to the Plt the sum of Four hundred and seventy eight
pounds of Tobacco by Bill under hand and seale dated the 16th of March 1687
which in his lifetime the said sum nor any part thereof hath paid wherefore he
hath brought his action against ELEANOR the relict and administratrix of the
Estate of the said Oares and prays Judgment for his said Debt And the said
Eleanor Oares by SAMPSON DARRELL her Attorney came into Court and confessed
Judgment ..

603.   ELEANOR OARES by SAMSON DARRELL her Attorney came into Court and confest
          judgment to JOHN PEAKE SENR. for the sum Three hundred and eighteen pounds
of Tobacco being due from her Husband NATHAN OARES .. Therefore tis ordered
that the said RICHARD HOLMES shall make present payment of Three hundred and
eighteen pounds of Tobacco unto the afsd John Peake Senr. being the full ballance of the assets of the aforesaid Nathan Oares Estate als Execution..

604.   ROBERT ROBERTS complains against WILLIAM WALLER in plea of Debt for that
          the said William Waller stands indebted to the Plt the sum of Three hund-
red and twenty five pounds of Tobacco in cask due to him by account .. And said
William Waller came into Court and discounted the sum of Forty pounds of Tobacco
..

605.   EDWARD WATTS complaineth against THOMAS CHAPMAN in plea of Debt for that
          the said Thomas Chapman stands indebted to the Plt the sum of Two thousand
three hundred and forty one pounds of Tobacco due to him by account .. Thomas
Chapman came into Court and legally discounted the sum of Two thousand and thirty
one pounds of Tobacco .. and that Edward Watts shall make a return of around
slave belonging to the aforesaid Thomas Chapman he the said Chapman paying costs
alias execution.

599 - 605

Page 23   Court held 13th March 1689/90.

606. GEORGE LUKE who married the widow and admx of Doctr. RALPH SMITH late of
      this County deced made humble suit to this Court that ROBERT ALEXANDER
stands indebted to the Plt in qualification the sum of One thousand nine hundred and seventy pounds of Tobacco and caske .. and the said Robert Alexander
comes into Court and legally discounted the sum of Seventeen hundred and six
pounds of Tobacco out of the aforesaid sum ..

607. Ordered that ZACHARY HAYNES shall make present payment of One hundred and
      fifty pounds of Tobacco unto ROBERT STREET, THOMAS MOSSE and JOHN COL-
CLOUGH per peice for their attendance at Court in a suit depending between him
and ROGER STONEING with costs als Execution.

608. Capt. GEORGE BRENT complains against PHILIP WILLEN in a plea of Debt for
      that the said Philip Willen stands indebted to the Plt the sum of Five
hundred pounds of Tobacco due to him by account .. And Philip Willen the deft
as afsd came into Court and could say nothing in Barr or preclusion of the said
Debt but that the same is Justly due as aforesaid .. ordered Philip Willen shall
make present payment ..

609. EDWARD MADDOX complains against GEORGE LUKE who married the widow and
      admx of Dr. RALPH SMITH late of this County deced in a plea of Debt for
that the said Ralph Smith stood indebted to the Plt at the time of his decease
the sum of eleven hundred ninety three pounds of Tobacco lent the afsd Smith in
his lifetime before his decease .. and George Luke came into Court and could
say nothing in Barr or preclusion of the afsd Debt .. ordered George Luke shall
make payment ..

610. RICHD. GIBSON complaining sheweth that EVAN JONES Tanner stands indebted
      to the Plt by a former Judgment of this Court the sum of Four hundred
ninety six pounds of Tobacco and caske which he hath not paid .. and the said
Evan Jones came in Cour propria

Page 24   Court held 13th March 1689/90

persona and could show no lawful cause to the contrary why Judgment should not
be tis ordered that Judgment shall be renewed ..

611. Ordered by this Court that THOMAS ODENELL shall have Judgment against
      GEORGE LUKE who intermarried with the widow and admx of Doctr. RALPH SMITH
late of this County deced for the sam of Four hundred and fifty pounds of Tobacco
due to him the said Thomas Odenell for five bushels of salt lent to the said
Dr. Ralph Smith in his lifetime and was never paid him nor any part thereof ..

612. Ordered by this Court that GERRARD BANKES the only son and orphan of ADAM
      BANKS late of this county deced shall be put and bounde as an apprentice
to RICHARD MARTYN of this County for and during the term of three years com-
mencing from the date of this order and that the said Richard Martyn shall
fully learn him the trade or occupation of a wear maker during the Term afsd
and shall also find and allow him good and sufficient meat apparel washing &
Lodging fit for such an apprentice & shall carefully look after him during the
Term aforesaid.

613. Whereas Capt. GEORGE BRENT Atturney of JOHN RAYLEY in Maryland obtaind a
      Judgment of this Worshipful Court the 11th day of December last against
DAVID DARNELL of this County for the sum of Twelve hundred eighty and seven
pounds of Tobacco due to him in qualification afsd Vizt Four hundred due by
Bill and Eight hundred eighty seven pounds of Tobacco by account which said

Page 24 (contd)   Court held 13th March 1689/90

Bill and account was fairly brought in and Exhibited to this Court by Capt.
George Brent as afsd only that the said David Darnell prayed he might have
Liberty granted to him till the next Court to produce receipts for the payment
of the aforesaid Tobacco to the said John Rayley which accordingly was granted
him .. and now forasmuch as the said David Darnell did by RICHARD GIBSON Atturney appear and produce receipts in Court against the aforesaid Bill of Four
hundred pounds of Tobacco and a certificate attested under the hand of NEHEMIAH
BLAGSTONE against the said Account of Eight hundred Eighty and seven pounds of
Tobacco so that the said sums of Tobacco nor any part thereof appear to this
Court to be justly due .. said David Darnell be fully and freely discharged
from the aforesaid Debt .. said Capt. George Brent shall be nonsuite and shall
make present payment of the sum of fifty pounds of Tobacco unto David Darnell
with costs als Execution.

614. GEORGE LUKE who Intermarried the widow and admx of Dr. RALPH SMITH late
      of this County deced complains against WILLIAM BALTHROP in a plea of
Debt for that he stands indebted to the Plt the sum of Five hundred and five
pounds of

Page 25 Court held 13th March 1689/90

Tobacco due to him by accompt in qualification .. And the said William Balthrop
the deft in propria persona came into Court and legally discounted the sum of
Two hundred pounds of Tobacco .. ordered make payment of ballance ..

615. THOMAS SWAINE complains against ROBERT JOHNSON in a plea of Debt for
      that he stands indebted unto the Plt the sum of Two hundred and Eighty
pounds of Tobacco & caske for work done for which he hath brought his action
against the said Robt. Johnson .. and the deft by RICHARD GIBSON his Attorney
came into Court and to the declaration pleads nill debet ..

616. Capt. GEORGE BRENT the Atturney of EDMOND JENNINGS Esqr. Atturney of
      their Majestys in General set forth and declared that WILLIAM GREENE late
of this County deced at the time of his death stood indebted to RICHARD LAWRENCE
late of James Citty Rebell by Bill under his hand the sum of Eleven hundred and
thirty one pounds of Tobacco & caske as by the said Bill dated the 20th of June
1675 will appear that the said Richd. Lawrence after the taking the said Bill
broke out into open rebellion whereby his Estate became forfeited to the Crowne
and amongst other the abovesaid Bill and Debt of the said Greenes which having
never yet been paid there Majesties have now brought their action against Capt.
MARTIN SCARLET who married the relict and Executrix of the aforesaid Greene and
demands Judgment thereon for the said Bill of Eleven hundred and thirty one
pounds of Tobacco and cask with costs of suit And the said Martin Scarlet came
into Court in propria persona and Exhibited an account to this Worshipful Court
brought by Coll. LAWRENCE WASHINGTON late deced against him as marrying the
relict and executrix of the afsd William Green which said account he made oath
that he had fully satisfied and paid Wherefore he humbly prays to be discharged
from the aforesaid action And now forasmuch as the said Martin Scarlet having
produced the aforesaid accompt and drawn adeption in this Court under his
hand and fairly sworne and signed thereto in this Court Therefore tis ordered
that Martin Scarlet shall be fully and freely discharged ᵽ. Capt. George Brent
Atturney of Edmund Jennings Esqr. Atturney General as afsd not being content
with the Judgment of this Court appeals to the fourth day of the General Court
to be held before his Excellency and the honourable Counsell of State at James
Citty.

614 - 616

Page 26   Court held 13th March 1689/90

617.   Ordered that RICHARD CARVER shall make present payment of one hundred and
        sixty pounds of Tobacco to BENJAMIN NEWTON for four days attendance at
Court and to GEORGE AYTREE Eighty pounds of Tobacco for two days attendance at
Court in a suit depending between him and JOHN NEWTON with costs als execution.
Ordered that John Newton shall make present payment of One hundred and sixty
pounds of Tobacco to EDWARD TAYLOR for his attendance at Court in a suit de-
pending between him and Richard Carver with costs als execution.

618.   RICHD. BRYANT complains against DAVID STRAWHAN in a plea of Debt for
        that the said Strawhan stands indebted to the Plt the sum of Twelve hund-
red pounds of Tobacco due per Bill .. And the said David Strawhan came into
Court in propria persona and legally discounted the sum of Eight hundred and
thirty pounds of Tobacco .. Therefore tis ordered the said David Strawhan shall
make present payment of the same ..

619.   XTOPHER RICHARDSON complains against RICHARD WILLIAMS in a plea of Debt
        for the said Williams stands indebted to the Plt the sum of Seven hundred
pounds of Tobacco due by Bill .. and Richard Williams did appear himself in
propria persona in this Court and confest Judgment unto the afsd Xtopher
Richardson ..

620.   EDWARD MADDOCKS complains against ADAM CURTIS in a plea of Debt for that
        the said Curtis stands indebted to the Plt the sum of Twelve hundred pounds
of Tobacco due unto him by Bill .. and the said Adam Curtis the deft did appear
in Court by JOHN WYTHERS his Atty confest Judgment ..

621.   Forasmuch as SAMPSON DARRELL did arrest ABRAM AMIS to this Court and the
        said Abram Amis did not appear to answer and alsoe that the Sheriff did
Justifie and avers in this Court that JOHN WEST became security for the said
Abram Amis appearance the Court doe accordingly order Therefore this ordered that
the afsd action shall be referred to next Court and that the said Abram Amis
doe not then make his personal appearance .. that then Judgment shall pass
against John West Security as afsd with all costs.

622.   SAMPSON DARRELL came into this Court and did assume to pay Capt. GEORGE
        MASON Churchwarden of the upper parish of this County the sum of Five
hundred pounds of Tobacco for DANIEL JEFFCOAT fine for committing fornication
with SUSAN SWAN according to the Judgment of this Court bearing date the 13th
of December last past.

623.   Ordered that JAMES MONKE shall make present payment of One hundred and
        sixty pounds of Tobacco unto THOMAS SHUTE and WILLIAM STURDY per peice
for their attendance four Court in a suit depending between him & WILLIAM
DOWNING with costs als Execution.

Page 27   Court held 13th March 1689/90

624.   Forasmuch as THOMAS JEFFRIES did arrest THOMAS HARRIS to this Court and
        did not appeare to prosecute his action Therefore tis ordered that Thomas
Jeffries shall be nonsuite and shall pay unto Thomas Harris fifty pounds of
Tobacco with costs.

625.   Forasmuch as DAVID DARNELL did arrest WILLIAM DAVIS ..

626.   Ordered that GEORGE LUKE who intermarried with the relict and admx of
        Doctr. RALPH SMITH late of this County deced shall make present payment
in qualification afsd the sum of Five hundred forty five pounds of Tobacco unto
JOHN WYTHERS being the full ballance of all Tobacco accounts between them ..

Page 27 (contd)   Court held 13th March 1689/90

627.   CHARLES BREBAND brought his action to this Court and complains against
       CHARLES BALDRIDGE in plea of Debt .. sum of Sixteen hundred and five
pounds of Tobacco .. Wherefore he by MALACHI PEALE his Atturney hath brought
his action .. ordered Charles Baldridge make payment ..

628.   MATTHEW THOMPSON complains against EDWARD SMITH in plea of debt ..

629.   STEPHEN SEBASTIAN made complaint to this Court that Coll. WILLM. FITZHUGH
       and the rest of the Execrs in Trust to the Estate of Majr. JAMES ASHTON
deced stands indebted ..

Page 28.   Court held 13th March 1689/90

630.   ROBT. HAMBLETON came into Court and confessed Judgment to JOHN WYTHERS
       for sum of Three hundred thirty five pounds of Tobacco ..

631.   Ordered that WILLIAM LOXHAM shall make present payment of the sum of one
       hundred and sixty pounds of Tobacco to JOHN COLCLOUGH, BENJAMIN COLCLOUGH
and PHILIP WILLEN per peice for their attendance four days at Court in suit
depending between him and CHARLES BALDRIDGE with costs ..

632.   Ordered that THOMAS HOWARD shall make present payment of the sum of
       Eighty pounds of Tobacco to BENJAMIN COLCLOUGH for his attendance two
daies at Court in a suit depending between him and THOMAS ODENELE with costs ..

633.   Forasmuch as THOMAS JEFFRIES did arrest JOHN CLARKE to this Court and
       did not appear to prosecute ..

634.   Forasmuch as RICHARD FOSSAKER did arrest MORRIS CLARKE to this Court and
       did not appear to prosecute ..

635.   Forasmuch as JOHN CLARKE did arrest THOMAS JEFFRIES to this Court and
       did not appear to prosecute ..

636.   JAMES MONKE the Atturney of ELIZABETH WILLIS complaineth against WILLIAM
       DOWNINGE in a plea of Trespass for that the said William Downinge of this
County did on or about June last was twelve month take and carry away a young
horse belonging to your Petr and the said young horse so taken away did brand
with his usual brand and doth keep and detaine the said horse contrary to Law
.. and William Downinge the deft came into Court by his attorney .. for plea
said not guilty .. Jury Enquire the fact, WILLIAM TODD, SIMON STACEY, JOHN
MATHEWS, JOSEPH HENSON, ROBERT HEDGES, HENRY WOOD, THOMAS DERRICK JUNR.,
RICHARD FOSSAKER, RICHARD RICHEE, THOMAS HOWARD, JOHN BREWTON, JOHN TURNER
which said Jurors do say we find for the Plt Eight hundred pounds of Tobacco
for the aforesaid horse and One hundred pounds of Tobacco for damages

Page 29   Court held 13th March 1689/90

Therefore tis ordered William Downinge shall make present payment of Nine hundred pounds of Tobacco for the said horse and damages unto James Monke .. Ordered
James Monke shall pay the Jury Seventy two pounds of Tobacco with costs ..

637.   AUGUSTINE KNEATON, RICHARD BRYANT, WILLIAM RUSTALL, THOMAS DERRICK JUNR.,
       JOHN ROWLEY, RICHARD CARVER, BRYANT BATTEY, RICHARD RICHEE, CHRISTOPHER
       BUTLER, WILLIAM WALLER, GEORGE AUSTREE, BENJAMIN NEWTON, JOSEPH EYRES,
EDWARD WATTS, BENJAMIN WEBB, SAMUEL KENT, WILLIAM PARKER, CHRISTOPHER HERRINGE,
JAMES MAN, STEPHEN SEBASTIAN, HENREY MEREST, ABRAHAM BECKINGHAM, GEORGE SHEPARD,
HENRY RIDGWAY was this day sworne of the grand jury for this County.

627 - 637

Page 29 (contd)   Court held 13th March 1689/90

638. SIMON THOMAS complains against CHRISTOPHER BUTLER in a plea of Debt ..

639. CHARLES BALDRIDGE complaining against RICHARD BRYANT and sheweth that
      in the month of July last past CHARLES RAROKE of this County deced played
at cards with JONATHAN BUCKLEY for a horse and twelve hundred pounds of Tobacco
that your Petr went halves with the said Raroke that the said Raroke did win the
horse and Twelve hundred pounds of Tobacco that the said Raroke being since
dead not having made your petitioner any satisfaction for his share of the said
Tobacco and horse Richard Bryant of the said County hath possessed himself of
the said Bill for Twelve hundred pounds of Tobacco and the horse and refuses
to pay your petr for his half .. Wherefore prays the said horse may be appraised
and that he may have Judgment against the said Bryant for half value of the
horse and six hundred pounds of Tobacco with costs And the said Richard Bryant
came into Court .. prays to be dismissed from the action .. And now forasmuch
as Charles Baldridge could not aver Justifie and maintain his action to be
true as before is alledged against Richard Bryant .. Therefore tis ordered
that Richard Bryant of and from this action shall be dismissed and that Charles
Baldridge pay costs ..

640. At a Court held for the County of Stafford March the 14th 1689/90

      Present Coll. Wm. Fitzhugh, Mr. Edwd. Thomason, Mr. Matt. Thompson, Mr.
      Samll. Hayward, Capt. Geo. Mason, Mr. Wm. Buckner, Justices

641. BENJA. COLCLOUGH complaineth against NATHAL. WEST in a plea of Debt ..

Page 30   Court held 14th March 1689/90

and for his assumpsed for DANIEL RICHMOND who stood indebted to him the said
Plt Eighty pounds of Tobacco for a pair of Drawers sold him all which he refuseth to pay .. and forasmuch as Nathaniel West hath absented himself out of
this County soe that the due process in Law could not be had against him
Therefore tis ordered that Benjamin Colclough the Plt came and prayed for an
order against the Sheriff according to Act of Assembly and WILLIAM WILFORD
came into Court and assumed payment of Three hundred and fifty pounds of Tobacco out of the Debt ..

642. WILLIAM LOXHAM complains against THOMAS ENGLISH in plea of Debt ..

643. Ordered that XTOPHER HEIRINGE shall make present payment of one hundred
      and twenty pounds of Tobacco to ELIZABETH WILLIAMS the wife of RICHARD
WILLIAMS for her attendance in Court three days in a suit depending between
him and EDWARD WATTS ..

644. Ordered that SAMPSON DARRELL shall make present payment of one hundred
      and twenty pounds of Tobacco unto CHRISTOPHER BUTLER for three days at-
tendance in Court in a suit depending between him and DANIEL BEACH ..

645. MALACHI PEALE High Sheriff complains against GERRARD LOWTHER in an action
      of the case for that HUGH FRENCH and GERRARD LOWTHER as aforesaid stands
bound unto your Petr in sum Ten thousand pounds of tobacco in caske as per bond
bearing date the 27th day of March anno 1688 for executing an execution on the
Estate of JOHN WHEATLEY and attachment being Executed on the Estate of the said
Wheatley before the Execution was served and the Estate was to remain in the
custody of the said French until your Worships Judgment which should take
priority and your Worships Judgment was that the attachment should take place
before the Execution it being first arrived as per the records will more fully

Page 30 (contd)   Court held 14th March 1689/90

appear and the said French the deft did contrary to your Worships order dispose of the said cattle which was soe attached by virtue of the aforesaid attachment served according to Law by which means your Petr could not deliver the cattle according to your Worships Judgment on the afsd attachment for which your Petr is damnified to the full value of the said bond .. And Gerrard Lowther appears in court .. for plea saith that the declaration is uncertain and knows not how to make his plea and prays a nonsuit

Page 31   Court held 14th March 1689/90

against the said Malachi Peale .. and forasmuch as Malachi Peale High Sheriff had not entered his declaration full so as the deft could in Law make a plea .. tis ordered Malachi Peale be nonsuited ..

646.   Ordered by this Court that MALACHI PEALE High Sheriff shall bring to the next Court the bonds passed by WILLIAM BOURNE and Capt. GEORGE BRENT to him in order to the prosecuting an Audita Querela formerly granted by this Court to the aforesaid William Bourne with the order of Court and all the papers relating to the aforesaid Audita Querela Juter the aforesaid William Bourne & RICHARD GIBSON.

647.   Ordered that JOSEPH NEWTON shall pay unto CHARLES BALDRIDGE and DAVID ANDERSON Immediately Eighty pounds of Tobacco per peece for their attendance two days at Court in a suit depending between him and ABRAHAM BECKINGHAM ..

648.   JOHN BREWTON humbly complaining sheweth that your Petr about two years agoe did deliver into the hands of JOSHUA DAVIS one of the undersheriffs of this County an attachment against the Estate of JOHN WHEATLEY in the hands of WILLIAM LOXHAM and as your Petr understands was served upon the said Estate in the hands of the said Loxham But as yet the said sheriff hath made no Legal return thereof to your Petrs great damage .. appear to this Court that Joshua Davis Hath not made any due and lawful return of the afsd attachment .. Therefore tis ordered that John Brewton shall have Judgment against Joshua Davis undersherrif or MALACHI PEALE High Sheriff for the sum of Eight hundred and fifty pounds of Tobacco in caske for cattle ..

649.   ZACHARY HAYNES humbly complaining sheweth that RICHARD LEE keeps and detains from him a cow and calfe which is truly and without fraud bounde to him by THOMAS DEANE for the security of Four hundred pounds of Tobacco and caske this said Beast being then when bounde a heifer swallow forked of the right ear and the left ear underkeeld as per the binding Instrument .. which Beast the said Lee hath mismarked and keeps together with the calfe .. Richard Lee by his atturney pleads not guilty .. and whereas Zachary Haynes could not answer Justifie and prove his said action to be true against Richard Lee

Page 32   Court held 14th March 1689/90

.. Therefore tis ordered Zachary Haynes shall be nonsuite ..

650.   EDWARD WATTS and ANNE his wife complaining that CHRISTOPHER HERRINGE of this County in August last past at the house of SYMON STACEY at Potomack Creek in this County and within the jurisdiction of this Court the Plt Anne then and there being in the peace of God and of our Sovereign Lord and Lady the King and Queen an assault did then and there make upon the body of her the said Anne and with force and Armes did her the said Anne kick beat and Evilly intreat so that by the said kicking and blows she the said Anne was greviously

Page 32 (contd)   Court held 14th March 1689/90

bruised and for a considerable time lame all which being contrary to the peace
of their Majesties that now in their Crowne and dignity and to the damage of
the Plts Ten thousand pounds of Tobacco .. that deft may be compelled to give
Security for his good behaviour .. and Christopher Herringe by RICHARD GIBSON
his Atturney .. and for plea saith that for the assault supposed to be done ..
their action ought not to have against him because the afsd Anne the day and
year afsd in and upon him the said Christopher Herringe at the place afsd an
assault did make and him the said deft to the uttermost of his power in Strength
Sence Malice Spight and Envy in the condition he then was did beat wounde and
Evill Intreate soe that the said Christopher Herringe did only keep off and de-
fend himself from the rage malice assault and battery of the Plt Anne and therefore if any damage did then happen to her it was by the assault then made upon
him .. which plea was overruled by the Court .. Therefore tis ordered that the
Jury Enquire the fact: SIGISMUND MASSEY, THOS. NORMAN, DAVID STRAWHAN, BRYANT
BATTEY, RICHARD WILLIAMS, WILLIAM PARKER, JOHN GATHER, SIMON STACEY, WILLIAM
BREWTON, RICE HOOE, GEORGE SHEPARD, RALPH WALKER which said Jurors find for
the Plt One hundred pounds Tobacco damages Therefore tis ordered that Judgment
shall be entered on the verdict of the Jury .. Ordered Edward Watts shall pay
the Jury Seventy two pounds of Tobacco with costs ..

651. Capt. GEORGE MASON Attorney of Capt. WILLIAM JONES Mariner complains
      against ROBERT BRENT in a plea of Debt .. and forasmuch as Robert Brent
did prove in this Court by the testimony and oath of JAMES BUTLER Examined and
Sworne .. and also Capt. George (sic) did averr and Justifie to this Court
that the

Page 33   Court held 14th March 1689/90

said Brent had paid Four hundred pounds of Tobacco out of the Debt unto William Jones .. Therefore tis ordered said Robert Brent shall make present payment of sum of Five hundred pounds of Tobacco to Capt. George Mason attorney ..

652. Ordered that JOHN SYMONS shall make present payment of the sum of one
      hundred and twenty pounds of Tobacco unto HENRY RIDGWAY for his attendance
three daies at Court in a Suite depending between him and EDWARD WATTS ..

653. WILLIAM PARKER complains against JOHN BLUNDALL in a plea of Debt ..

654. Whereas ZACHARY HAYNES did summon ROGER STONING of this County and his
      wife to this Court to give in their Evidence of the Truth of what they
knew in an action between Zachary Haynes and RICHARD LEE and the said Stoning
and wife did faile to appear .. Zachary Haynes shall have Judgment against the
aforesaid Roger Stoning and his wife for sum of Seven hundred pounds of Tobacco
according to Act of Assembly ..

655. Capt. GEORGE BRENT humbly complaining sheweth that JOHN GUYATT late of
      this County stood indebted unto him ..

656. JOSEPH NEWTON complains against ABRAHAM BECKINGHAM in a plea of Debt ..

Page 34   Court held 14th March 1689/90

657. Whereas Capt. GEORGE BRENT did arrest JOHN JEANES late of this County to
      this Court and the Sheriff returned him .. Therefore tis ordered Capt.
George Brent shall have an attachment granted him against Estate of John Jeanes
Estate ..

Page 34 (contd)   Court held 14th March 1689/90

658.   RICHD. GIBSON humbly complaining sheweth that WILLIAM BOURNE of this
       County sometime in March last was Twelve month did contract and agree with
your Petr to work along with two of your Petrs servants to make a cornfield
fence sufficient and plant corne along with the said servants for that year
and the said servants did then take in his charge and custody but afterwards
his said contract and bargain not minding did neglect to perform the said cornfield fence according to bargain afsd whereby your Petr not only lost his corne
but the work of his servants to his damage at least Four thousand pounds of
Tobacco for which he hath brought this action .. and forasmuch as Richard
Gibson could not aver Justifie and maintaine against William Bourne Therefore
tis ordered (he) be nonsuited ..

659.   JOHN SYMONS humbly complaining sheweth that JACOB HUBBARD late of this
       County stood indebted sum of Five barrells of Indian Corne at the time
of his decease being for corne delivered to Jacob Hubbard in his lifetime upon
consideration that the said Plt live with Jacob Hubbard one year and which the
said Hubbard refused to comply according to agreement .. Wherefore the Plt hath
brought his action against EDWARD WATTS who intermarried with the Widow and
Executrix of Jacob Hubbard .. Therefore tis ordered that Edward Watts shall
make present payment of Four hundred twenty and five pounds of Tobacco to John
Symons for the corne put in partnership with Jacob Hubbard deceased ..

660.   JOHN COLCLOUGH complains against RICHARD MARTYN in plea of Debt ..

661.   RICHARD RICHEE complains against HERMAN SALLEE for Debt of two (later
       Two hundred) pounds of Tobacco due to him for take up a horse of the
said Sallee ..

Page 35   Court held 14th March 1689/90

Court finding that the sum Two hundred pounds of Tobacco was too an Expensive
and Exhorbitant price for the taking up of the said horse Therefore tis ordered
that Herman Sallee shall make payment of one hundred pounds of Tobacco with
costs ..

662.   Forasmuch as RICHARD GIBSON and EDWARD MASON late of this County deced
       entered themselves as Securities with RICHARD NIXON for the due and
faithful administration of THOS. HOLMES Estate late of this County deced and
whereas the said Richard Nixon after he had obtained administration of the said
deced Holmes Estate did by virtue of said administration wast embezzle and con-
sume the said Estate and afterwards run away out of this County without paying
the Just debts of the aforesaid Holmes deced .. and whereas ROBERT HANKS one
of the choicest creditors of the deced Holmes obtained an order of this Court
to enter his action against Richard Gibson and Edward Mason .. and now forasmuch
as Richard Gibson one of the Securitys did appear in this Court and alledged
that Edward Mason the other Security was since dead and that he doubted not but
could find many things in this County which did of right belong to the aforesaid Nixon Estate .. Therefore tis ordered Richard Gibson shall between this
and next court make a thorough search and Inspection into the Estate of the
aforesaid Holmes deced and that if he find any part thereof to return an account
of what he finds and in whose hands he finds it to the next Court and that the
aforesaid action be referred until then.

663.   JOHN MATHEWS complaining sheweth that WILLIAM LYNNE stands indebted to
       him one good fat hogg of three years old for which your Petr hath brot
his action .. forasmuch John Mathews did prove by sufficient testimony of three

Page 35 (contd)   Court held 14th March 1689/90

Lawful witnesses .. Therefore tis ordered that William Lynne shall at or upon
the last of December next ensueing make payment of a hogg about one hundred
and twenty weight ..

664.   Whereas WILLIAM MINTORNE did summons JAMES THEARLE of this County to this
        Court to give in Evidence in action depending between him and JOHN JONES
in a plea of trespass and forasmuch as James Thearle did faile to appeare ..
Therefore tis ordered William Mintorne shall have Judgment ..

665.   WILLIAM BOWRNE complaineth against RICHARD GIBSON in a plea of detinue
        for that he the said Plt having been a Sojourner in the house of Mr.
Richard Gibson for some time and at his going away left in the said Gibsons
house sundry household goods and other moveables with design in a short time
to have fetched or sent for

Page 36   Court held 14th March 1689/90

them Vizt one bed and bolster one chest and two boxes two guns one table one
chair one Scotch cloth shirt one horne comb one razor and hone one set of wedges
one pair of small Stilliards one Iron spit one pair of pot hooks one pewter
bason four pewter dishes four books Vizt the Holy Pilgrim, St. Austins Medita-
tions, the History of King Charles the second and a Phisick book Entitled the
Gentlewomans Delight all which goods he did send for not long after his departure and within the terme of one year from this date but Gibson refused to deliver them .. to damages of two thousand pounds of Tobacco .. Therefore tis
ordered the Sheriff together with William Bowrne shall go to the dwelling house
of Richard Gibson and that the sheriff shall put the said Bowrne in possession
of what goods doth of right belong to him ..

666.   WM. MINTORNE complaineth against JOHN JONES in plea of Trespass for that
        the said John Jones in December last was Twelve month shot your Petrs
horse in the Loynes of which shot he dyed and to your Petrs damage of two
thousand pounds of Tobacco and caske .. John Jones pleads not guilty .. forasmuch as William Mintorne could not prove his action to be true against the said
John Jones .. Therefore tis ordered William Mintorne shall be nonsuit ..

667.   Ordered that JOHN MATHEWS shall make present payment of One hundred and
        twenty pounds of Tobacco to BRYANT BATTEY, ROBERT JOHNSON and WM. HAMBLE-
TON per peece for their attendance in a suit depending between him and WILLIAM
LYNNE ..

668.   GEORGE BRENT humbly complaining sheweth that the Plt having obtained a
        Judgment in this Worshipful Court against CHARLES BALDRIDGE as the Attur-
ney of Capt. GERRARD SLYE for the sum of Six thousand Eight hundred and Eleven
pounds of Tobacco and caske and intending to take execution thereon against the
body of the said Charles Baldridge, JOSEPH NEWTON to save the said Baldridge
from charge and imprisonment as alsoe he was indebted to the said Charles Baldridge in the month of March last and at several times since did assume and
promise to pay to the Plt the sum of Four thousand pounds of Tobacco in caske
towards the payment of the said

Page 37   Court held 14th March 1689/90

Baldridge Debt by means of which promise and assumption the Plt hath not taken
Execution against the said Baldridge nor any other course and now the deft
Joseph Newton refusing to perform his promise the Plt hath brought his action
.. Capt. George Brent did prove to this Court by the testimony of ROBERT COLSON

Page 37 (contd)   Court held 14th March 1689/90

undersheriff that Joseph Newton did assume to pay .. Therefore tis ordered
Joseph Newton shall make payment of Four thousand pounds of Tobacco in cask ..
Whereas Capt. George Brent Atturney for Capt. Gerrard Slye obtained a Judgment
in this Court against Joseph Newton for Four thousand pounds of Tobacco ..
Therefore tis ordered Charles Baldridge shall be freely and fully discharged
of the said sum ..

669. Whereas JOHN DIXON did arrest WILLIAM JOHNSON to this Court and did not
     appear to prosecute his action .. ordered John Dixon shall be nonsuite ..

670. Ordered that RICE HOOE shall make present payment of One hundred and
     twenty pounds of Tobacco to HENRY MEREST, WILLIAM PARKER and JOHN MINNI-
FEE for their attendance three days per peice at Court in an action depending
between him and JOHN DAVIS ..

671. Ordered that THOMAS WALKER and PETER DAWSON shall pay unto RALPH WALKER
     & RICE HOOE One hundred and twenty pounds of Tobacco per peece for their
attendance at Court five days in a Suite depending between them and FRANCIS
DADE.

672. JOHN DAVIS humbly complaining sheweth that your Petr was sold unto THOMAS
     HOWARD deced and predecessor to Mr. RICE HOE by Capt. Davis for the Terme
of four years that at the expiration of the said Terme your Petr demanded his
freedom from the said Rice Hoe which the said Rice Hoe denied him and restrained
him from coming to Court to procure his freedom so that your Petr was constrained
to serve five years which was compleated about twelve month since in all which
time Rice Hoe refused to make your Petr satisfaction for the years service or
for his Corne and cloaths whereby your Petr saith he is damnified to the value
of Four thousand pounds of Tobacco for which he hath brought his action .. And
now forasmuch as John Davis did by Testimony and Oaths of three Lawful and sufficient Evidences prove that he had served Rice Hooe one whole year more than
he was first really sold for Therefore tis ordered that

Page 38   Court held 14th March 1689/90

the said Rice Hooe shall make present payment of One thousand pounds of Tobacco
.. and one Kersey coat and breeches being the remaining part of his freedom
cloaths ..

673. SAMUEL HAYWARD complaineth against THOMAS MONTJOY for that the said Mont-
     joy as Atturney for JAMES CRAVEN Merchant stands indebted the sum of
Seven hundred and sixty pounds of Tobacco for Clerks fees .. Thomas Montjoy
Attorney as aforesaid did appear in this Court by JOSHUA DAVIS his attorney
and confest judgment ..

674. MORRIS CLARK came into Court and acknowledged a Bill of his which he for-
     merly gave to THOMAS MASTERS for Seven hundred pounds of Tobacco which
he did signe seale and deliver to the said Masters in the month of September
last before THOMAS NORMAN and CHRISTOPHER BUTLER witnesses subscribed to the
said Bill. Ordered that Thomas Masters shall make present payment of one hundred & twenty pounds of Tobacco to THOMAS NORMAN and XTOPHER BUTLER per peece
for their attendance three days in Court in a suite depending between him and
Morris Clark.

675. WM. DOWNING complaineth against JOHN RICHARDS in a plea of Debt .. for
     his assumpsed for JOHN JEANES .. Therefore tis ordered John Richards make
payment ..

669 - 675

Page 38 (contd) Court held 14th March 1689/90

676. WM. WALLER complains against EDWARD WATTS in a plea of debt ..

Page 39   Court held 14th March 1689/90

677. EDWARD ONIS complaining sheweth that JACOB HUBBARD at the time of his
      decease stood indebted sum of two thousand two hundred pounds of Tobacco ..

678. Capt. GEO. BRENT Attorney of GERRARD SLYE complaineth against CHARLES
      BALDRIDGE in a plea of debt ..

679. JOHN WITHERS Attorney of ROBERT HEWIT complains against RICHARD CARVER
      in plea of debt for that the said Carver and SAMUEL SMITH stands bounde
Joyntly and Severally by Bill the sum of Four hundred and twenty pounds of
Tobacco in caske ..

Page 40   Court held 14th March 1689/90

680. WM. WALLER complains against JOHN DRAPER in a plea of debt that the said
      John Draper stands indebted to the Plt the sum of Seven hundred and ten
pounds of Tobacco in cask .. John Draper shall make payment ..

681. ROBT. BRENT complains against JOHN DRAPER in a plea of debt that the said
      John Draper stands indebted to the Plt the sum of Eight hundred pounds of
Tobacco .. John Draper shall make payment ..

682. SAMLL. HAYWARD complains against WILLIAM PARKER in plea of Debt that the
      said William Parker stands indebted to the Plt the sum of Four hundred
seventy eight pounds of Tobacco .. Parker shall make payment ..

683. SAMLL. HAYWARD complains against RICHARD CARVER in plea of Debt that the
      said Richard Carver stands indebted to the Plt the sum of Five hundred
forty two pounds of tobacco .. said Carver did appear in Court by GERRARD LOW-
THER his Attorney appointed by him as appeared by the Testimony of JOSHUA DAVIS
here in Court given and confest Judgment .. Richard Carver shall make payment ..

684. SIGISMUND MASSEY Atturney of NICHOLAS HAYWARD complaining against THOMAS
      HOLDING in plea of Debt for that the said Holding stands indebted to the
Plt in Qualification afsd the sum of Nine hundred and sixty pounds of Tobacco
and cask ..

Page 41   Court held 14th March 1689/90

and the said Holding the Deft by his wife did appear in this Court and for plea
saith Nil debet and there prayed to be dismissed from this action with costs
And now forasmuch as it doth appear to this Court that Thos. Holding doth not
stand indebted to the afsd Sigismund Massey .. Therefore tis ordered that Thomas Holding of and from the said action shall be dismissed .. Sigismund Massey
pay costs ..

685. JAMES HERSE Attorney of WILLIAM THOMPSON of Westmoreland County Clerk
      complains against WILLIAM FREZER of this county in plea of debt for that
the sd Frezer at and to the Plt in Qualification afsd the sum of Four hundred
pounds of Tobacco in cask due to him for his marriage in Anno 1680 for which
he hath brought his action .. And the said Frezer did in proper person appear
in this Court and for plea saith that the said debt here in Court prayed for
by the deft is to Large and he presumes that the said Fee for marriage is very
Exhorbitant & contrary to the Act of Assembly in that case made and provided
but that he is willing to pay what by act is provided he did never yet refuse
and he humbly conceives that by Law he ought to be dismissed of this action and

Page 41 (contd)   Court held 14th March 1689/90

that the Plt pay costs And the Court having fully and maturely considered of the premises do accordingly order Therefore tis ordered that William Thompson shall make present payment of sum Two hundred pounds of Tobacco to James Herse according to act of assembly concerning marriages ..

The balance of this page and part of page 42 contains a summary of the previous actions giving Attorney and his clients.

Page 42   Court held 14th March 1689/90

This Court is adjourned till the first Monday in April next God save their Majesties.

686.   At a Court held for the County of Stafford April the 7th Anno 1690

Present Collo. William Fitzhugh, Mr. Samll. Hayward, Mr. John Withers, Mr. Edwd. Thomason, Capt. Geo. Mason, Mr. Wm. Buckner, Mr. Matt. Thompson, Justices

687.   Coll. ISAAC ALLERTON by Mr. ROBERT BRENT his Attorney made humble suit in this Court that he might have administration granted him of the Estate of JOHN COLLOME Late of Plymouth Devon in England which said Collome stands indebted to the aforesaid Coll. Isaac Allerton the sum of Thirty pounds Sterling .. And now forasmuch as it doth appear to this Court that John Collom stood Justly indebted to Collo. Isaac Allerton and that there doth not appear to this Court any greater creditor Therefore tis ordered that Collo. Isaac Allerton shall have administration granted him of the said Estate he giving Security to this Court .. Capt. GEORGE MASON and Mr. Robert Brent became Securities with Collo. Isaac Allerton to perform what the law requires ..

688.   Probat of the Last Will & Testament of ROBERT KING late of this county deced is granted to MARY the wife of the aforesaid Robert King she having fully proved the same by Sufft Oaths & Testimonies of WILLIAM HEAD, JOHN BREWTON, RICHARD AYLIFF, ELIZA. BREWTON and WILLIAM SMITH witnesses to the aforesaid Will thereunto subscribed Richard Ayliff and John Brewton did come into Court and give bond as her the said Mary Kings Secty for the performance of what the Law requires of her touching her husbands estate.

Page 43   Court held 7th April 1690

Ordered that John Brewton, Richard Ayliff, William Head and Richard Wall or any three of them shall appraise the Estate of Robert King late of this county deced upon the 20th of this Instant April and that Coll. WILLIAM FITZHUGH do accordingly swear them.

689.   JOHN WYTHERS complains against JOHN HODGEN in plea of debt for that he stands indebted to the Plt the sum of Nine hundred pounds of Tobacco in cask .. ordered John Hodgen shall make payment ..

690.   Ordered that THOMAS NEWS shall forthwith deliver into the custody and possession of THOMAS KNIGHT the only son and orphan of GEORGE KNIGHT all the cattle which he hath now in his hands belonging to his Brother JOHN KNIGHT late deced which is four breeding cattle with their calves if any ..

691.   JONAH REVET complains against JOHN HAWKIN in plea of debt for that the said Hawkin stands indebted to the Plt Seven hundred twenty eight pounds of Tobacco .. and forasmuch Jonah Revet did not appear in this Court to maintain and Justifie his said action against John Hawkin Therefore tis ordered that John Hawkin of and from this suit be dismissed .. Jonah Revet pay costs ..

Page 43 (contd)   Court held 7th April 1690

692. RICHD. GIBSON did appear in this Court Attorney of JOHN HALEY now of
      Westmoreland County and did assume to pay what damages might accrue to
JOSEPH EYRES of this County concerning a Bill in chancery put in and Exhibited
to this Court by the said Haley against Joseph Eyres and whereas there hath
been an action in Chancery Long Lain in this Court between John Haley Plt and
Joseph Eyres the deft and that there has been a long time of respite granted
to the afsd Eyres the deft to bring in his answer to the aforesaid Bill in
chancery by the said Haley the Plt Exhibited against him Therefore tis ordered
by this Court that if Joseph Eyres shall faile to bring in his answer to the
next Court to the said Bill .. that then the said Bill shall be taken as pro
confesso and Judgment shall passe against him for the same with all costs ..

693. SAMPSON DARRELL complains against SIMON STACY in a plea of Trespasse that
      whereas the Plt by right of his Wife the only Surviving child and heir
of her Father Capt. JOHN NORGRAVE late of this County deced is possest in fee
simple of certaine tract or parcel of land about six hundred acres upon Potomack
Creek on some part of which land Simon Stacey of this County is seated and unjustly claims right to most part of the six hundred acres or tract of land by a

Page 44   Court held 7th April 1690

pretended lease from THOMAS WATTS late of this county deced for Sixteene years
this being the second year the consideration as yet unpaid and forasmuch as
there hath been neither part nor parcel of the said six hundred acres directly
nor indirectly survaied nor divided either by Estimation condition nor appoint-
ment by or betweene the said Watts who intermarried with FRANCES the other
daughter of Capt. John Norgrave and whereas Capt. John Norgrave the Testator
and Father did by his last will & testament devise the said tract of six hundred acres equally to the Survivors of his children That therefore the Plt humbly conceives there was neither right Title nor quality in the said Watts Lease
each Moiety of land for want of Survey and division being then unknown Yet such
hath been the Plt civility to the said Stacey to have offered several times
since the Plts arrival the same messuage or Tenement of land upon reasonable
terms he refusing all manner of Terms under sixteen years and persisting in
Scurrilous and base language soe that the Plt is debarred from either Seating
building or manureing either part or parcel of the said land to the Plt damage
of Forty thousand pounds of Tobacco and cask for which he brings his suit ..
And Simon Stacey the deft did appear in Court by GERRARD LOWTHER his attorney
.. and for plea saith not guilty .. and now forasmuch as the said Sampson Darrell
the Plt could not Justifie prove and maintaine his said action of Trespass ..
Therefore tis ordered that Sampson Darrell shall be nonsuit and pay ..

694. Ordered that the action depending in this Court between Capt. GEORGE BRENT
      Plt and JOHN JEANES the deft be referred till next Court and then if the
said Jeanes shall then faile to appear at the next Court to answer the complaint
.. that then Judgment shall passe against him ..

695. Ordered that the action depending in this Court between THOMAS BARTON Plt
      and FRANCIS HAMMERSLEY the deft shall be referred to next Court to the
intent that the said Hammersley a true and perfect account of the Estate of
JAMES GERRARD that Judgment may pass against him as far as assets or else for
him to obtain a Quietus for the said Estate.

696. Whereas the grand jury of this County have made their presentments into
      this Court of severall offenders whose names are hereunder written and
set downe for Severall misdemeanours by them committed Vizt for speaking

Page 44 (contd)   Court held 7th April 1690

Blasphemy as also for persons committing adultery and for fenceing in their
majesties road Therefore tis ordered that the Sheriff summon all such offenders
and likewise the informers as is hereafter nominated to make their personal
appearance at the Court House before their Majesties Justices of the Peace the
next Court held for this County to answer the same and likewise all such other
matters & things

Page 45   Court held 7th April 1690

as by the grand jury of this County alledged for their neglect in not observing
and obeying the several good laws of this Countrey and if any such offenders
or informer shall faile to appear at the time afsd that then they shall have
such fine or fines imposed upon him or them as the Laws in such cases doth
provide and direct

    1. ANNE the wife of RICHARD AYLIFF for Speaking Blasphemy .. JOHN CRAF-
FORD, RICHARD AYLIFF SENR., RICHARD AYLIFF JUNR., GEORGE SPILLAR and JAMES
STANTON informers.

    2. JAMES LUNSFORD for living in adultery with SARAH THORNBY having gotten
her with child he having a wife and three children in Lancaster County in
Virginia and for all that he said all the Justices of Stafford County shall
not make him goe to his wife againe. RICHARD BRYANT, JOHN ROWLEY, WILLIAM
RUSTALL and WILLIAM VINE informers.

    3. GEORGE ANDREWS for living in adulterie with another mans wife he
having got Two children by her. JOHN TONEY informer.

    4. Mr. THOMAS GREGG SENR. for goeing to fence in their majesties cleared
road.

    5. ROBERT ALEXANDER hath fenced the road about from the old way so that
it is not passable for strangers in the night. AUGUSTINE KNEATON, BRYANT
BATTEY, ABRAM BECKINTON, RICHARD BRYANT, HENEREY MEREST, STEPHEN SEBASTIAN,
GEORGE OSTREE, JOHN ROWLEY, CHRISTOPHER HERRINGE, THOS. DERRICK, WILLIAM
PARKER, HENRY RIDGWAY, RICHARD RICHEE, BENJAMIN WEBB, WILLIAM RUSTALL grand-
jurymen informers.

697.   Ordered that the Sheriff summon ELIZABETH the widow and admx of NICHOLAS
        BURNARD late of this County deced to the next Court to bringe in a True
and perfect account of her Husbands Estate and that she may then make oath to
the same.

698.   ROBERT BRENT the attorney of GILBERT CLARKE of the Province of Maryland
        complains against STEPHEN SMITH of this County in plea of debt for that
the said Smith stands justly indebted to the Plt in qualification afsd in sum
of Twelve hundred ninety six pounds of Tobacco in cask .. And Stephen Smith by
RICHARD GIBSON his Attorney .. for plea saith non est factum which plea is
overruled by the Court .. Therefore tis ordered Stephen Smith shall make payment ..

699.   Whereas PATRICK MICKLEROY brought his action in this Court against JOHN
        GANNAWAY for the sum of Seven hundred and five pounds of Tobacco in cask
who not appearing Thereupon order passed against the Sheriff to bring the body
of the said John Gannaway to this Court according to act of assembly and because the Sheriff did not bring the body of the said

Page 46   Court held 7th April 1690

John Gannaway according to the said order Therefore tis ordered that Patrick
Mickleroy shall have Judgment against MALACHI PEALE High Sheriff for the pay-

Page 46 (contd)   Court held 7th April 1690

ment .. Whereas Patrick Mickleroy obtained an order of this Court against
Malachi Peale high sheriff .. and forasmuch as MATTHEW OSEE of this County became Security with the said John Gannaway for his appearance at Court .. There-
for tis ordered Malachi Peale high sheriff shall have judgment against the
said Matthew Osee for payment of said Seven hundred and five pounds of Tobacco
in cask with costs ..

700.   Whereas Capt. GEORGE MASON brought his action in this Court against ABRAM
        AMIS for sum of Four hundred pounds of Tobacco in cask who not appearing
Thereupon an order passed against the sheriff to bring the body of the said
Abram Amis to this Court according to act of assembly and because the sheriff
did not bring the body of the said Abram Amis according to their order Therefore
tis ordered that Capt. George Mason have Judgment against Malachi Peale high
sheriff .. and whereas Capt. George Mason obtained an order of this Court
against Malachi Peale high sheriff for nonappearance of Abram Amis .. Therefore
this ordered Malachi Peale high sheriff shall have Judgment against Abram Amis
for payment of the sum of Four hundred pounds of Tobacco ..

701.   SAMPSON DARRELL complains against ABRAM AMIS in plea of debt for that the
        said Amis stands indebted to him the Plt in the sum of Fifteen hundred
pounds of Tobacco in cask .. and whereas JOHN WEST became Security with the
said Abram Amis to answer the complaint .. and forasmuch as Abram Amis did not
appear to answer .. Therefore tis ordered Sampson Darrell shall have Judgment
against John West Bayle as aforesaid for the sum of Eight hundred Eighty two
pounds of Tobacco in cask being the full ballance of account due from Abram Amis.

702.   Ordered that the high sheriff bring the body of JOHN CARR to next Court
        to answer the complaint of JOSEPH EYRES according to act of assembly and
pay costs.   Attachment according to act of assembly granted the sheriff against
the Estate of John Carr for his nonappearance to answer the suit of Joseph
Eyres with costs.

Page 47   Court held 7th April 1690

703.   RICHD. GIBSON did appear in this Court the Attorney of PHILIP EVANS and
        did assume to pay all costs and charges that might accrue to DAVID DAR-
NELL in an action depending in this Court between the said Philip Evans and
David Darnell the deft and pay all costs.

704.   SAMLL. HAYWARD complaining sheweth that NICHOLAS BURNARD at the time of
        his decease stood indebted to the Plt the sume of Four hundred and ninety
pounds of Tobacco .. for which he hath brought his action against ELIZABETH the
relict and admx of Nicholas Burnard deced .. and now forasmuch as Samuel Hayward did produce here in Court the aforesaid Bill .. Therefore tis ordered
Elizabeth Burnard shall make payment ..

705.   MALACHI PEALE high sheriff complaining sheweth that NICHOLAS BURNARD at
        the time of his decease stood indebted to the Plt the sum of Five hundred
and two pounds of Tobacco .. for which he hath brought his action against
ELIZABETH the relict and admx of Nicholas Burnard deced .. and now forasmuch
as Malachi Peale did produce in Court the aforesaid Bill .. Therefore tis ordered Elizabeth Burnard shall make payment ..

706.   JOHN PORE came into Court and confessed Judgment unto RICHARD GIBSON for
        sum Four hundred pounds of Tobacco and cask Therefore tis ordered John
Pore shall make payment ..

Page 47 (contd)   Court held 7th April 1690

707. JOHN WITHERS the Attorney of ROBERT HEWIT complaining sheweth that NICO.
      BURNARD late of this County deced at the time of his death stood indebted
to the Plt the sum Four hundred ninety and six pounds of Tobacco due per a former Judgment of this Worshipful Court .. brought against ELIZABETH the widow
relict and admx of Nico. Burnard deced .. And now forasmuch as Elizabeth Burnard
did by GERRARD LOWTHER her attorney appear in Court and could say nothing in
Barr of Judgment .. Therefore tis ordered Elizabeth Burnard shall make payment ..

Page 48   Court held 7th April 1690

708. ROBT. CROPPER complains against JOHN CHAMPE in a plea of Debt for that
      the said John Champe stands indebted to the Plt the sum of Seven hundred
pounds of Tobacco .. and John Champe confessed Judgment .. Therefore tis ordered John Champe make payment .. Whereas Robert Cropper did arrest John Champe
to this Court and there did appear no cause of action Therefore tis ordered
Robert Cropper shall be nonsuit and pay John Champe fifty pounds of Tobacco ..

709. ROBERT BRENT complains against ROBERT DUNNE in a plea of debt that the
      said Robert Dunne did by deed under his hand and seale bearing date 28th
day of May 1687 become bound and obliged to the Plt to doe soe much worke of
and belonging to his Trade of Bricklayer or Mason as should be really worth
one thousand pounds of Tobacco and cask when thereunto required by the Plt as
by the above recited deed or Instrument Obligatory doth and may appear the sum
being due for the consideration of the said sum of one thousand pounds of Tobacco by the said Dunne reced before the passing of the said deed which said
worke the Plt did often request and Importune the deft to doe and perform but
never could get him to do it nor any part thereof until in or about the month
of August 1688 at which time the deft came and promised the Plt to do work to
the value aforesaid and in order thereunto set to making of Bricks for backs
of Chimneys fire hearths and one oven and had for his assistance therein three
servants of the Plts for the space of one week in which time he made what
bricks the Plt had occasion of and then pretended he would goe elsewhere to
work for 2 or 3 days while the bricks dryed but never came more to use them so
that they were all washed away with the raine and the Plts worke remains yet
undone by reason whereof he is damnified Two thousand pounds of Tobacco and
cask and Whereas by the Statute of the 5th of Queen Elizabeth it is provided
that if any Artificer or Labourer that shall be retained for the performing or
finishing of any work and shall depart from the same before it is finished shall
pay to the owner of the worke the sum of Five pounds Sterling over and besides
such ordinary costs and damages as may be or ought to be recovered by the Common Laws for any such offence the Plt hath then brought his action against the
deft for the said sum of Five thousand pounds of Tobacco and cask and five
pounds Sterling and humbly prays Judgment .. And now forasmuch as it doth appear to this Court that there is due from Robert Dunne only the sum of Seven
hundred and fifty pounds of Tobacco unto Robert Brent Therefore tis ordered that
he shall make payment (of said sum) with costs ..

Page 49   Court held 7th April 1760

710. Whereas RALPH ELKIN made humble petition to this Court that he became
      bound together with FRANCIS DADE of this County as Security for CHARLES
BALDRIDGE touching the Estate of JOHN HERBERT late of this County deced and now
considering he the said Elkin is very antient as also sick and weak doth therefore humbly pray that he may be discharged from the said bond and Securityship
and that Charles Baldridge may bring another in his Room and stead And the Court

do accordingly order and Therefore tis ordered that Ralph Elkin of and from
his Bonde and Securityship for Charles Baldridge shall be fully and freely discharged and that the Sheriff shall take Charles Baldridge into his custody until he bring a good and sufficient Security to be bounde in the Room and place
of Ralph Elkin touching the aforesaid Estate.

711. WILLIAM DAVIS complaining sheweth that DAVID DARNELL of this County in
      May last did Inveagle persuade and Entertaine your Petitioners Servant
by name MARTIN SPENCE and pretending he would set him free and that he was no
servant to your Petr did there persuade the said Servant to stay with him and
there did Employ him to Worke for the Space of Ten dayes in which time the only
Season for planting hapned & at that time your Petr being from home upon business in the Province of Maryland left the planting of his crop besides he is
damnified and hath damage to the value of Five thousand pounds of Tobacco for
which he hath brought his action .. And the said David Darnell by his Wife came
into Court .. for plea saith not guilty .. And now forasmuch as the said William Davis could not aver Justifie and maintaine his said action against David
Darnell and that it doth appear to this Court that the Servant did voluntarily
runaway and absent himself from William Davis his afsd Master Therefore tis
ordered that David Darnell shall pay unto William Davis Seven days worke in the
month of May and that each party pay his own costs and charges ..

712. JOHN BREWTON complains against ROBERT BRENT in a plea of Debt for that
      he stands Indebted to the Plt the sum of Two hundred and eighty pounds
of Tobacco .. and forasmuch as it doth appear to this Court that there is due
from Robert Brent (the said sum) .. Therefore tis ordered Robert Brent shall
make payment .. and Robert Brent not being content with the Judgment of the
Court doth therefore appeale to the 6th day of the General Court .. at James
Citty.

Capt. George Brent became security with Robert Brent to prosecute his appeale
and HENRY THOMPSON became Security with John Brewton to answer the appeale.

713. HENRY MEREST complains against RICHARD GIBSON in a plea of debt for that
      the said Gibson stands indebted to the Plt the sum of One thousand and
seventy pounds of Tobacco .. and forasmuch as it doth appear to this Court the
sum is due .. Therefore tis ordered Richard Gibson make payment ..

714. PHILIP EVANS complains against DAVID DARNELL for that David Darnell did
      some time in June last past did Employ your Petr to work for the Space
of six weeks at twenty per diem after the said worke done did not only refuse
to pay your Petr his wages but did also stop and detain all your Petrs cloaths
Whereby he is damnified at the least three thousand pounds of Tobacco and cask
.. and the said David Darnell by his Wife appears in Court .. for plea saith
not guilty .. and for Tryal puts himself upon the Country and the Plt Likewise.
Therefore tis ordered the Jury Enquire the Fact: SIGISS. MASSEY, BRYANT BATTEY,
WILLIAM HAMBLETON, JOHN MATHEWS, BENJAMIN WEB, WILLIAM DOWNING, JAMES MONKE,
AUGUST KNEATON, HENRY THOMPSON, DAVID WAUGH, SIMON THOMASON, WILLIAM BOWRNE
which said Jurors Elected Tryed and sworne to say the Truth of the Premises do
say upon their oaths we find for the Plt and doe allow him one thousand pounds
of Tobacco for the Coat and suit with work done and that the deft is to have
the coat. Therefore tis ordered Judgment shall be entered on the Verdict of
the Jury .. Ordered Philip Evans shall pay the Jury Seventy two pounds of To-

Page 50 (contd)   Court held 7th April 1690

bacco with costs .. Ordered Philip Evans shall make payment of Eighty pounds of
Tobacco per peece unto CHRISTOPHER HERRINGE and his wife for their attendance
two daies at Court in suit depending between him and David Darnell with costs ..

715. MALACHI PEALE High Sheriff complains against HUGH FRENCH in a plea of
      Debt that the said Hugh French stands indebted to the Plt the sume of
Four hundred twenty five pounds of Tobacco due him for sheriffs fees for

Page 51   Court held 7th April 1760

which he hath brought his action .. And now forasmuch as Malachi Peale did here
in Court produce his account of fees .. and doth appear sum is due .. Therefore
tis ordered Hugh French make payment ..

716. JOHN WEST complaining sheweth that ABRAHAM BECKINGTON about seven years
      since gave to your Petrs Son a browne pide yearling cow calfe then un-
marked runing on the plantation of your Petr and then did order your Petr to
marke the said Beast which he did cropt and slit on the left and apeece taken
from under the right eare and two nicks on the upper side of the Eare which
Beast so given and so marked hath ever since run for the said JOHN WEST JUNR.
together with her increase until lately that the said Abram Beckington hath
taken into his possession the said Beast and two of her increase Wherefore the
Plt brings his suit .. and now after the Court hearing a full debate of the
matter doe order Therefore tis ordered that Abram Beckington shall give to
John West Junr. Sonne of John West of this County Immediately one two year old
heifer with all her future female increase and that Abram Beckington shall
presently marke the afsd heifer in a proper marke for John West Junr. and shall
keep her with her female increase unto John West Junr. shall come of age of
twenty one years old and that each party pay their own costs.

     The balance of this page contains a summary of the previous actions
giving Attorneys and clients.

     The Court is adjourned till the Second Wednesday in June next

Page 52 At a Court held for County of Stafford June the 11th 1690

717. Present Lt. Coll. Wm. Fitzhugh, Capt. Geo. Mason, Mr. John Withers,
      Mr. Samuel Hayward, Mr. Matthew Thompson, Justices

718. WM. FITZHUGH Gent complaineth against FRANCIS DADE in a plea of Trespasse
      for that Francis Dade with force and Armes keeps and detaines from your
Petr messuage Tenement and large orchard thereto belonging and the land thereto
adjoining situate lying and being on Mochotack Creek in Stafford County and
generally called by the name of SIMMES PLANTATION and yet continues to keep and
detain the same although he was therefrom forewarned the 15th day of May last
past to your Petitioners damage three hundred pounds Sterling and divers other
harms to your Petr .. which said land and appurtenances is a part of a greater
dividend of 1300 acres granted by patent unto GERVASE DODSON the 13th of Octo.
1653 according to the condition of plantations and therein mentioned to be situate
lying and being in Northumberland now Westmoreland which then was Westmoreland
at the granting thereof in the year 1653 afsd and by Gervase Dodson sold to
one JOHN SMITH by a Sort of a Deed on the backside of the said Patent bearing
date 17th August 1658 which deed follows in these words These presents witnesseth
that I Gervase Dodson doe engage myself my heirs and assigns to warrant and
firmly possess John Smith of a patent of 1300 acres of land Specified according
to the contents of the within specified patent and shall further Ensure the same
unto the said Smith his heirs and assigns upon a valuable consideration already

715 - 718

Page 52 (contd)   Court held 11th June 1690

reced as witness my hand this 17th of August 1658. The contents of the above
specified engagement I do oblige myself my heirs or assigns to perform or pay
unto the said Smith his heirs or assigns 30000 lb Tobacco upon demand Witness
my hand the day and year abovesaid and as pretended to be acknowledged in
Northumberland County when the land at the first pattenting as by the words of
this pattent appeares was situate lying and being in Westmoreland County by
JAMES POPE Attorney of the said Dodson Two years and one month after the date
of the sale as aforesaid to say the 5th of September 1660 neither is there any
proof of the procuration afsd which acknowledgment follows in hoc verba 5th
September 1660. This sale of land was acknowledged to the above named John
Smith was acknowledged in Northumberland County Court by James Pope Atturney
of the said Gervase Dodson and ISABEL his wife and is recorded per me RICHARD
FLYNT where note he has not nominated himself Clerk of the sd County of Northumberland and non Constat whether he was or noe according to the first Rules
of Law it ought not to be helpt by averment which said land soe to the said
Smith conveyed was by the said Smith for the valuable consideration of 12000
lb Tobacco in hand paid conveyed by a good authentick deed considering the
unskilfulness and Brevity of those times to HUGH DOWDINGE of Gloucester County
by deed bearing date the 15th day of July 1659 which said deed follows in these
words These presents Witnesseth that I John Smith of Westmoreland County for
and in consideration of 12000 lb Tobacco and cask to be paid according to

Page 53   Court held 11th June 1690

the Tens. of a Specialty bearing date with these presents have sold and do
hereby assigne and set over from me and my heirs to Mr. Hugh Dowding of
Glocester his heirs or assignes forever all my Right Title and Interest to and
in the within mentioned land Patent and Bill of Sale with the warranty therein
mentioned as witness my hand this 25th of July 1659 (Note a year and two months
after this Sale from Smith was the Northumberland acknowledgment made to him
Vizt September 1660) which sale from Smith to Dowdinge was acknowledged in
Stafford County Court where the land then lay by the Division of the Counties
by Mrs. BEHETHLAND GILSON by name of the late relict of the aforesaid John
Smith 12th June 1667 to Endeavour a full confirmation of that sale which she
perhaps might know was honestly bought and justly paid for as your Petr believes
and Supposes which acknowledgment follows in these words This assignment was
by Mrs. Behethland Gilson the late relict of John Smith by atturney acknowledged
in Court and recorded the 12th June 1667 and then also was recorded in the said
Court of Stafford the originall patent to Dodson the said sale from Dodson to
Smith fully as it is above expressed which said land so conveyed as aforesaid
to the afsd Dowding one half thereof was by the said Dowding assigned and made
over to Mr. JOHN BUCKNER of Glocester County as your Petr is informed and some-
thing thereof by division upon record bearing date the 11th of April 1663 doth
appeare and as your Petr believes by a further deed and Instrument though not
Authentick according to the Strict Rules of Law yet considering the ignorance
and Summary methods of those times your Petr conceives to be valid and then 100
acres of part of the said dividend of 1300 acres was by the said Dowding and
Buckner assigned and made over to one BLAGRAVE for seating of it in their be-
halves no deed upon the records or elsewhere appearing for the same yet having
been 30 years or thereabouts possest quietly by the said Blagrave and his assigns Colclough and his heirs your Petr Esteems that likewise valid the remainder the said Dowding possest and Enjoyed himself during his natural life and
left the same by Will to his Son HUGH DOWDING and his heirs forever but if he
dyed without heirs then to the children of ROBERT BUTTERFIELD his wives daugh-

Page 53 (contd) Court held 11th June 1690

ters children and their heirs by whose death and the Will afsd his Wife ANNE
DOWDINGE was seized and possessed of the house and Plantation where he lives
upon the said land together with the one third thereof which sd Dowding quietly
enjoyed during his life and she her thirds quietly and peaceably after his decease till her death which was about the 12th or 13th of May 1690 which wants
but 2 months of 31 years of quiet possession since the first purchase and the
said Dowding thereon dyed before he attained the age of twenty one years by
whose decease the said Land descended and came to RICHARD DOWDINGE of London
Mariner the Brother and heir of Hugh Dowding the Father and unkle and heir of
Hugh Dowding the Son who came in and pursuant to his right and claim took possession thereof about 8 or 9 years since Mr. ANTHONY BUCKNER deced and your
Petr being present when he took the possession aforesd and when he made the
assignation of the one third to ANNE SIMMS the widow and relict of his Brother
Hugh Dowding deced and the said Buckner and your Petr swore

Page 54 Court held 11th June 1690

Employed by the said Richard Dowding by virtue of a procuration to them granted
to oversee the occupation and possession of the other two thirds part of the
land belonging to the said Dowdinge as afsd who forthwith sent up a Servant to
live upon and manure part of his 2 third parts which he had then in actual possession to wit one JOHN REYNOLDS by which actual possession of Richard Dowding
heir as afsd the pretensions of the said Butterfields children are taken away
since which time the said Richard Dowding is dead without Will or heir or any
way disposing the same by deed or otherways in his lifetime Whereby the said
land became escheat to the right Honble Lord Culpepper as Chief Lord of the Fee
as appears by divers deeds and grants made to his Lordship whereon he is Intitled to the same which said right of the land so escheated his Lordship by
deed hath granted to your Petr for a valuable consideration by your Petr paid
for the same by vertue whereof your Petr is in the actual Seisin and possession
of the 2 third parts that was in the actual possession of the said Richd.
Dowding deced and is kept out with force and Armes as afsd and against the
peace of our Sovereign Lord and Lady King William and Queen Mary of the other
part by the said Dade therefore prays for the damages of Three hundred pounds
Sterling afsd and that the Sheriff may put him in possession without that that
the said Francis Dade made any Lawful or Just claim to the same who pretends
himself as your Petr is informed Son and heir of John Smith the purchaser of
Dodson and vendor to Dowding and farther saith the said Smiths Sale to Dowding
was invalid and ineffectual in Law for that there was no acknowledgment within
six months according as the Law directs and consequently the right never devested
out of the said Smith and so by consequence he as his son and heir the right
proprietor of the said land not considering when he said soe that he himself
petitiond 25th May 1664 to Sr. WILLIAM BERKLEY then Governour for the benefit
of the Escheat of a Tract of 600 acres of land lying in Stafford County formerly
granted to Major Jno. Smith deced which your Petr doth aver to be the same John
Smith aforementioned and is ready to prove the same if it be Denyed and lately
found to Escheat to his Majestie by an Inquisition in the Secretarys office
under the hand and seale of Coll. PETER ASHTON by vertue of adeputation from
Coll. MILES CARY his Majesties Escheator General for this country and the Jury
sworn before him for the purpose dated 11th January 1664/5 as may appeare and
is now granted to Francis dade who hath now made his composition to be paid
according to act so that then it appears by the oaths of 12 men that the afsd
John Smith dyed without heir and this found and made appeare at the motion and
intercession and for the benefit and behoofe of the said Francis Dade who if

Page 54 (contd)   Court held 11th June 1690

had been his son and heir where was the possibility of the Land to Escheat also
not considering the 81 years quiet possession as aforesaid and himself being
now upwards of 30 years old and not in all this time make any Legal claim to
the Title nor any Interruption to the quiet possession as aforesaid if he had
been Legall heir as he pretends or the deed had been ineffectual or invalid as
he folishly fancies your Petr humbly conceives he is barred by the 30th act of
assembly in the Printed Booke Intituled Land 5 years in possession and further
to demonstrate his nonclaims to the said Land and his acknowledgment of the
Right to those in possession in June last 1689 he took a Lease and became tenant
to the said Ann Sims the widow and relict of the aforesaid Hugh Dowding deced

Page 55   Court held 11th June 1690

Her for the same the yearly rent of 1200 lb Tobacco and 4 barrells of Indian
Corne for her right to the same afsd as by the deed upon the records doth appear and for his pretensions to the Illegallity and Invalidity of the deed for
want of timely acknowledgment or recording your Petr supposes he must ground
that advantage either upon the 27th H 8 Cap 16 Intituled a Statute of Imple-
ments of Bargains and contracts of land and tenements or upon the 73d printed
act of assembly Intituled against fraudulent conveyances but may it please your
Worships one cannot the other must not be binding in this case as your Petr
shall plainly make appeare for the English Statute the words are except the
same bargaine and sale be made by writing indented and Inrolled in any of the
Kings Courts at Westminster or else in the same Court where the land lyes and
the same Inrollment to be had within Six months next after the date of the same
writing Indented The Clerk of the peace shall sufficiently inroll in parchment
so that by this act ineffectual if it be not inrolled in parchment or one day
after the 6 months is Expired or recorded in the same County makes all fruitless
though all the other branches of the act had been duly pursued as may be fully
seen by the Statute itself and my Lord Cookes Learned Commentary thereupon in
his 2d Institute fo 674 besides this Statute requires noe acknowledgment from
the Vendor but that the Vendee take care to have it inrolled as the Law directs
that is recorded pursuant to all the circumstances of the said Act if it should
be of force here and Titles questioned thereby your Petr dares and does confi-
dently affirme that there is hardly one good Title to land in Virginia Therefore
this Statute must not take place as to our own act of assembly that noe person
whatsoever shall passe over by conveyance or otherwaies any part of his Estate
whether land whereby his Creditors might be defrauded of their Just debts unlesse
such conveyance or other deeds be acknowledged before the Governour and Council
at the General Court or before the Justice of the County Courts and there regis-
tered in a booke made for that purpose within six months after such alienation
and whoever shall make and alienate any part of his Estate otherwise than is
here Expressed the same shall not be accounted valid in Law nor shall it barr
any creditor by seizing the same by Law for satisfaction of the debt the property
of the Estates not being Legally but in the first Vendour This seems positive
at first view but upon consideration of the whole scope and drift of the act
appears to be for prevention of frauds used by Debtors by clandestinely conveying away their Estates to defraud their creditors and therefore perhaps notwithstanding this act a deed made bone fide upon good consideration where the
Vendor has sufficient besides to Satisfie all creditors though this act were
not pursued in the Sale I humbly conceive the deed might be good enough that
the said Smith at the time of making the afsd deed to Dowdinge had sufficient
to answer all creditors and a plentiful Estate besides is well known to all the
antient Inhabitants and if occasion were is Easily proved But may it please

Page 55 (contd)   Court held 11th June 1690

your Worships this deed of Dowdings as per the date thereof appears was made
in the year 1659 and this act of assembly was made in the year 1662 soe that
this act cannot have relation to a deed that was made three years before the
making of the said Laws for that would be making Laws Expost facto, and this
in a word your Petr conceives clears the deed from any defect by that Law
farther may it please your Worships that the Stat of H 8 was strictly to be

Page 56   Court held 11th June 1690

pursued and by consequence Dowdings deed void by that Law then by the same
Law or same Reasons would Smiths deed from Dodson be utterly void as materially
failing in all points by that Statute required as Dowdings or farther admitting
that the said act of assembly made in 1682 for acknowledgment of deeds within
six months as one reason why it shouts stop there and could not looke some
months farther and Espy Smiths deed so far from being acknowledged in the
General Court where the land lyes within the six months prescribed by the Law
that it stayes two years one month before it is acknowledged at all and then
acknowledged in a remote county where the land lay not by an attorney which is
not all proved to case. Therefore I say if the other be faulty this is absolutely vitious and ineffectual and consequently the right would againe vest in
Dodson the first proprietor who also is dead without heir and by that means my
Lord Culpepper would be intituled to the whole tract and then your Petr. having
his right as aforesd would be betterd in his Estate which your Petr neither
covets nor desires as Esteeming those deeds good considering the time they were
made in but however your Petr submits to your Worships Judgment assuring himself
that upon the Laws aforesaid your Worships must either Judge both of the deeds
good or bad for they are both of one Stampe, if good then your Petrs right to
Dowdings part that he left undisposed is good as he has above declared if bad
then your Petr has a greater right then he could think or hope for in his own
poor weak Judgment and either way your Petr conceives the said Dade a Trespasser
as afsd Wherefore your Petr prays that he may be by the Sheriff removed immediately and pay the damages aforesaid with costs of suit and further your
Petr humbly moves that according to the 84 act of assembly in the Printed Booke
Intituled the Defendt to put in his answer for the reasons therementioned to
say that for the better regulating and keeping the records and transferring the
presidents to posterity as also for the prosecution of new Suites upon mistakes
of the grounds of others that as the plaintiff both in General and County Courts
files his declaration so the deft in both courts shall alsoe put in his answer
in writing & that the deft may be ordered to put his And the said Francis Dade
by GERRARD LOWTHER his Attorney comes into Court and craves Licence of Imparlance till the next Court for to put in his answer to the Plts declaration which
unto him is granted and that then his plea be not wanting.

719.   JOHN HARVEY complaining sheweth that WILLIAM JOHNSON and CHARLES SLEDGE
       stand indebted unto the Plt the sum of Nineteen hundred and sixteen pounds
of Tobacco in caske due him by accompt who hath absented himself out of this
county and your Plt tooke out an attachment against their Estates according to
Law .. and now forasmuch as John Harvey did Exhibit his accompt to this Court
and Justly made appear his debt to be due Therefore tis ordered (he) shall
have Judgment against the Estates of William Johnson and Charles Sledge .. And
EDWARD HUDSON by ROBERT COLLIS his Attorney came into Court and prayed a Replevin of a cow and calfe with a yearling bull which belongs to him that

719

was attached by the sd JOHN HARVEY in the lands of HENRY HARVEY as afsd and
Esteems to be the Estate of the aforesaid Johnson and CHARLES SLEDGE which unto
him is granted until the next Court he the said EDWARD HUDSON giving security
to the Court to provide that the cattle soe attached may be forthcoming to the
next Court & then he may bring in a good and sufficient proof that the said
cattle is his as he above declares and prayes for & that he faile not to bring
in his Evidence to the next Court as afsd or else pay his cost. WILLIAM BURTON
became Security with the sd Edward Hudson to perform what the Law requires
touching the said Estate.

720.   JOHN GRIGSBY complaining sheweth that WILLIAM JOHNSON and CHARLES SLEDGE
         stand indebted to the Plt the sum of nine hundred pounds of Tobacco in
cask due him by Bill .. And now forasmuch as the said John Grigsby did produce
the aforesd bill in this court under the hands and Seales of the afsd William
Johnson and Charles Sledge .. Therefore tis ordered that John Grigsby shall
have Judgment against one hhd Tobacco and one Bushell and half of Indian Corne ..

721.   MARY MASSEY complaining sheweth that THOMAS ENGLISH late of this county
         stood indebted to the Plt the sum of four hundred and thirty two pounds
of Tobacco in cask due per bill .. And forasmuch as Mary Massey did Exhibit in
this Court the afsd bill .. Therefore tis ordered that Mary Massey shall have
Judgment against the Estate of Thomas English soe attached in the hands of
THOMAS HOWARD for the afsd sum ..

722.   HENRY CARPENTER of Maryland came into Court and confessed Judgment to
         Capt. MALACHI PEALE Attorney of EVAN JONES for the sum of twelve hundred
pounds of Tobacco in caske due per bill .. Therefore tis ordered Henry Carpenter shall make payment ..

723.   WM. YOUNG the oldest son of Mr. VINCENT YOUNG late of this County deced
         and appointed one of the Executors of the afsd Vincent Young appointed
in his last will & Testament came into Court in propria persona and relinquished
his part of the Executorship of the said Will. Probate of last will & Testament of Vincent Young late of this County deced is granted to ELIZABETH the
wife of Vincent Young she having fully proved the same by the Oaths and Testimonies of JAMES NELSON and JOHN PORTER Witnesses to the afsd Will thereunto
subscribed she giving Security to perform what the Law requires touching her
said Husbands Estate.

Page 58   Court held 11th June 1690

Mr. SAML. HAYWARD and JOHN WILLIAMS came into Court and became Securities with
the afsd Elizabeth Young to perform what the Law requires touching the said
Estate. Ordered that PHILIP BUCKNER, JOHN WILLIAMS and JAMES BURNARD shall
appraise the Estate of Mr. Vincent Young late of this County deced upon the
26th of this Instant June or any two of them and that Mr. JOHN WITHERS shall
swear them accordingly. Ordered that Elizabeth Young shall make present payment of the sum of forty pounds of Tobacco unto JAMES NELSON and JOHN PORTER
per peece for their attendance in Court for to prove her Husbands will with
costs ..

724.   Ordered that there shall be an Orphans Court for this County at the Court
         House on second Wednesday in July next and that the Sheriff summon all
manner of persons whatsoever that are concerned with Orphans Estates then and
there to make their personal appearance and to render a Just and True Accompt
of the said Estates committed to their charge and Trust.

Page 58 (contd)   Court held 11th June 1690

725. Ordered that THOMAS CHAPMAN shall have Judgment against EDWARD WATTS for
      the sum of two hundred pounds of tobacco and that he shall make present
paymt of the same with costs .. ·

726. Ordered that EDWARD WATTS shall make present payment of forty pounds of
      Tobacco unto JAMES MONKE for his attendance one day at Court in a Suit
depending between him and THOMAS CHAPMAN with costs ..

727. Ordered by this Court that JOSEPH NEWTON shall make present payment unto
      MARY BUTLER his late Servant her freedom Cloaths according to the custom
of the country in the like kind and one barrel of Indian Corne and if that she
can bring sufficient Evidence to the next Court that she was free in free in
February Last that then the said Joseph Newton shall pay her Two barrels of
Indian Corne more with costs ..

728, Ordered that the Sheriff shall take the body of JAMES LUNSFORD into his
      Custody for him to give bond with good sufficient security for his ap-
pearance at the next Court to answer the complaint of the grand jury then and
there to be made against him.

729. Upon humble petition made to this Court by EDMOND KELLEY of this County
      that he has lived to the age of sixty one years and having a great family
of children and almost past his Labour he therefore humbly prays this Worshipful Court that he might be fully and freely discharged from paying any further
levy and the Court having fully considered the Truth of the premises doe accordingly order Therefore tis ordered that the said Edmond Kelley shall for the
future be fully and freely discharged from paying any farther Levy.

730. EDWARD HUDSON came into Court and confessed Judgment unto GEORGE LUKE
      for the sum of six hundred and twenty five pounds of Tobacco due per
Bill ..

731. JOHN MATHEWS came into Court and became Security with CHARLES BALDRIDGE
      for the Estate of JOHN HEABERD to perform what the Law requires touching
the said Estate.

Page 59   Court held 11th June 1690

732. THOS. CHAPMAN came into Court and confessed Judgment unto XTOP. HERRINGE
      for sum of eight hundred pounds of Tobacco in caske due per Bill ..

733. ELIZA. BURNARD widow and relict of NICHOLAS BURNARD late of this County
      deced humbly petitioned to this Court that her Husband at the time of
his death left her in a very poore condition as likewise destitute of relief
wherefore she humbly prays this worshipfull Court to allow her one flock bed
one sheet one blanket and Rugg one Iron Pot two pewter dishes and two plates
a small table two chairs one old Trunke and one chest being that part of her
Husbands Estate wch was not appraised for her paraphalenia And the Court having
taken into their most charitable consideration accordingly orders Therefore tis
ordered that Elizabeth Burnard shall be allowed the recited goods for her paraphalenia.

734. JOHN HALEYS, JOSEPH EYRES in Chancery upon reference from the 12th Xber
      1689 And now until when the deft had Lycence to put in his plea and for
plea saith by GERRARD LOWTHER his attorney not guilty And forasmuch as the Court
having fully heard the matter debated between them as well on the behalfe of
Joseph Eyres the deft as on the other parte of John Haley the Plt and maturely
weighed and Throughly considered of the premises doe accordingly order There-

725 - 734

Page 59 (contd)   Court held 11th June 1690

fore tis ordered that Joseph Eyres shall make present satisfaction of the said
Mare with her increase which he has now in his custody and belonging to the said
Haley in the like good condition as she was delivered to him Each party paying
their own costs.

735. JOHN BLUNDALL complaining sheweth that NICHOLAS BURNARD late of this County
      deced stood indebted to the Plt the sum of Eleven hundred pounds of To-
bacco in caske due per bill .. Wherefore he brought his action against ELIZABETH
the late widow and relict of Nicholas Burnard deced .. And now forasmuch as it
doth appeare that Elizabeth Burnard hath paid out of her deced husbands Estate
as farr as assetts all to the sum of Eight hundred eighty four pounds of Tobacco Therefore tis ordered that John Blundall shall have Judgment against
Elizabeth Burnard for the afsd sum ..

736. Whereas RICHARD GIBSON made humble complaint to this Court shewing that
      he hath a Servant woman named MARY MASON who hath run away & absented
herself at several times to the number of thirty two daies and the Trouble
charges and damages for looking after her amounts to the sum of nine hundred
pounds of Tobacco and caske Wherefore your Petr hath brought his Servant to
this Court and Exhibited his Just accompt against her and therefore prays the
Judgment of this Worshipfull Court against Mary Mason for the aforesd Lost

Page 60   Court held 11th June 1690

Time and damages for looking after her according to act of assembly in that
case made and provided .. Therefore tis ordered Mary Mason shall serve Richard
Gibson her afsd Master the full end & Term of one year after the Expiration of
her time by Indenture & a former order of this Court bearing date the 12th of
March 1690 for her so fugitively running away ..

737. JOSEPH EYRES complaining against JOHN CARR in a plea of Debt .. sum of
      seven hundred sixty and five pounds of Tobacco in caske .. Therefore tis
ordered John Carr shall make payment ..

738. THOS. BARTON complaining sheweth that FRANCIS HAMMERSLEY as Trustee to
      the Estate of JAMES GERRARD deced stands indebted to the Plt the sum of
sixteen hundred pounds of Tobacco and Caske for funeral charges accomodation
Trouble & attendance of him the said Gerrard in his Languishing Sickness which
the said Hammersley hath not paid the Plt .. and now forasmuch as it doth appeare to this Court that the said Hammersley hath paid out of the said James
Gerrards Estate almost as far as assets Therefore tis ordered that Francis
Hammersley make payment of eight hundred pounds of tobacco in cask ..

739. JOSHUA DAVIS Attorney of MICHAEL WELLINGTON the attorney of ANNE CHEWINGE
      the widow and Executrix of THOMAS CHEWINGE late deced complains against
FRANCIS BOX in a plea of Debt for that the said Box stands indebted to the Plt
.. Five thousand one hundred ninety four pounds of Tobacco in cask .. Francis
Box did discount sum .. appears to be due upon ballance only the sum of three

Page 61   Court held 11th June 1690

Thousand one hundred and sixty four pounds of Tobacco .. make payment for aforesaid with costs ..

740. ROBERT BRENT complains against THOMAS TUSTIN in plea of Trespass for that
      whereas by the 12 fifth act of Assembly it is enacted and provided that
whosoever shall steal or unlawfully kill any hogg which is not his owne and

735 - 740

Page 61 (contd)   Court held 11th June 1690

the said fact being proved by sufficient Evidence he or they so offending shall
pay to the owner of the said Hogg one thousand pounds of Tobacco and one thousand pounds of Tobacco to the Informer and if the owner inform he to have both
the fines and in case of Inability to pay and satisfie now so it is the deft
Thomas Tustin did in or about the months of October or November and December
1687 upon the Plts Plantation in this County unlawfully steal and kill divers
hoggs of the Plt three of which the Plt is ready to prove by Sufficient Evidence
.. And the said Thomas Tustin by GERRARD LOWTHER his attorney comes into Court
.. for plea saith not guilty .. Therefore this ordered that the Jury Enquire
the fact: Capt. WM. DOWNING, WILLIAM BURTON, JOHN MATHEWS, THOMAS HOWARD,
FRANCIS HUNT, SIMON THOMAS, THOMAS BARTON, WM. HAMBLETON, THOMAS DERRICK JUNR.,
BENJAMIN WEBB, JOHN BREWTON, HENRY THOMPSON which said Jurors Elected Tryed and
sworn do say upon their oaths we find for the defendant no cause of action
Therefore tis ordered that Judgment shall be entered on the verdict of the Jury
and Thomas Tustin of and from this action shall be dismissed and Robert Brent
shall pay costs. Ordered that Thomas Tustin shall pay the Jury seventy two
pounds of Tobacco with costs. Mr. MATH. THOMPSON absent and the said Robert
Brent not being content with the Verdict of the Jury appeals to be heard before
the Honble the Governour and Councel of State for Virginia the 6th day of next
General Court. Capt. GEORGE BRENT became security with Robert Brent to prosecute his appeale. Ordered by this Court that Thomas Tustin shall be summoned
by the Sheriff to the next Court there to give in Security to answer the appeale ..

741. Whereas ADAM WAFFENDALL did arrest ROBERT HEDGES to this Court to answer
      in a plea of debt and did not appeare to prosecute his action Therefore
tis ordered Adam Waffendall shall be nonsuit ..

Page 62   At a Court held for Stafford County the 12th day of June 1690

742. Present Collo. William Fitzhugh, Mr. Samuel Hayward, Capt. George Mason,
      Mr. John Withers Justices

743. FRANCIS HAMMERSLEY complains against JONATHAN BUCKLEY in plea of Debt ..
      sum of eight hundred pounds of Tobacco and cask due per Bill .. Jonathan
Buckley confessed Judgment .. Therefore tis ordered he shall make payment ..

744. EDWARD TAYLOR JUNR. complaineth against RICHARD PARKINSON in a plea of
      Debt .. the sum of five hundred and seventy pounds of Tobacco due per
accompt which he refuses to pay altho often fairly & legally demanded .. Therefore tis ordered Richard Parkinson shall make payment .. Ordered Edward Taylor
shall make payment of eighty pounds of Tobacco to JOHN BEACH for two daies attendance at Court in a suit depending between the said Edward Taylor and Richard
Parkinson with costs. Ordered that John Beach shall make payment of eight
pounds of Tobacco to Edward Taylor Junr. for his two days attendance at Court
in a suit depending between him the said John Beach and THOMAS DERRICK JUNR.
with costs ..

745. Ordered that the Sheriff shall bring the body of THOMAS NEWS to the next
      Court to answer the complaint of EDWARD TAYLOR JUNR. or else be Lyable
according to act of assembly and pay costs. Attachment according to act of
assembly is granted to the sheriff against Estate of Thomas News for his nonappearance at this Court to answer the suit of Edward Taylor Junr. with costs ..

741 - 745

Page 62 (contd)   Court held 12th June 1690

746. Whereas ROBERT BRENT did summons WILLIAM BEARD of this County to this
      Court to give Evidence to the Truth of what he knowes in an action depen-
ding between him and Robert Brent and THOMAS TUSTIN in a plea of Trespasse and
forasmuch as William Beard did faile to appeare and Robert Brent lost his cause
in this Court by reason of his nonappearance Therefore tis ordered that Robert
Brent shall have Judgment against William Beard for sum three hundred and fifty
pounds of Tobacco with costs according to act of assembly in that case made
and provided ..

Page 63   Court held 12th June 1690

747. RICHARD GIBSON complaining sheweth that RICHARD RICHEE of this county
      did some time in July last past at the house of BURR HARRISON in this
county and within the Jurisd. of this Court falsly maliciously and scandalously
contrary to the peace of their Majesties King William & Queen Mary abuse scan-
dalize and defame your Petr by saying your Petr is a rogue a pitiful rogue and
had cheated him in his accompts all which he would prove and much other such
bad and abusive language is hereby your petitioner is damnified five thousand
pounds of Tobacco Wherefore he hath brought his action .. and Richard Richee
by GEORGE BRENT his attorney comes and for plea saith that the words are not
actionable & therefore pleads to the uncertainty of the declaration and humbly
prays a nonsuit .. And the Court having fully and maturely weighed and considered
the premises do accordingly order Therefore tis ordered that Richard Gibson
shall be nonsuite and shall pay Richard Richee fifty pounds of Tobacco with
costs .. Ordered Richard Gibson make payment of eighty pounds of Tobacco unto
THOMAS MARLEY for his attendance Two daies at Court in a Suit depending between
him and Richard Richee with costs ..

748. RICHARD GIBSON complaining sheweth that RICHARD RICHEE of this county
      stands indebted to the Plt the sum of Fourteen hundred and sixteen pounds
of Tobacco and cask twelve hundred forty six of which being due per Bill the
remainder by account .. to which the deft pleaded that the said Bill or some
part thereof was for a debt due from the Estate of THOMAS MARLEY as by the
order therein will appear Now soe it is may it please your Worships that your
petitioner humbly presumes it was by some misanimadversion of the matter that
his plea was allowed against the Bill for by Law that plea could noeways Excuse
him from the payment thereof .. and your Petr having now brought his action
against the said Richee as marrying the administratrix of the said Marley humbly prays Judgment for seven hundred forty six pounds of Tobacco in cask being
the remainder of his debt .. and Richard Richard by GEORGE BRENT his attorney
pleads to the uncertainty of the declaration .. And now after full debate of
the matter heard by the Court .. the Court find that

Page 64   Court held 12th June 1690

the said Richard Gibson had noe cause of action .. Therefore tis ordered Richard
Gibson shall be nonsuit ..

749. JOHN AMEE complaineth against ROBERT HAMBLETON of this County in a plea
      of Trespass for that Robert Hambleton by force of Arms and contrary to
Law and the peace of our Sovereign Lord and Lady the King and Queen hath about
the middle of October last past killed one of the Hoggs of Capt. WILLIAM DOWNING
of this County .. (cites 125th act of assembly) .. And Robert Hambleton by his
Attorney comes into Court and for plea saith not guilty .. Therefore tis ordered
that the Jury Enquire the fact: AUGUSTINE KNEATON, XTOPHER HERRINGE, JOHN

Page 64 (contd)   Court held 12th June 1690

MATHEWS, WILLIAM RUSTALL, WM. HAMBLETON, JOHN MAN, JAMES MONKE, WILLIAM BURTON, GEORGE SHEPARD, JOHN BEACH, THOS. PORTER, HENRY THOMPSON which Jurors Elected Tryed and sworne to say the Truth of the premises We find for the defendant no cause of action Therefore tis ordered that Judgment shall be entered upon the Verdict of the Jury and that the Plt JOHN AMEE shall be nonsuit and shall pay ROBERT HAMBLETON fifty pounds of tobacco with costs .. Ordered Robert Hambleton pay unto the Jury seventy two pounds of tobacco with costs .. Ordered John Amee shall make payment of one hundred and twenty pounds of Tobacco unto HENRY RIDG-WAY and CHRISTIAN WADDINGTON per peece for their attendance at Court three daies in a suit depending between him and John Amee with costs .. (sic)
Ordered Robert Hambleton shall make payment of one hundred and twenty pounds of Tobacco unto WILLIAM DOWNING and HENRY TAYLOR per peece for their attendance at Court three daies in suit depending between him and Robert Hambleton .. (sic)

750.   Whereas ROBERT BRENT brought his action in this Court against JOHN WADDING
        for three barrels and a half of Indian Corne and four hundred pounds of Tobacco in caske due per bill who not appearing thereupon order passed against the Sheriff to bring the body of John Wadding to this Court according to act of assembly and because the Sheriff did not bring the body of John Wadding according to the afsd order Therefore tis ordered Robert Brent shall have Judgment against MALACHI PEALE high sheriff for the payment (of the debt) .. Whereas Robert Brent obtained an order of this Court against Malachi Peale high sheriff of this county for the nonappearance of John Wadding (for amount above) ..

Page 65   Court held 12th June 1690

and forasmuch as JONATHAN WHITTALL of this County became Security with John Wadding for his personal appearance at Court to answer the complaint of the aforesaid Brent Therefore tis ordered that Malachi Peale high sheriff shall have Judgment against John Whittall Security for payment (sum of debt) ..

751.   Capt. GEORGE BRENT the Attorney of HENRY BRENT complaineth against ROBT.
        DUNNE in plea of debt .. sum three thousand pounds good Tobacco and cask due per Bill under hand and seale dated the 28th of May 1687 .. Robert Dunne could say nothing in Barr or preclusion of said Debt .. Therefore tis ordered that Robert Dunne shall make payment ..

752.   RICHD. GIBSON complaining sheweth that STEPHEN STEPHENS stands indebted
        to the Plt sum Two hundred pounds Tobacco and cask for a retaining fee councell and advice against Mr. Scarlet which formerly he promised to pay but since hath denied .. forasmuch as Richard Gibson could not justly make appeare his debt to be due Therefore tis ordered Stephen Stephens of and from this action be dismist and Richard Gibson pay costs ..

753.   CHRISTOPHER BUTLER complaining sheweth that FRANCIS HAMMERSLEY Executor
        of his own wrong of the Estate of MARTHA BARTON who was Executrix of the Will of her Husband NATHAN BARTON stands indebted to the Plt the sum of three thousand three hundred and seventy pounds of Tobacco and cask by a former order of this Worshipfull Court against said Nathan Barton deced which Nathan Barton in his lifetime hath not paid .. and forasmuch as Francis Hammersley did make it plainly appear in this Court that he hath paid as farr as assetts of the Estate of Nathan Barton deced Therefore this ordered that Francis Hammersley of and from this action shall be dismissed and that Xtopher Butler pay costs ..

Page 65 (contd)   Court held 12th June 1690

754. ROBT. HANKS complaining sheweth that THOMAS HOLMES late of this County
      deced at time of his death stood Indebted to the Petr by Two Bills the
sum of two thousand seven hundred pounds of Tobacco and caske that the said
Holmes dyed intestate and RICHARD GIBSON (sic should be RICHARD NIXON) marrying
his widow obtained admn. upon the Estate and before the Plt could bring his
action wasted the said Estate and run away so that the Plt could not proceed
against him Whereupon the Plt by his petition made humble suit to your Worships
that he might be qualified to sue Mr. Richd. Gibson and Mr. EDWD. MASON the
Securities of the said Nixon for his faithful admr. which your worships

Page 66 Court held 12th June 1690

was pleased to grant him order for Whereupon he hath now brought his action and
prays Judgment against Mr. Richard Gibson and Mr. Edward Mason as Security of
the said Nixon And now forasmuch as it doth appear to this Court that RICHARD
NICKSON admr upon the Estate of Thomas Holmes and that Richard Gibson and Edward Mason became security with him.. whereas Edward Mason is since dead Therefore tis ordered by this Court that Richard Gibson the other Security shall
make payment ..

755. RICHD. MARTIN complains against AUGUSTINE KNEATON in a plea of Debt for
      that the said Kneaton is Indebted to the Plt the sum of four hundred
pounds of Tobacco and cask due per account .. Kneaton discounted .. Therefore
tis ordered he shall make payment the ballance ..

756. JOHN ATTERTON came into Court in propria persona and confessed Judgment
      unto Collo. WILLIAM FITZHUGH for sum of five hundred pounds of Tobacco
due per Bill Therefore tis ordered said Atterton shall make payment ..

757. RICHD. BRYANT complains against THOMAS FOLIO in plea of Trespass for that
      whereas by the 125th act of assembly (re killing hogs) .. Now as it is
Thomas Folio of this County Planter on or about the 28th of December last killed
a hog which hog was seen dressing at his dwelling house within this County ..
And the said Thomas Folio by RICHARD GIBSON his attorney .. for plea saith not
guilty .. Therefore tis ordered that the Jury Enquire the Fact: AUGUSTINE
KNEATON, XTOPHER HERRINGE, JOHN MATHEWS, WILLIAM RUSTALL, WM. HAMBLETON, JAMES
MAN, JAMES MONKE, WILLIAM BURTON, GEORGE SHEPARD, JOHN BEACH, THOMAS PORTER,
HENRY THOMPSON which said Jurors Elected Tryed and Sworn to say the Truth of the

Page 67   Court held 12th June 1690

Premises doe say upon their Oaths we find for the Deft noe cause of action
Therefore tis ordered that Judgment be Entered on the Verdict of the Jury and
that Richard Bryant be nonsuit and pay fifty pounds Tobacco unto Thomas Folio
with all costs .. Ordered Thomas Folio pay the Jury seventy two pounds of Tobacco with costs. Ordered Thomas Folio shall make payment sum forty pounds of
Tobacco unto FRANCIS HUNT for one days attendance in Court in a Suit depending
between him and Richard Bryant with costs .. Ordered Richard Bryant shall make
payment of one hundred and twenty pounds of Tobacco unto DANAH SMITH, EVAN
JONES, THOS. KILBOURNE, JOHN ROWLEY and ANNE his wife, EDWARD ROAD and his wife
per peece and eighty pounds of Tobacco to WILLIAM VINE for their attendance in
Court in a Suit depending between him and Thomas Folio with costs ..

758. ROBERT BRENT complaining sheweth that Mr. MATTHEW THOMPSON of this County
      and your Petr doe (as tenants in common) hold a certain dividend or tract
of land containing one thousand and forty acres Scituate in this County and

Page 67 (contd)   Court held 12th June 1690

whereas its provided by the Statute of the 1st of Henry the 8th Capt. that any
person holding Land as Tenants in common may sue division to be made by the
writ Departicipatione facienda and forasmuch as Matthew Thompson doth refuse
to make division of the tract of land your Petr hath therefore brought his action
.. for writ directed to the sheriff of this county to make partition of the said
one thousand and forty acres of land. And the Court having fully considered ..
Therefore tis ordered that Robert Brent the Plt shàll have the aforesaid writ
granted and that the Sheriff shall immediately summons an able Jury of his
Balyiwick to make a just and lawful division .. and return an account thereof
to the next Court.

759. JOHN TURNER humbly complaining sheweth that your Petr did in May Court
      last obtain an order for the returning home of his Wife wheresoever and
in whose company so ever she should be found in order for her living and remaining with her husband now so it is that notwithstanding the said order of
restraint from keeping and entertaining his Wife THOMAS THOMPSON of this County
in whose company and by whose allurements she hath lived and frequented several
years in Levity and Idleness did carry your said Petrs wife over to Maryland
within some few days after the May Court and Longe before your Petr hath not
heard nor seen his wife and further your petitioner complains that the said
Thompson hath several times with force and Armes without any or the least Just
claim of right or Lawful Pretence thereto taken and wrested away out of your
Petrs house several or indeed most of all of your Petrs goods and necessaries
whereby to live and keep house Vizt his feather bed bolster and pillow with
coverlid Rugg cotton blanket and matchcoat a carbine a Bible Testament with
other things not leaving your Petr able to subsist he continually abusing and
threateninge your

Page 68   Court held 12th June 1690

petitioner so that he is in great fear of his life .. And THOMAS THOMPSON by
RICHARD GIBSON his attorney comes into Court .. for plea saith not guilty ..
and after full debate and hearing the matter in Court on both sides .. the Court
doe order that Thomas Thompson shall presently surrender and deliver up to the
Sheriff all the goods that of right doth belong to John Turner .. and Thomas
Thompson pay costs .. Ordered John Turner shall make payment of one hundred
pounds of Tobacco unto THOMAS PEARSON for his attendance in Court .. Ordered
Thomas Thompson shall make payment of forty pounds of Tobacco unto Thomas
Pearson for his attendance in Court ..

760. JOHN PEAKE SENR. complains against JOHN COTTON in a plea of Debt .. the
      sum of six hundred and ten pounds of tobacco and cask by account .. And
the said John Cotton came into Court and for plea saith Nil Debet which plea
was overruled by the Court .. After full debate appears John Cotton stands indebted to John Peake Senr. the sum three hundred and ten pounds of Tobacco by
account .. Therefore tis ordered John Cotton shall make payment of said sum ..

761. RICHD. GIBSON complains against JAMES MONKE in plea of Debt .. the sum of
      three hundred eighty nine pounds of Tobacco and cask due per accout which
he denies to pay .. And James Monke comes into Court and legally discounted the
sum .. Therefore tis ordered James Monke make payment to Richard Gibson of
two hundred pounds of Tobacco being due to him for a retaining fee from the
said Monke as attorney of Mrs. ELIZABETH WILKES with costs ..

759 - 761

Page 68 (contd)   Court held 12th June 1690

762. RICHARD ASHWORTH complains against HENRY HARVEY for that the said Harvey
        stands indebted sum of Fifteen hundred and four pounds of Tobacco one
per account which he refuses to pay ..

Page 69   Court held 12th June 1690

And the deft comes into Court and for plea saith Nil debet which plea was overruled by the Court .. after full hearing it appears to this Court that Henry
Harvey stands justly indebted .. Therefore tis ordered he shall make payment
of twelve hundred and twenty six pounds of Tobacco in caske ..

763. GEORGE SHEPHARD complains against HENRY THOMPSON in plea of Debt .. sum
        of twelve hundred pounds of Tobacco in cask .. and Henry Thompson comes
into Court and could say nothing in Barr or preclusion of the debt .. Therefore
tis ordered Henry Thompson shall make payment of said sum ..

764. Ordered that the Sheriff shall bring the body of WILLIAM PAGE to the next
        Court to answer the complaint of WILLIAM BREWTON or else be Lyable ac-
cording to act of assembly and pay costs. Attachment according to act of assembly is granted the sheriff against Estate of William Page for his nonappearance
at this Court to answer complaint of William Brewton with costs. William Page
complains against William Brewton in plea of Debt .. the sum of two thousand
four hundred and eighty pounds of Tobacco in cask due per account .. And now
forasmuch as William Page did not appeare in this Court to prosecute his suite
.. Therefore tis ordered William Page shall be nonsuit and pay unto William
Brewton fifty pounds of Tobacco with costs ..

765. GERRARD LOWTHER complains against WILLIAM PARKER in a plea of debt .. sum
        of four hundred and fifty pounds of Tobacco in cask per Bill .. and Wil-
liam Parker came into Court and could say nothing in Barr or preclusion of the
said debt .. Therefore tis ordered he shall make payment of afsd amount ..

766. JOHN PEAKE SENR. complains against RICHARD NEVET for that about five or
        six years ago Richard Nevet did borrow of your Petr one mare which said
Mare the said Nevet doth detaine and never did deliver to your Petr according
to his promise to the great damage of at least four thousand pounds of Tobacco
and cask ..

Page 70   Court held 12th June 1690

And the said Nevet by RICHARD GIBSON his attorney comes into Court and craves
Licence of Imparlance herein till next Court which unto him is granted and
that then his plea be not wanting.

767. GERRARD LOWTHER the attorney of RICHARD BRYANT came into Court and became
        Security of Richard Bryant for the payment of fifty pounds of Tobacco for
a nonsuit formerly granted by this Court to THOMAS JEFFRIES against JOHN CLERK
with costs. Richard Bryant complaining sheweth that Thomas Jeffries stands
indebted the sum of five hundred and fifty pounds of Tobacco and caske due per
Bill dated 12th March 1683/4 unto RICHARD MINTHORNE late of this County deced
and from the said Minthorne in his lifetime transferred to John Clerk of Rappa-
hanock County and from the said Clerk assigned and made over to Richard Bryant
the 2d day January 1689 .. and Thomas Jeffries by RICHARD GIBSON his attorney
comes in Court and craves Licence of Imparlance till the next Court to put in
his plea which unto him is granted and that then his plea be not wanting.

768. ROBERT BRENT complains against BURR HARRISON of this County that whereas
        Your Petr did attach of the Estate of RICHARD NICKSON late of this County

Page 70 (contd)   Court held 12th June 1690

upon or near the said Nixon plantation in this county three head of cattle of
the said Nixon being all cows big with calf and at Court held for this County
the 11th of December 1689 obtained Judgment against the said Estate soe attached for a debt of fifteen hundred thirty five pound Tobacco due from the
said Nixon to the Plt but soe it is may it please your Worships the deft hath
since the said Judgment obtained removed and drove away the three head of cattle
from their wanted and accustomed place of feeding as the Plt is informed and
doth believe hath drove them out of the County so that Execution cannot be levied
upon them .. And Burr Harrison by Gerrard Lowther his attorney comes in Court
and craves Licence of Imparlance till the next Court to put in his plea which
unto him is granted and that then his plea be not wanting.

769.   ROBERT BRENT complains against JOHN POER in a plea of Debt .. the sum of
       seventeen hundred and thirty pounds of tobacco and caske Vizt fifteen
hundred pounds thereof by Bill bearing date 24th August 1687 .. and John Poer
by RICHARD GIBSON his attorney comes in Court and confessed Judgment .. Therefore tis ordered John Poer shall make payment ..

Page 71   Court held 12th June 1690

770.   MATTHEW KEENE complains against WILLIAM DOWNHAM of this County in a plea
       of Trespass for that whereas the plt together with EDMOND HOLDER of this
County deced did Joyntly purchase in fee simple of JOHN PEAKE of this County a
certain dividend or Tract of land containing by Estimation 750 acres Scituate
lying and being in this County of Stafford near the head of Potomack Creek and
on the northwest side thereof by deed bearing date the 14th day of November
1672 more at Large doth and may appear and the said lands so purchased in Joint
Tenancy as aforesaid they the said Joint Tenants did hold in Joint Tenancy for
and during the natural life of Edmond Holder and until the time of his death
without partition or Severation of the said Premises and the said Edmond Holder
dyeing or Severation of the said premises or Jointure as afsd the Plt by right
of Survivorship became intirely seized in his demesne as of fee of in and unto
the 750 acres of land with all and singular its rights members and Jurisdictions
and appurtenances But now so it is may it please your Worships the deft William
Downham has by force and arms Entered into and upon a certain plantation of the
plts part of the aforesaid premises and hath by the Space of five years kept
possession of the same and thereon doth commit many Trespasses & Enormities by
breaking up planting & tending of the same cutting downe and destroying much
Timber and other trees to the utter ruine and destruction of the said plantation
and to the plts damage forty thousand pounds of Tobacco and caske for which he
brings his suit against the deft humbly prayes Judgment .. directed to the
Sherif of this County to put the plt in Quiet and peaceable possession of his
land & premises And William Downham by RICHARD GIBSON his attorney comes in
Court and craves Licence of Imparlance therein till the next Court for to
bring in his plea wch unto him is granted and that then his plea be not wanting.

771.   BOWRNE v GIBSON in Audita Querela from February 14, 1688. And now the
       parties coming into Court and each producing his account which being
throughly Examined by the Court and after a full Examination and the utmost
allegations heard that was made by each party it did appear to the Court that
two thousand three hundred forty and three pounds of Tobacco was due and unpaid
of the Execution of five thousand and eighty seven pounds which Richard Gibson
had against WILLIAM BOWRNE and upon which the said Bowrne obtained the said
Writ of Audita Querela Therefore tis ordered and adjudged by this Court that
Capt. GEORGE BRENT who became security with William Bowrne for the obtaining
and Effectual prosecution of the said writ of Audita Querela afsd shall pay to
the said Gibson the afsd sum of two thousand three hundred and forty three pounds
of Tobacco with costs and damages according to Law which sum so adjudged against

Page 71 (contd)   Court held 12th June 1690

George Brent as afsd the said George Brent then in Court submitted to the Judgment and Tendered the Toba. so ordered in open Court to Richard Gibson and desired the Tender aforsd might be entered with the said Judgment.

772. GEORGE BRENT humbly complaining sheweth that he the plt was ordered by this Worshipful Court to survey and lay out a peice of land for WILLIAM LYNNE that he had bought of JOHN MATHEWS at Pasbitanzy that pursuant to your Worships order and at the instance and request of William Lynne the plt went in company with the said Lynne and all other persons concerned in the grand pattent and did in March 1688 survey and lay out to every man his due and full proportion in such part and place of the

Page 72   Court held 12th June 1690

land as by the respects then present was mutually agreed where each mans land should lye yet notwithstanding William Lynne refuseth to pay the plt his fee due by act of assembly wherefore he hath brought action and prays Judgment against the said Lynne for four hundred pounds of tobacco and cask for his fee for surveying one hundred acres of land for him out of the pattent of John Mathews abovesaid and that he pay costs and now forasmuch as it doth appear to this Court that William Lynne stands indebted unto Capt. George Brent the sum four hundred pounds of Tobacco for a Surveyors fee Therefore tis ordered William Lynne shall make payment .. with costs ..

773. FRANCIS DOUGHTY complains against JOHN CHADWELL in a plea of debt .. the sum of five hundred pounds of tobacco and caske for which he hath brought his action .. And now forasmuch as Francis Doughty could not Justly make appear his debt to be due Therefore tis ordered that John Chadwell the deft of and from this action shall be dismissed and that Francis Doughty pay costs.

774. Ordered that the Sherif shall bring the body of DANIEL HUNTSMAN to the next Court to answer the complaint of JOHN BLUNDALL or else be Lyable according to act of assembly and pay costs. Attachment according to act of assembly is granted the sherif against the Estate of Daniel Huntsman for his nonappearance to answer the complaint of John Blundall at this Court with costs ..

775. Ordered that the sherif shall bring the body of EDWARD HUDGSON to the next Court to answer the complaint of JOHN ATTERTON or else be Lyable according to act of assembly and pay costs. Attachment according to act of assembly is granted to the sherif against the Estate of Edward Hudgson for his nonappearance to answer the complaint of John Atterton at his Court with costs ..

776. Whereas GEORGE KING did arrest AMBROSE FARLOW to this Court and did not appear to prosecute his action Therefore tis ordered that George King be nonsuite and shall pay unto Ambrose Farlow fifty pounds of tobacco with costs ..

777. Whereas ROBERT MASON did arrest DAVID STRAWHAN to this Court and did not appear Timely to prosecute his action Therefore tis ordered Robt. Mason shall be nonsuite and shall pay David Strawhan fifty pounds of tobacco with costs ..

778. Whereas HENRY THOMPSON did arrest HENRY MARTIN to this Court and did not appear Timely to prosecute his action Therefore tis ordered Henry Thompson shall be nonsuit and shall pay Henry Martin fifty pounds of Tobacco with costs ..

Page 73   Court held 12th June 1690

779.   HENRY THOMPSON complains against AUGUSTINE KNEATON in plea of Debt .. sum
        of sixteen hundred and fifty pounds of Tobacco and caske due by Bill
which he refuses to pay .. and Augustine Kneaton comes in Court in propria
persona and legally discounts sum of eight hundred pounds of Tobacco out of sum
.. Therefore tis ordered that Augustine Kneaton make payment of eight hundred
and fifty pounds of Tobacco and cask ..

780.   ABRAHAM BECKINGTON complains against GEORGE ANDERSON for that said Ander-
        son stands Indebted .. sum five bushels Indian Corn and refuseth to pay
the same .. And after full hearing it appears to this Court that George Anderson stands indebted (as charged) .. Therefore tis ordered that George Anderson
shall make payment of two hundred pounds of Tobacco or five bushels of Indian
Corne ..

781.   Whereas it is provided by act of assembly that each respective Inhabitant
        do give in his Just number of Tithables to such persons appointed by the
County Court to take the same under a great penalty to those that shall not
fully perform the same and whereas the said Law is in the affirmative and not
in the negative and soe consequently leaves the said Law as it was formerly
for taking Tithables which was anciently by the Constables taking the whole
tithables in their precincts & whereas the said Method by act is both severe
and uncertaine if that they Justly deliver in their due Lists and Severe upon
a discovered defalcation & to the end that the great severity of the said Law
may not fall upon any individual person in this respective County and yet that
the same may be a full & perfect account of the Tithables in this County Therefore tis ordered that the respective Constables of each precinct take a full &
just account of every Tithable in their respective districts and deliver the
same in at October Court next to be held for this County and that whatsoever
Constable shall be defective or not fully perform and give due obedience to this
order shall be Esteemed as contemners of authority and accordingly proceeded
against and it is further ordered that the Clerke take care by the 30th day of
this present month to give out as many copies of these orders as there shall be
Constables in this County and it is also further ordered that the sherif himself
by his deputy or deputys take care by the Tenth day of the next month at farthest
to deliver the same several orders to the respective Constables of this said
County and to the end there may be no pretence or Evasion to avoid the due Exe-
cutions of the same by pretence of not delivery by the Clerke to the Sheriff or
Sheriffs or by the sherif or sherifs to the respective

Page 74   Court held 12th June 1690

Constables Therefore tis further ordered that the Clerke take a receipt for
delivery of the said orders within the time profixed and that the sheriff or
sheriffs take a Severall receipt from each Constable for delivery of each respective order to the severall Constables and produce the same at the next
Court to be held after for this County that it may be known where the default
lies if any such be that the delinquent herein may be proceeded against accordingly.

        (There follows a resume of the suits giving lawyers and clients.)

782.   At an Orphans Court held for Stafford County the 9th July 1690
        Present Collo. William Fitzhugh, Mr. Samuel Hayward, Capt. George Mason,
        Mr. Willm. Buckner, Mr. Edward Thomason, Justices.

Page 74 (contd)   Orphans Court held 9th July 1690

783.   THOMAS SMITH being summoned by the sherif unto this Court to give bond
         and security touching the Estate of MARY MALLET deced FRAS. HAMMERSLEY
and AUGUSTINE KNEATON became security with the said Thomas Smith and did enter
into Bond accordingly to perform what the Law shall require concerning the same.

Page 75 Orphans Court held 9th July 1690

784.   JOSEPH NEWTON being summoned by the sheriff to this Court to give bond
         and security touching the Estate of JAMES PRICE and WILLIAM KAY deced
Mr. JOHN WAUGH and FRANCIS HUNT became security with Joseph Newton and did enter
into Bond accordingly to perform what the Law shall require concerning their
estates.

785.   Whereas Docter EDWARD MADDOCKE by the sheriff summoned unto this Court
         to bring security and give bond concerning the Estate of Capt. JOHN NOR-
GRAVE deced but forasmuch as Docter Edward Maddocke was not proved with the
same Therefore tis ordered that he shall be summoned to next Court to bring
security to perform the will of Capt. John Norgrave deced according to Law
which has since been done as the Law directs.

786.   Whereas RICHARD RICHEE was by the sheriff sumoned unto this Court to bring
         security and give bond concerning the Estate of THOMAS MARLEY late deced
and forasmuch as Richard Richee did come into Court and declare upon Oath that
there was no Estate left Therefore tis ordered that he shall be fully and freely
discharged from the same.

787.   Whereas DANIEL JOYNER was by the sheriff sumoned unto this Court to bring
         his security and give bond concerning the Estate of JOHN COURTNAY deced
But forasmuch as the said Daniel Joyner did not appear according to summons
with his security Therefore tis ordered that Daniel Joyner shall be summoned
to the next Court and bring Security with him to enter into Bond to perform what
the Law shall require touching the said Estate.

788.   Whereas EDWARD WATTS was sumoned by the sheriff to this Court to bring
         his security and give bond concerning the Estate of JACOB HUBBARD deced
but forasmuch as Edward Watts did not appeare with his security according to
sumons Therefore tis ordered that Edward Watts shall be sumoned to the next
Court to bring security to perform the will of Jacob Hubbard according to Law.

789.   Whereas Mr. JOHN WITHERS was sumoned by the sheriff to this Court to bring
         his security and give bond concerning the Estate of JOHN SIMSON deced
but forasmuch as John Withers did not appear with security according to summons
Therefore tis ordered Mr. John Withers shall be summoned to the next Court and
bring security with him to Enter into Bond to perform what the Law shall require
touching the said Estate.

790.   Whereas CHARLES BALDRIDGE was summoned by the sheriff unto this Court to
         give Bond and further security concerning the Estate which Capt. WM.
HEABERD gave unto WM. HEABERD the Son of JOHN HEABERD deced one of the Bonds-
men being dead and the other being Mr. FRANCIS DADE did prefer a petition to
this Court to be freely and fully discharged from his Securityship and forasmuch as Charles Baldridge was not provided with security and the Court thinking
and adjudging it not convenient for the said Estate to be kept any longer in
his hands doe accordingly order Therefore tis ordered that Chs. Baldridge shall
between this and the next Court deliver the aforesaid Estate into the hands of
THOMAS GREGGE JUNR. and that Thomas Gregge shall bring an account thereof

Page 75 (contd)   Orphans Court held 9th July 1690

to the next Court and likewise good security and enter into Bond concerning the same.

Page 76   Orphans Court held 9th July 1690

791.   ELIZABETH BURNARD being summoned by the sheriff to this Court to give security and enter into Bond touching the Estate of NICHOLAS BURNARD her late deced husband JOSHUA DAVIS and HENRY MEREST became security with Elizabeth Burnard and did enter into bond accordingly to perform what the Law shall require touching the same.

792.   Whereas RICHARD ELKIN was sumoned by the sheriff to this Court to bring security and enter into bond concerning the Estate of DAVID THOMAS deced his Father RALPH ELKIN being lately dead and the former security prayed for a full discharge from his securityship who comes into Court and offers JOSEPH NEWTON and JOHN HAWKIN to be his security for the said Estate who was accepted and entered into bond with him accordingly with Richard Elkin concerning the said Estate.

793.   Mr. GERRARD LOWTHER did appear in this Court the attorney of Doctor EDWARD MADDOCKE concerning the Estate of Capt. JOHN NORGRAVE deceased.

794.   At a Court held for the County of Stafford July the 9th 1690
        Present Coll. William Fitzhugh, Mr. Samuel Hayward, Capt. George Mason, Mr. William Buckner, Mr. Edward Thomason Justices

795.   ELIZABETH the Widow and Executrix of Mr. VINCENT YOUNG late deced sheweth that having delivered up a True & perfect Inventory of the Estate of her Husband deced she therefore having craves an order of this worshipful Court for her paraphenalia as hath been usually granted to other widows and which having taken into their Serious and Charitable consideration doe therefore accordingly order that the said Elizabeth Younge shall be allowed out of her husbands Estate and keep for her own proper use one bed and furniture one old small chest three chairs one old warming pan one old pair of Bellows one Iron pot old Frying pan two spoons two porringers Two pewter dishes one old table cloth two old Towels three napkins one old pillion, one pewter Tankard one box Smoothing Iron for her paraphenalia as aforesaid.

796.   EDWARD TAYLOR JUNR. complaining against THOMAS NEWS in a plea of debt .. the sum of five hundred and sixty pounds of Tobacco due per account which he refuses to pay altho often fairly and legally demanded .. And now forasmuch as Edward Taylor did by his account here in Court produced Justly made appeare his debt to be due Therefore tis ordered Thomas News shall make payment .. being full ballance of all demands between them.

797.   Whereas WILLIAM WILLFORD deputy sheriff made complaint to this Court that EDWARD PLATT one of the Constables for the Lower Parish of this County that the said Platt doth in contempt of authority and contrary to an order of this Court neglect and refuse to receive an order of Court for the Impowering of him the said Platt

Page 77   Court held 9th July 1690

to take the List of Tithables in his precincts and to give in a True and Perfect account of the same at October Court and forasmuch as the said Edward Platt doth refuse to take the same order as afsd Therefore tis ordered that the sherif sumons him to the next Court then and there to receive the afsd order and then if he shall refuse to come it shall be Esteemed as a Contempt

Page 77 (contd)   Court held 9th July 1690

of Authority by him and he shall be proceeded against accordingly.

798. GEORGE LUKE made humble petition to this Court showing that your peti-
          tioner by virtue of a grant made to him made by Collo. WM. FITZHUGH doth
hold and enjoy the two thirds in three parts to be divided with HENRY MEREST
in Right of MARY his wife of a certain Dividend plantation and tract of land
in this County of Stafford Therefore your petitioner humbly prays division of
said premises according to Law .. And the Court having considered the premises
and the equity and reasonableness thereof Therefore tis ordered that the said
land be divided according to the quality and quantity as the Law directs in
such cases and that Henry Merest in right of his wife shall have first choice
of one third part together with the housing orchard and pasture ground.

799. JAMES THEARLE made humble petition to this Court that your petitioner
          was supeaned to this Court by WILLIAM MINTORNE to give in his Evidence
to the Truth of what he knew in an action depending between the said Mintorne
and JOHN JONES and your petitioner being at that time sick and weak was not
able to appear at Court Wherefore the said Mintorne out of a covetous and
Malicious humour craved an order against your petitioner for three hundred and
fifty pounds of Tobacco for his nonappearance according to Law which was granted
accordingly now forasmuch as your Petr is ready here to prove to this Worshipful Court that he was sick and weak at the afsd time he therefore humbly prays
that you will be pleased to take the said Fine from your petitioner And forasmuch as James Thearle did sufficiently prove in this Court by the Oath and
Testimony of CHARLES ELLIS that he was sick as afsd .. Therefore tis ordered
that James Thearle of and from this find shall be freely and fully discharged
he paying this costs.

800. Ordered that EDWARD TAYLOR JUNR. shall make payment of eighty pounds of
          Tobacco unto JOHN BEACH for his attendance Two daies in Court in a Suit
depending between him & THOMAS NEWS with costs ..

801. JOSHUA DAVIS complains against THOMAS NEWS in a plea of Debt .. the sum
          of Eleven hundred and eighty nine pounds of Tobacco in caske .. Thomas
News legally discounted the sum of nine hundred and twenty pounds of Tobacco ..

Page 78   Court held 9th July 1690

Therefore tis ordered Thomas News shall make payment of two hundred and sixty
nine pounds of tobacco in full the ballance ..

802. EDWARD HUDGSON humbly sheweth that your petr has a replevin granted him
          at the last Court for this County for a cow and calf and yearling Bull
which were attached by Mr. JOHN HARVEY in the hands of HENRY HARVEY as the Estate of WILLIAM JOHNSON and CHARLES SLEDGE and your Petr by good and sufficient
Evidence here in Court ready to prove that the cattle are bone fide his and
that the property was never altered by Sale or otherwise but still remains his
own proper Estate .. prays attachment be declared void .. appears to Court that
they are his own proper Estate Therefore tis ordered that the sherif shall
immediately put Edward Hudgson into possession of the said cow and calfe and
yearling Bull ..

803. JOHN LEWIS made humble petition to this Court shewing that JOHN LEWIS
          having lived a great while in this County and being old and lame so that
he is incapable of getting his livelihood anymore doth therefore humbly pray
discharge him from paying any further Levy .. Court doe accordingly order ..

Page 78 (contd)   Court held 9th July 1690

804. Ordered that the action Inter ZACHARY HAYNES and ROGER STONING the deft
      be referred till the next Court for JOSHUA DAVIS to bring in then and
there good and sufficient evidences to make proof that he Joshua Davis did take
a bond of Roger Stoning according to Zachary Haynes consent and direction or
else that Judgment shall passe against him for sum of one thousand pounds of
Tobacco with costs.

805. THOMAS NEWS came into Court and confessed Judgment unto RICHARD GIBSON
      for sum of four hundred pounds of Tobacco and caske due per bill ..

806. JOSHUA DAVIS subsherif sheweth that the complainant Executed an attach-
      ment on the Estate of JOHN WHEATLEY for JOHN BREWTON and after was Execu-
ted for Mr. French per Execution and was to have remained in the custody of
him in whose hands it was attached until your Worships Judgment was obtained
which should take priority .. and the said Estate was disposed of by the said

Page 79   Court held 9th July 1690

French soe that the sherif was made incapable for to deliver the said Estate
unto John Brewton but Judgment is past against your complainant for the value
of the Estate soe attached and wholly omitted in the said Order which should
priority your complainant therefore prays your worships that the said order
may by the Clerke be made more full and large that your complainant may be rendered in a capacity to recover the said value and damages against the said
French in the County where he lives And the Court having fully considered the
premises doe accordingly order Therefore tis ordered that for the better Expla-
nation and more fully and clearer understanding of the said former order it
was and is the Judgment of this Court that the attachment took priority and
that Execution of the said Estate ought to have been made on behalfe of HUGH
FRENCH.

807. JAMES HARRISON on behalf of ELLEN MOTT one of the Orphans of Mr. GEORGE
      MOTT deced complaining sheweth that PATRICK HUME is possest with a young
stone horse to the said Ellen Mott without having the property Transferd
either by her or her Guardian and detains the horse though demanded pretending
he cannot safely deliver him without this Worshipful Court order that he may be
reimbursed by the party of whom he saith he bought him Your complainant therefore humbly craves an order to be possest of the horse in behalf of Ellen Mott
who hath the undoubted right to the horse as afsd And now forasmuch as it doth
appear to this Court that the horse did of right belong to Ellen Mott and was
taken up by RICHARD MARTIN a Ranger in this County and carried before a Justice
of Peace but forasmuch as Richard Martin did not take out a certificate from
the Clerke of the Legall taking up of the horse as the Law in such cases doth
direct Therefore tis ordered that Richard Martin shall make present payment of
the sum of five hundred pounds of Tobacco in cask to Ellen Mott with costs ..

808. Whereas Capt. GEORGE BRENT brought an action of covenant in this Court
      against ROBERT DUNNE and did here Exhibit the said condition of Covenant
whereto the defendant did plead non Est Factum and the Plt not having his Evidence here in this Court to prove the same Therefore tis ordered that the said
action shall be referred till the next Court for Capt. George to bring his Evidence there to prove that the same is the afsd Robert Dunne own act and deed.

809. Coll. WM. FITZHUGH and FRANCIS DADE upon Imparlance from the 12th of
      June 1690 unto the 9th of July Anno Dom 1690 And Francis Dade the deft
by GERRARD LOWTHER his attorney comes into Court and defends .. and for plea

Page 79 (contd) Court held 9th July 1690

saith that the messuage Tenement and Orchard whereas the Trespasse is Supposed
is part of a greater dividend of thirteen hundred acres granted by patent to
GERVASE DODSON the 13th of October 1653 and by the said Dodson for a valuable
consideration then reced sold to JOHN SMITH by deed of Sale dated the 17th of
August 1658 which deed

Page 80 Court held 9th July 1690

was acknowledged by JAMES POPE attorney of the abovesaid Gervase Dodson as by
the record certified under the hand of RICHARD FLINT Clerke of the afsd Court
appears Whereupon this deft entered the 20th day of May Anno Dom 1687 and
continues his possession thereof as Son and heir of the afsd John Smith which
he hopes being ready to prove was Lawful for him to doe and that without that
he is not guilty of the Trespasse alledged against him and for further plea
saith the said John Smith his Father never acknowledged any sale of the Land
in Question to Mr. HUGH DOWDING nor had any consideration for the same as by
the Plt is alledged and as to what the Plt alledges as he seems for his advantage that the deft the 25th May 1664 petitioned an Escheat of six hundred acres
that was not part of the said dividend of 1300 acres and admit it had it cannot
prejudice this deft being then an infant of the age of four years and about six
months but this deft presumes the said Escheat of the said six hundred acres
was made by those who designed to have the use and benefit thereof till this
deft came to age which was almost seventeen years but admitting this deft had
been of full age at the time of the said Escheat and it had been the land in
Question was soe escheated this deft humbly conceives he may be remitted to his
better Title so that notwithstanding the said Escheat he now is En Sonprimeur
Estate or Enson meloor droit for the first and most ancient Title is the most
sure and most worthy Quod prius Est verius Est quod prius Est Tempore potius
Est Jure Co. on Lit 347 and in as much as the Plt seems to alledge that the
deft Francis Dade cannot be son and heir to John Smith tis answered he may
inasmuch as he can prove himself oldest Son to the said John Smith for although
the person and place cannot be changed their names may be for if a man be
baptized by the name of Thomas and his name of Confirmation John he may purchase
by his confirmation name and this was the case of Sir FRANCIS GAWDY Chief Justice of the Common Pleas but to come nearer all purchases are generally good by
a knowne or reputed Sirname or name of Baptism or by a certain description of
the person without either Sirname or name of Baptism as a woman Covert may purchase by the name of uxori FS or primogenito JS Co. on Lit for 3d Co Rep 6th
part Sir MOYLE FINCHES case so that the deft appearing to be the only son of
John Smith which was the Fathers name of purchase if his name were Francis Dade
it shall not barr this defendant

And as touching the acknowledgment made by this defts Mother Mrs. BEHETHLAND
GILSON that cannot be any barr to this defendts Title to the lands in Question
inasmuch as she is not a party to the pretended sale from Smith to Dowden as
if she had been a party to the said deed it could amount to no more than a conveyance of her third part for her life besides her acknowledgment is by Atty
being then under Coverture contrary to an act made at James City the 21st of
Sept. 1674 and this deft for further plea saith that in all the time the said
HUGH DOWDEN lived was in the Infancie of this deft and when the said RICHD.
DOWDIE made claim to the said Land if any such claime were made as the Plt
alledges about 8 or 9 years the same cannot conclude this defts Title by the
said act intitled 5 years possession there being sundry presidents to the contrary in Case this deft had lapst his time by the said act and this deft for
further plea saith that

Page 81   Court held 9th July 1690

as the possession of the said ANNE SIMS she held the same by your petitioners
permission in favour to her poverty and age and to the acknowledgment made by
this defts said Mother which this deft was unwilling to invalidate or make void
this deft coming to a plentiful Estate but after this deft was informed the
Plt had Escheated the lands in Question being willing rather to gain a peaceable
possession than to wage Law with the Plt knowing the said Mrs. Sims to be mighty
ancient and infirm took a lease from her of the lands in Question for her life
whereby he gained his possession and hopes he may be remitted to his better
Title as heir to his said Father John Smith and for further plea saith that admitting the possession of Hugh Dowding, Richard Dowding and Anne Sims to be
one Entire possession by the plts own shewing it is Two months short of thirty
one years which availeth nothing to the plts advantage and admit it was thirty
one years yet the deft is not barred from his Title being but twenty nine years
of age the Seventh of November next by the Stat. of 21st of King James and for
further plea saith that the plt had noe occasion to Insist upon the Circumstances specified in the Stat of the 27th of King Henry the 8th Cap 16 Touching
Bargains and Sales of land pursuant to the said Statute for that this deft
humbly conceives himself not within the said Statute having noe occasion thereof
to corroborate his Title whereby inasmuch as before the said act of assembly to
Impower Femes Covert to make acknowledgment of land no other observation is
made upon a Bargain and Sale for conveying of lande from one to another more
than that the same be acknowledged in the General Court or County Court where
the land lies by the Vendor to the Vendee which acknowledgment made to Smith
was pursuant thereunto as appears by the said act which cannot be alledged
Expost Facto for that the Law as by the said act appears was the same before
the making the said act or the said conveyance from Dodson to Smith whereas tis
objected by the plt that the said Lands were acknowledged in Northumberland
County where its said to be in Westmoreland County at the time of the sale from
Dodson to Smith this deft conceives the said acknowledgment from Dodson to Smith
to be good and valid in Law inasmuch as the said County of Westmoreland was but
newly divided and separated from Northumberland and tis possible no court held
or records kept at the time for Westmoreland County and admit there were Courts
then held the acknowledgment in Northumberland was good being the lands sold
are said to be in Northumberland as well as Westmoreland County but admitting
of Dowdings possession to have gained a Title and that for want of heirs to
Richard Dowding the land in Question could Escheat yet this deft does not conceive this grant to the plt to be valid in Law inasmuch as my Lord Culpepper
was dead before the same was made and inasmuch as the said grant is not pursuant to the Statute made the 18th year of King Henry the Sixth which said Statute
provides that no land shall be granted before the Kings Title thereunto be
found by Inquisition nor within a monthe after by all which it appears the plt
has noe Title to the Land in Question and therefore craves Judgment and to be
dismissed with costs

     Wherein it is the Judgment of this Court that Dodsons deed to Smith

Page 82   Court held 9th July 1690

And Smiths to Dowdy are good in law considering the time wherein they were made
and that the cause be referred till the next Court for William Fitzhugh to prove
his Title.

810.   Whereas the Proprietor of this Northern Neck have by Coll. PHILIP LUDWELL
       their agent and attorney prohibited all Pens to be made in the woods under

Page 82 (contd)   Court held 9th July 1690

pretensions of catching wild horses as also all Rangers to say those that make
it their business to Range for wild horses & whereby it appears by the said
prohibition put upon Record divers inconveniences and prejudices happen to
several of the Honest Inhabitants as therein doth fully appear and hath been
also submitted the order and direction for Rangers wholly to the consideration
and discretion of this Court the Court doth therefore concur therein and accordingly order that all Rangers from henceforth do cease their said ranging
Let their pretensions be from whence they will also that they desist from making
any more pens in the woods remote from habitations under pretence of catching
wild horses and that those that are already made be with the first conveniency
Throwne down and demolished That for the future whoever has any pretensions
or claims to wild horses & doe first make application to this Court for an al-
lowance for the same that the Court may have their reasons and pretensions
therein and order as shall be most Just for them and convenient for the rest
of the Inhabitants and it is further ordered that this order be publickly read
at the beginning of each Court held for this County.

There follows a summary of Lawyers and their clients.

The Court is adjourned till the Second Wednesday in August next
God Save their Majesties

811. At a Court held for County of Stafford Septr the 9th 1690

Present Coll. Wm. Fitzhugh, Mr. Samuel Hayward, Capt. George Mason,
Mr. John Withers, Mr. Edward Thomason, Mr. William Buckner, Mr. Math.
Thompson, Justices

812. MATHEW THOMPSON by GEORGE BRENT his attorney complains against THOMAS
TUSTIN in a plea of debt .. the sum of Four thousand and forty three
pounds of Tobacco and caske being for goods sold him and for payments made
for him to sundrys besides his diet and some other accounts that he the plt
in due time reserves his charge the said Tustin hath fugitively absented himself from this County so that

Page 83 Court held 9th September 1690

the ordinary proceedings of law could not be had against him wherefore the Plt
took out an attachment against Thomas Tustin which being served and duely returned he therefore prays Judgment against the said Tustin and condemnation of
the Estate so attached with costs And the said Thomas Tustin the deft did
appear in propria persona in this Court and did replevin his Estate so attached
and forasmuch as it doth appear to this Court that the sum of Four thousand and
forty three pounds of Tobacco is due from Thomas Tustin unto Mathew Thompson he
having proved it by his accompt here in Court produces as afsd Therefore tis
ordered that Thomas Tustin shall make payments .. with costs.

813. RICHARD ELKIN the son of RALPH ELKIN late of this County deced made humble
petition to this Court for a Probate of the Last Will & Testament of his
Father deced he being Execr. appointed in the will which unto him is granted
Therefore tis ordered that Richard Elkin the son of Ralph Elkin deced shall
have probate granted him of the Last Will & Testament of his deced Father he
having fully proved the same by the Oaths & Testimonies of STEPHEN GARDNER and
GEORGE LODGE to the will subscribed & George Lodge and JOHN HAWKIN became Security with Richard Elkin to perform the will of his Father Ralph Elkin deced
and entered into bond accordingly. Ordered that George Lodge, JOSEPH SUMNER
and JOHN GRIGSBY shall upon the 26th of this Instant appraise the Estate of Ralph
Elkin deced and that Coll. WILLIAM FITZHUGH swear them accordingly.

Page 83 (contd)   Court held 9th September 1690

814.   MARTHA FOLIO the Widow and relict of THOMAS FOLIO late of this County
        deced made humble petition to this Court by ROBERT COLLIS showing that
your Petrs Husband Thomas Folio departing this life without making any will
Therefore humbly prays administration may be granted her of her Husbands Estate she being ready to give Security according to Law which being duly considered by the Court of the Reasonableness and Equity thereof doe order Therefore tis ordered that Martha Folio shall have Letters of administration granted
her of her deced Husbands Estate she giving Security and enter into Bond
accordingly for to perform what the Law doth require touching the said Estate.

815.   Ordered that the whole remainder of Major JAMES ASHTONS Estate shall
        be appraised between this and next Court by Doct. EDWARD MADDOCKS,
JOSEPH SUMNER and ROBERT ALEXANDER or any two of them Vizt horses hogs and
other goods which are now in the hands of JOHN HAWKIN and that Mr. WILLIAM
BUCKNER swear them accordingly also it is further ordered the Estate soe
appraised shall be left in the custody of John Hawkin that he may have the
advantage of the appraisement of the Estate provided he bring in the accompt
of the Estate so appraised with good and sufficient security and enter into

Page 84   Court held 9th September 1690

Bond accordingly at the next Court to render the value of the Estate to the
Execrs. in Trust of Major James Ashton deced provided that the former Inventory of Major James Ashton is not capable of paying his Debts also ordered
that Mr. WILLIAM BUCKNER shall swear the appraisers accordingly.

816.   JOHN BATTAILE complains against RICHARD BRYANT in a plea of debt for
        that (he) stands Indebted to the Plt the sum of Five hundred pounds
sweet Tobacco due to the Plt by account which he refuses to pay altho often
demanded .. And Richard Bryant the deft did appeare in Court in propria persona and could say nothing in Barr or preclusion of the Debt .. Therefore
tis ordered Richard Bryant shall make payment with costs ..

817.   ANNE the widow and relict of THOMAS OD'NEAL late of this County deced
        being appointed one of the Executors of Thomas Odeneal Last Will &
Testament therein nominated did voluntarily and of her own consent come into
Court & relinquish her part of the Executorship in Thomas Odeneal last Will
and Testament and prayed it might be Entered on Record that she might be
fully discharged of the same.

818.   Capt. GEORGE BRENT in behalf of his Son George Brent who had a legacy
        given him in the Last Will & Testament of THOMAS ODENEAL late of this
County deced made a petition to this Court that whereas ANNE wife of Thomas
Odeneal being nominated & appointed one of the Executors in the said last
Will and Testament did voluntarily come into Court and relinquish her part
of the Executorship and forasmuch as HENRY COLDSTREAM the other Executor in
the will nominated and appointed came into Court and prayed admon of the will
cum Testamento annexed which was accordingly granted Therefore the said Capt.
George Brent in behalf of his son humbly prayed the Court that the said will
might be fully proved by the Oaths and Testimonies of the witnesses to the
will Subscribed according to Law which was accordingly done by the Oath of
Mr. SAMUEL HAYWARD one of the witnesses thereunto subscribed and whereas
WILLIAM TODD one of the witnesses thereto did not appear at this Court it is
further ordered by this Court that the Sherif shall summons William Todd to
the next Court to give in his Evidence And forasmuch as it doth appeare to
this Court that JOHN BASFORD who did then write the will and Testament as

814 - 818

Page 84 (contd)   Court held 9th September 1690

afsd and being the other witness thereunto Subscribed hath absented himself
and is gone out of this Countrey so that he cannot appeare at this Court to
give his Evidence according to Law but considering that John Basford did for
some considerable time officiate in the office of a Deputy Clerk to this Worshipful Court and for that very reason the Court doth accordingly adjudge
and accord that having well viewed the will and finding it to be Basford hand
as Likewise that he was alsoe witness thereunto do therefore order that the
clerke shall accordingly enter it

Page 85   Court held 9th September 1690

upon the records of this County to Capt. George Brents motion to the Court
herein. Henry Coldstream one of the Execrs. of Thomas Odeneal late of this
County deced of his last Will & Testament made humble petition to this Court
that he might have administration cum Testamento annexed may be granted him
of the Estate of Thomas Odeneal deced by which the True Value of the Estate
may be Certainly Knowne and each concerned in the will have Justice done them
for which your Petr is ready to give good Secty & enter into Bond according
as the Law directs And now forasmuch as Anne the widow and relict of Thomas
Odeneal deced and one of the Execrs in the last will & testament nominated
and appointed did personally appear in this Court and did freely and voluntarily relinquish and absolutely refuse to take the great charge and burthen
of the Executorship of her late deced Husband all which being Truely and
Seriously weighed and considered by the Court and the Equity Justice and
reasonableness thereof doe accordingly order Therefore tis ordered that
Henry Coldstream shall have comocon of the decedends Estate he giving security
to perform what the Law required of him Touching the said Estate. WILLIAM
BUCKNER and Doct. EDWARD MADDOCKS became Security with Henry Coldstream and
did here in Court enter bond accordingly.

819.   The Court taking into consideration the great Necessity of having good
        roads in this County whereby their Majesties Subjects may have free
and safe passage about their occasions which by act of assembly is Enjoyned
to be forty foot wide and whereas by our Remissnesse in performing the said
act the grand jury for the whole body of the Colony and Dominion of Virga.
have formerly presented to our County for not keeping and clearing according
to Law whereupon an Order of the General Court passed the 20th of April anno
1688 for putting the laws into due Execution in Obedience whereunto and for
the freer and safer Passage of their Majesties subjects it is ordered that
Coll. WILLIAM FITZHUGH, Mr. JOHN WITHERS, Mr. WILLIAM BUCKNER and Mr. WILLIAM
BUNBURY (be in the room of RALPH ELKIN which is dead) be Surveyors of the
Highways for the Lower Parish precincts and that Mr. JOHN WAUGH, JOSEPH NEW-
TON, Capt. GEORGE MASON, Mr. EDWARD THOMASON, Capt. GEORGE BRENT, Mr. RICHARD
GIBSON and Mr. ROBERT COLSON be Surveyors of the highways of the upper parish
precincts also it is further ordered that Mr. MARTIN SCARLET be Surveyor from
the head of Oquoquon to Neapsco that they take care of clearing highways
according to the order of the General Court within their precincts and because the roads ways Bridges and Swamps may be the better and more Expeditiously
cleared made good and repaired it is therefore ordered that the Surveyors may
make choice of and appoint such persons as they shall think fit to be overseer in their respective places and precincts who are hereby authorized to
Summons & warne the Inhabitants every one according to the number of Tyth-
ables he hath in his family to send men upon the first of October next and
other daies they shall appoint to helpe them to clear the waies or making or

Page 85 (contd)   Court held 9th September 1690

repairing the bridges according to the afsd act and if the Surveyors shall
neglect to appoint overseers the overseers to Sumon and warne the Inhabitants
to

Page 86 Court held 9th September 1690

send help according to the Summons the Surveyors or overseers or persons summoned shall pay such penalty or penaltys as the Court shall think fit and
that the roads be cleared bridges made and repaired by the Twentieth day of
October next at Farthest and the overseers are hereby strictly required to
cause persons delinquent to be summoned to the next Court to answer their
contempt of this order and to be proceeded against accordingly.

820.   Forasmuch as there was an order of Westmoreland Court bearing date
        30th day of July 1690 presented to this Court this day wherein was
represented in the afsd order the speedy necessity for the repairing of the
two bridges called Ayliffs Bridge and Jordans Bridge lying upon the great
Swamp which divides the two counties of Westmoreland and Stafford and in the
main and great Roads leading to and from the said Counties are soe decayed
Ruinous and broken that their Majesties Liege People and Subjects with their
horses cannot passe and Travel that way without great damage to the great
damage and common hurt of all their Majesties Liege people and Subjects that
way going passing and Travelling and this Court fully considering the great
& absolute necessity of having the said bridges well repaired (and know themselves to be Equally concerned with the Inhabitants of Westmoreland in the
making or repairing of said bridges) doe accordingly order and therefore tis
ordered that WILLIAM BUNBURY who is appointed Surveyor of those precincts
shall sumons in all the Inhabitants and Tithables of his precinct against
the 1st day of October next by 9 of the clock in the morning at the said
Bridges to meet the Surveyor and Inhabitants of those precincts in Westmoreland County in order to the repairing of the Bridges and clearing the highways in those precincts and the Clerk of this Court is hereby Ordered to
transmit a copy hereof to the Worshipful Court of Westmoreland to the end
that the Surveyors Inhabitants and others within the upper precinct of your
County may have timely notice from the Worshipful Court for the meeting of
our men at the time and place appointed.

821.   SAMPSON DARRELL who married the sole Daughter now living of Captain
        JOHN NORGRAVE petitioned this Court for a cow and Signet of Armes
which was left by the will of Capt. John Norgrave to one or either of his
children according as his Execrs appointed in his will should see fit to be-
stow as appears more fully by the Will here in Court produced and forasmuch
as Sampson Darrell complains that FRANCES the Widow and Executrix appointed
in Capt. John Norgraves will doth as yet unjustly keep and detain from him
one cow and Signet of Armes in right of MARGARET his wife Therefore humbly
prays that Dr. EDWARD MADDOCKS who intermarried with Frances the Executrix
of Capt. John Norgrave may be ordered by this Court to deliver the cow and
Signet of Armes And Dr. Edward Maddocks comes into Court and proves that the
Signet of Armes was disposed on by Frances his wife according to the Tenor
of the Will .. and forasmuch as it doth plainly appear to this Court that
there is yet one cow due Sampson Darrell in right of his wife Therefore tis
ordered that Dr. Edward Maddocks who intermarried with

820 - 821

Page 87   Court held 9th September 1690

Frances the widow and relict of Capt. John Norgrave deced shall Immediately
deliver to the afsd Sampson Darrell one good able cow in his right to the
aforesaid according to the full True intent and meaning of the Last will and
Testament of the said Capt. John Norgrave.

822.   SAMSON DARRELL who married the sole daughter now Living of Capt. JOHN
         NORGRAVE Petitioned this Court that Docter EDWARD MADDOCKS who married
the relict and Exectx of the said John Norgrave deced might give security for
the performance of the said Will according to the Tenor thereof and further
alledged that Coll. Mason in his lifetime and all the time of his life gave
Security and that Since his decease one of his Securitys are dead alsoe
Therefore he prays the said Coll. Mason being dead as afsd and his Security
dead Likewise that the said Docter Maddocks who Since intermarried as afsd
and hath by the said Intermarriage the possession and Enjoyment of the said
Norgraves Estate may be compelled to Enter into bond with good and Sufficient
Securitys to be accountable for the same according to the request of the
deced and as the Law enjoynes which said motion of Darrells is approved of by
this Court and doe accordingly order that the said Doct Edward Maddocks doe
immediately give good Security and Enter into bond for the same as the Law
directs And he comes by GERRARD LOWTHER his Attorney and put in these reasons
And Gerrard Lowther the attorney of Doct Edward Maddocks comes and puts in
his plea in writing against Sampson Darrell and gives these reasons whereby
he humbly presumes that he ought not nor is Liable to give Security Vizt. as
to the Cattle they are paid Secondly the Ring is given to the Legatees according to, as to the negroes they are a personal Chattle and a remainder
Limitted in the will of a Chatle personal is void because if given for an hour
they are given forever but they are given to Mrs. Maddock for her life so
that the remainder after her decease is void Therefore for them no Security
ought to be given 4thly no Execr named by the Testator in his will are by
Law compellable to find Security for the performance of the Testators will
but we are Execrs therefore unless the Law will dispose and Intrust his Estate
of the Testator otherwise than he designed we are not obliged to find Security
for performance of the Testators will and this appears by the provision made
by the Laws of this Country that admrs shall finde Security but no Law doth
oblige Execrs 65 Act of assembly 21 Hen 8:15 Vide Title probate of Testaments
in Wingates abridgment Lastly there has been Security already found in this
matter and if the Court have discharged them without others we are not daily
bound to finde new Securitys. With which Judgment of the Court as afsd he
the said Edward Maddocks the deft not being content doth appeale to the Sixth
day of the next General Court there to be heard before the honourable the
Governour and Council of State at James City.   SAMUEL HAYWARD became Security
with the said Edward Maddocks to present his appeale And ROBERT BRENT with
Sampson Darrell to answer.

Page 88   Court held 9th September 1690

823.   WM. FITZHUGH in a plea of Trespass on June the 11th 1690 and to which
the said DADE comes in and Justifies as by his plea brought into Court in
Writing by GERRARD LOWTHER his attorney appears for that his Father had a
right and had not legally departed from the same which said deed of Dodsons
to Dades father Smith and the said Smith deed to DOWDY under which the said
Fitzhugh claims being duly considered and maturely weighed by this Court
they doe unanimously adjudge both the deeds good and effectual considering
the times they were made in and therefore doth adjudge Dades Special Justi-

Page 88 (contd)   Court held 9th September 1690

fication grounded upon his afsd Title Void in Law and doe accordingly order
the cause to be referred to the next Court for William Fitzhugh to prove his
Title.

824.   CHRISTO. HERRING complains against JOHN DRAPER in plea of Debt that he
          stands Indebted to the Plt the sum of Four hundred pounds of Tobacco
in caske due per bill .. and John Draper the deft did appear in this Court in
proper person and could say nothing in barr or preclusion of the debt but
that the same appears justly due Therefore tis ordered that John Draper shall
make payment ..

825.   Coll. WM. FITZHUGH and FRANCIS DADE in a plea of Trespass from the 9th
          of July Anno 1690 upon Imparlance from the 9th of September anno 1690
and now at this Court William Fitzhugh having made it appear that the claim
of DOWDY was Extint and that the right appertained and belonged to the right
Honble the Lord Culpepper who has by his grant the benefit of all Escheats
in this Northern Neck of Virga. and did in this Court produce a deed from
the said Culpepper granted by his attorney NICHOLAS SPENCER Esqr. dated the
20th of August 1688 wherein it appearing that the said Land was granted to
William Fitzhugh for a valuable consideration and noe other right nor pretensions of right appearing Therefore the Court doe adjudge the said Fitzhugh Title by the said Deed good and the said Dade a Trespasser and do order
that the sherif do forthwith deliver possession of the Messuage tenement and
the lands thereto belonging to William Fitzhugh and that Francis Dade be
immediately Ejected from the same And Mr. Francis Dade not being content with
the Judgment of this Court doth appeale to the Sixth day of the General Court
next then and there to be heard before the Honble Governour and Councel of
State at James City in Virginia and Mr. JOHN WITHERS became Security for
Francis Dade to prosecute his appeale and SAMUEL HAYWARD with Coll William
Fitzhugh to answer the same.

826.   Ordered that JOHN McCULLOUGH Servant to JOSEPH HENSON shall serve his
          Master two months after his service by Custom or Indenture is Expired
for the running away and fugitively absenting himself out of his Masters
Service the said JOSEPH NEWTON (sic) paying this costs ..

Page 89   At Court held 9th September 1690

827.   THROUGHGOOD PATE came into Court and confessed Judgment to WILLIAM
          LOXHAM for the sum of five hundred pounds of Tobacco due per bill ..
Therefore tis ordered (he) shall make payment with costs ..

828.   ZACHARY HAYNES complaining sheweth that ROGER STONING stands indebted
          to the Plt by a certain Instrument under his hand to looke after and
feed all and singular the Plts stock at the Plantation where Stoning lives
for which doing he is to have one third part of the increase of the stock
as in the said Lease or Instrument will appeare .. said Stoning hath refused
to neglect to feed and look after his stock to his great losse and detriment
and refuses also to pay the Plt sixteen hundred pounds of Tobacco and six
barrells of Corn which he owes him by account .. And now forasmuch as it doth
appear to this Court that Roger Stoning hath fugitively absented himself out
of this County and Zachary Haynes justly making it appear his debt to be due
Therefore tis ordered Roger Stoning shall make payment of said sixteen hundred
pounds of Tobacco in cask and six barrells of good Indian Corne with costs ..

Page 89 (contd)   Court held 9th September 1690

829.   JOSHUA DAVIS complains against ZACHARY HAYNES in plea of debt .. sum
        seven hundred and eighty pounds of Tobacco due per bill .. and Zachary
Haynes the deft did come into Court in propria persona and could say nothing
but the same appears to be due Therefore tis ordered Zachary Haynes shall
make payment ..

830.   Coll. WILLIAM FITZHUGH made a motion to this Court that whereas an
        order of this Court passed the 11th day of July 1690 for the division
of a certaine messuage Tenement and tract of land that lyes between him and
HENRY MEREST and now all in the Tenure and occupation of GEORGE LUKE Gent.
and the said Merest and forasmuch as Coll William Fitzhugh made complaint to
this Court that the order of Court was never duly executed according to the
Tenor thereof Therefore tis ordered by this Court that JOHN HARVEY and PHILIP
BUCKNER shall time betwixt this and the next court lay out and divide the
messuage Tenement together with the housing and fencing orchard pasture and
rough' ground according to Quantity and Quality thereof and that after a
Just and true Division of the same made by John Harvey and Philip Buckner
that they delever the first part of the aforementioned premises to Henry
Merest in right

Page 90   Court held 9th September 1690

of his wife and the other two third parts together with the housing orchard
pasture Fencing and Rough ground according to Quantity and Quality as the
Law directs unto Mr. George Luke in behalf of Coll. William Fitzhugh ..

831.   In the action depending between RICHARD GIBSON Plt and HENRY MEREST
        the deft it is ordered by this Court that Richard Gibson and Henry
Merest shall meet at the house of Mr. SAMLL. HAYWARD on the Monday before the
next Court then and there to be adjusted and made up by Mr. Samuel Hayward
and Mr. WILLIAM BUCKNER who is Likewise required to be there to the intent
that all their accounts may then be audited between them and that they return
an account of their audit to the next Court and the action to be referred to
the next Court.

832.   In the action that was depending Inter RICHARD MARTIN Plt and HENRY
        THOMPSON the deft concerning a horse race and after in another action
Inter Henry Thompson and Richard Martin the deft it was mutually agreed and
concluded by and between the parties that both actions should fall and that
Richard Martin should pay all costs which did accrue upon the actions and
did appeare in Court and acknowledge the same and desired it might be entered
upon the County records accordingly. Ordered that Richard Martin make payment of one hundred and twenty pounds of Tobacco per peice to SIMON THOMASON
and JAMES MAN for their attendance three daies at Court ..

833.   RICHD. GIBSON complaineth against GILES VANDACASTAILL in a plea of
        Debt .. the sum of 5 hundred and fifty pounds of Tobacco and cask due
for attorney fees councel and advice in Two actions at the Suit of JOHN DRAPER
which he did assume to pay the plt on demand but doth now deny .. And Giles
Vandacastil did appear in Court by GEORGE BRENT his attorney and pleaded nil
debet which plea was overruled by this Court And now forasmuch as it doth
appeare to this Court that there is the sum of three hundred pounds of Tobacco
due for two attorneys fees Therefore tis ordered Giles Vandagastail shall
make payment ..

Page 90 (contd)   Court held 9th September 1690

834.   WILLIAM BENNET by JOSHUA DAVIS his attorney complaining sheweth that
        THOMAS GULLOCK and WILLIAM PARSONS stand Indebted unto the plt the
sum of nine hundred pounds of tobacco in cask due per bill .. and now forasmuch as it doth appear to this Court that Thomas Gullock hath absented himself out of this County and whereas William Parsons did appear in this Court
by himself in person and Capt. GEORGE BRENT his attorney and could say nothing
but that the same appears to be

Page 91   Court held 9th September 1690

Justly due Therefore tis ordered William Parsons shall make payment ..

835.   JOHN GODDARD came into Court and confessed Judgment unto THOMAS POOLE
        for the sum of four hundred and seventy pounds of Tobacco due per ac-
count Therefore this ordered that John Goddard shall make payment ..

836.   At a Court held for County of Stafford September 10th 1690
        Present Coll William Fitzhugh, Mr. Samuel Hayward, Capt. George Mason,
        Mr. John Withers, Mr. Edward Thomason, Mr. William Buckner, Mr. Math.
        Thompson, Justices

837.   Ordered that the Sherif bring the body of THOMAS JEFFRIES to the next
        Court to answer the complaint of RICHARD BRYANT or else be Lyable
according to act of assembly and pay costs. Attachment according to act of
assembly is granted the sherif against the Estate of Thomas Jeffries for his
nonappearance at this Court to answer complaint of Richard Bryant ..

838.   Ordered that the Sherif bring the body of JOHN HAWKIN to the next
        Court to answer the complaint of JOHN MARTIN or else be Lyable according
to act of assembly and pay costs. Attachment according to act of assembly
is granted the sherif against the Estate of John Hawkin for his nonappearance
at this Court to answer complaint of John Martin ..

839.   Ordered that the Sherif bring the body of FRANCIS DADE to the next
        Court to answer the complaint of Capt. GEORGE BRENT or else be Lyable
according to act of assembly and pay costs. Attachment according to act of
assembly is granted the sherif against the Estate of Francis Dade for his
nonappearance at this Court to answer complaint of Capt. George Brent ..

840.   Ordered that the Sherif bring the body of JOHN JONES to the next Court
        to answer the complaint of RICHARD AYLIFF SENR. or else be Lyable ac-
cording to act of assembly and pay costs. Attachment according to act of
assembly is granted the sherif against the Estate of John Jones for his nonappearance at this Court to answer complaint of Richard Ayliff Senr. ..

841.   Ordered that the Sherif bring the body of JOHN JONES to the next Court
        to answer the complaint of SARAH MATHENEY or else be Lyable according
to act of assembly and pay costs. Attachment according to act of assembly is
granted the sherif against the Estate of John Jones for his nonappearance at
this Court to answer complaint of Sarah Matheney ..

842.   Ordered that the Sherif bring the body of ADAM WAFFENDALL to the next
        Court to answer the complaint of GERRARD BANKS or else be Lyable ac-
cording to act of assembly and pay costs. Attachment according to act of
assembly is granted the sherif against the Estate of Adam Waffendall for his
nonappearance at this Court to answer complaint of Gerrard Banks ..

Page 92   Court held 10th September 1690

843.   Ordered that the Sherif bring the body of THOMAS TUSTIN to the next
        Court to answer the complaint of ROBERT BRENT or else be Lyable ac-
cording to act of assembly and pay costs. Attachment according to act of
assembly is granted the sherif against the Estate of Thomas Tustin for his
nonappearance at this Court to answer complaint of Robert Brent ..

844.   Probate of the Last Will & Testament of EDWARD MASON late of this
        County deced is granted to MARGARET MASON his wife Executrix of the
said Will nominated and proved by the oaths and Testimonies of Captain
George Mason and Capt. George Mason witnesses to the Will subscribed.

845.   Ordered that the sherif shall four days before the next Court take
        the body of THOMAS NEWS into his custody and bring him to the next
Court to the intent that he may be punished for his disobedience and contempt of the Court order in goeing away being Summoned upon the Jury to try
a cause Inter RICHARD MARTIN plt and HENRY THOMPSON defendant before the
Jury had returned their Verdict.

846.   WILLIAM LOXHAM complains against THOMAS WALTERS in plea of debt ..
        the sum of 800 pounds of Tobacco due per bill under hand and Seale
dated the 7th of March 1686 and two hundred and seventy five pounds of
Tobacco more due per acct .. And Thomas Walters by WILLIAM WILFORD his attorney came into Court and legally discounted three hundred pounds of Tobacco
.. Therefore tis ordered Thomas Walters shall make payment (ballance) ..

847.   ROBERT BRENT complaining against BURR HARRISON of this County sheweth
        that whereas your petitioner did attach of the Estate of RICHARD NIXON
late of this County upon or near the said Nixons plantation in this County
three head of cattle of the said Nixon being all cows big with calfe and at
a Court held for this County 11th of Xber 1689 obtained Judgment against the
said Estate soe attached for a debt of fifteen hundred and thirty five pounds
of tobacco due from the said Nixon but so it is that the Deft hath since the
Judgment obtained removed and drove away three head of cattle from their
wanted and accustomed place of Feeding and as the Plt is informed and doth
believe hath drove them out of this County so that Execution cannot be levied
to the damage of two thousand pounds of tobacco and cask for which he brings
suit And the deft by GERRARD LOWTHER his attorney for plea saith not guilty

Page 93   Court held 10th September 1690

And now forasmuch as Robert Brent the Plt could (clerk appears to have omitted
the word "not") Justify and maintain his allegations to be true against Burr
Harrison the deft Therefore tis ordered that Robert Brent shall be nonsuit
and pay Burr Harrison sum of fifty pounds of Tobacco with costs ..

848.   Ordered that WILLIAM DOWNING shall pay unto WILLIAM BROWNE forty pounds
        of Tobacco for his attendance one day at Court in suit depending Inter
him and MATTHEW KEENE with costs. Matthew Keene and William Downing upon Imparlance from the 11th of June unto the 10th September 1690 And now until
when the deft had Licence to Imparle and comes to William Downing by RICHARD
GIBSON and SAMPSON DARRELL his attorneys and for plea saith not guilty according to the Statutes of Limitation which plea was overruled .. And now
forasmuch as the plt hath legally prov'd Justified and maintained his action
in this Court .. after a full hearing of the matter on both sides .. appears
that the said Downing the deft is guilty of the said Trespasse against Matthew
Keene Therefore tis ordered that the sheriff shall at or upon the 20th day

843 - 848

Page 93 (contd)   Court held 10th September 1690

of February next Eject and oust William Downing of and from the Land orchards housing and Fencing which he now lives on and shall immediately deliver the same into the peaceable and full possession of Matthew Keene and that William Downing pay ten pounds of Tobacco damages unto Matthew Keene with costs.

849.   JOHN MATTHEWS complaining sheweth that JAMES MAN of this County hath doth and will contrary to Law and the good peace of this their Majesties Government (Viat Armis) fall cleare occupy and Trespasse on and upon your Petrs dividend and Seat of land whereon your Petr now dwells and claims not withstanding your Petrs continual civil forwarning of him whereupon the said Man hath constrained your Petr to bring his Suit .. and James Mann comes in and Vouches JOHN WAUGH to be his Landlord of whom he fairly rented the beforementioned premises and that he was by him put into the possession of the same And forasmuch as John Waugh did also appear in Court and vouch and Justifie the same and did also pray for a Survey and full division of the said land now in dispute between them the Court adjudging it fit and Equitable to be done doe accordingly order Therefore tis ordered that Capt. GEORGE BRENT shall with an able Jury of the unconcerned Vicinage upon the 25th of this Instant be summoned by the sheriff to lay off the Lands Messuage and premises that is now in dispute between John Matthews Plt and John Waugh the deft and that they return an account of the Survey to the next Court to the Intent that each party may be by the next Court put into a Quiet and peaceable possession of their own part.

Page 94   Court held 10th September 1690

850.   WILLIAM PERKINS complains against THOMAS TUSTIN of this County in a plea of debt .. the sum of one thousand pounds of Tobacco and cask by bill and accompt for which he hath brought his action .. And Thomas Tustin comes into Court and legally discounted the sum of two hundred pounds of Tobacco out of afsd sum .. Therefore tis ordered that Thomas Tustin shall make present payment of the sum of eight hundred pounds of Tobacco being the full ballance between them ..

851.   RICHARD GIBSON complains against THOMAS TUSTIN in a plea of debt .. the sum of eight hundred pounds of Tobacco and caske .. and Thomas Tustin did appear in propria persona in this Court and could say nothing in barr or preclusion of the debt .. Therefore tis ordered Thomas Tustin shall make payment ..

852.   BURR HARRISON complains against THOMAS TUSTIN in a plea of debt .. the sum of eight hundred pounds of Tobacco and cask due per bill .. and Thomas Tustin did appear in propria persona in this Court and could say nothing in barr or preclusion of the debt .. Therefore tis ordered that Thomas Tustin shall make payment ..

853.   JOHN ATTERTON complains against EDWARD HUDGSON in a plea of debt .. the sum of two hundred and fifty pounds of Tobacco due per account .. And now forasmuch as John Atterton could not Justifie and maintain his action against Edward Hudgson Therefore tis ordered that Edward Hudgson of and from this action shall be dismissed and John Atterton pay this costs ..

854.   JOHN TONEY complains against ADAM ROBINSON in plea of Trespass for that your petitioner having a horse not long since Running at Mr. Alexanders pasture within a close fence in this County Adam Robinson of this

849 - 854

Page 94 (contd)   Court held 10th September 1690

County did contrary to the plts order or knowledge in the month of May last
past take and ride the horse on several Journeys as shall be made appear and
to the plts damage two thousand pounds of Tobacco and caske which the plt
hath brought his action

Page 95   Court held 10th September 1690

and the deft did appear in propria persona in this Court and for plea saith
not guilty and for Tryal puts himself upon the country and the plt likewise.
Therefore tis ordered that the Jury Enquire the fact: BURR HARRISON, JOHN
MATHEWS, SIMON STACEY, RICHARD AYLIFF SENR., WILLIAM PERKINS, FRANCIS WAD-
DINGTON, JOHN BREWTON, CHRISTOPHER HERRING, HENRY RIDGWAY, RICHARD BRYANT,
JOSEPH NEWTON, JOHN BEACH which Jurors Elected Tryed and Sworn to say the
Truth do say upon their Oaths we find for the Plt eight hundred pounds of
Tobacco damages and to have his horse returned again Therefore tis ordered
that Judgment shall be entered on the Verdict of the Jury and Adam Robinson
shall make payment and return horse .. Ordered John Toney shall pay the Jury
seventy two pounds of Tobacco with costs .. Ordered John Toney shall make
present payment of the sum four hundred and twenty pounds of Tobacco apeece
unto SIMON THOMASON and John Mathews for BALSAM JAMES for their attendance
three days at Court ..

855.   Ordered that RICHARD AYLIFF SENR. shall make present payment of sum
        of one hundred and twenty pounds of Tobacco to JAMES STANTON, JOHN
WRIGHT and JONAH DENTON for their attendance three daies at Court in suit
depending between him and JOHN JONES with costs.

856.   ISAAC ALLERTON Esqr. complains against JOHN WITHERS in Chancery in
        most humble wise your daily Orator sheweth that whereas at Court held
for this County the 7th of April 1690 your Orator obtained administration as
greatest creditor of the goods of JOHN COLLOM late of Plymouth in the County
of Devon in the Kingdom of England deced and whereas John Collom at his last
departure out of this Colony of Virginia did constitute authorize and appoint
the said Withers his lawful attorney for him and in his name and to the said
Colloms use to demand receive and all such Effects as were any waies due to
him in this Colony and forasmuch as your orator has no way to discover or
find out the goods and chattels of the sd Collom but by the Oath of the said
Withers your orator hath therefore supened the said Withers in Chancery and
humbly prays he may render an account upon his Oath of all and Singular the
goods and chattels wares, bills bonds and accompts due to or the said Collom
dyed possessed of in this Colony of Virginia that are in the hands or Custody
or otherwise come to the knowledge of the said Withers to the end your Orator
may take such measures for the recovery thereof as the Law directs and be
Enabled fairly to acquit himself in the administration of the goods as the
Law in such cases requires And John Withers did appear himself in person and
made answer to the bill in Chancery that he is ready to give an account of
all the goods and chattels of the said Colloms that he had left in his hands
or hath come to his hands since

Page 96   Court held 10th September 1690

his decease by Vertue of the Letter of Procuration granted to him by the said
Collom and this is what he hath given upon Oath to this Court being the goods
here undemenconed A horse running in the woods which Collom in his lifetime
said properly belong to himself one half of a shallop with tackle and furniture one hogshead Tobacco at four hundred pds or thereabouts which was left

Page 96 (contd)   Court held 10th September 1690

in the hands of Mr. ROBERT COLSON up the River I am not sure that the hhd of
Tobacco is Mr. Colloms neither was I ordered by him to call him to acco. for
it this is what I know to be his   to the best of my knowledge I have
likewise in my hands due to Mr. JOHN ADDIZ and ABRAM BEALE who I believe were
the Employers of Collom due from me to the sum of two thousand and forty nine
pounds of Tobacco of which sum thirteen hundred and thirty pounds of it is
due by bill the rest by account the Bill I suppose is in England & this is
all to the best of my knowledge John Withers Jurat in Curia Sept the 10th
Anno Dom 1690 And Coll Isaac Allerton by ROBERT BRENT his attorney comes
in Court and prays an order for the speedy appraisement of the shallop Tackle
and furniture now in the hands of John Withers and properly belonging one
half to the Estate of John Collom deced which accordingly is granted. Therefore tis ordered HENRY MEREST and ADAM ROBINSON on Monday next being the 15th
Instant repair to the house of John Withers and shall there Truely and faithfully appraise the shallop Tackle and furniture and that Mr. SAMUEL HAYWARD
swear them accordingly and that the appraisers doe return a Just and True
accompt of the appraisement unto Mr. Samuel Hayward.

857.   RICHARD GIBSON complains against JOSEPH NEWTON in a plea of debt ..
        the sum of twelve hundred pounds of Tobacco and caske by a note drawn
on him by CHARLES BALDRIDGE dated Sept the 20th 1689 which he hath several
times promised and assumed to pay but hath not paid .. And now forasmuch as
it doth appear to this Court that Richard Gibson could not aver Justifie and
maintain his action as is before alledged Therefore tis ordered that Joseph
Newton of and from the action shall be dismissed and that Richard Gibson pay
costs ..

858.   In the action depending in this Court Inter EDWARD THOMASON plt and
        ADAM ROBINSON the defendant It is ordered by this Court that Mr.
RICHARD GIBSON who was formerly subsherif to Edward Thomason shall bring all
the books papers and accompts to the next Court which shall any waies relate
to any account which is betweene Edward Thomason and Adam Robinson in the
time of his Shrievalty and that this action be referred to next Court.

859.   JOSHUA DAVIS attorney of MOSES HUBBARD complains against STEPHEN SE-
        BASTIAN in a plea of debt .. the sum of nine hundred pounds of Tobacco
due per bill ..

Page 97   Court held 10th September 1690

And Stephen Sebastian did appear in Court in propria persona and for plea
saith Nill debet but forasmuch as it appears to this Court that Joshua Davis
could not aver Justifie and maintain his action against the deft as is alledged
Therefore tis ordered Joshua Davis shall be nonsuite and shall pay Stephen
Sebastian fifty pounds of tobacco with costs.

860.   WILLIAM PAGE by SAMSON DARRELL his attorney complaining sheweth that
        whereas WILLIAM BREWERTON Cooper of this county hath been a retainer
to my house by agreemt with him made for his dyet at forty pounds of Tobacco
so long as he should continue which agreemt was made & his commencement thereupon begun on the beginning of March 1686 the said Brewerton having reced the
same in full satisfaction according to agreement from the time abovesaid until
Xmas last without any objection which is full twenty months and that likewise
your petitioner hath carefully and well looked after the said Brewertons stock
of cattle and wintered the same by his request who promised me satisfaction

for soe doing to content with several other charges and services by your Petr
done for the said Brewerton as will more fully appear by my acco^t .. your
Petr in all Justice and right constrained to bring his action for the same of
two thousand four hundred and eighty pounds of Tobacco and caske and craves
Judgment But now forasmuch as William Page Senr. could not aver prove Justifie
and maintain his action against William Brewerton Therefore tis ordered that
William Brewerton of and from this action be dismissed and that William Page
Senr pay costs .. William Brewerton by GEORGE BRENT his attorney complaining
sheweth William Page Senr. of this County Carpenter stands indebted to him
the sum of nine hundred pounds of Tobacco and cask for so much paid for him
to Mr. RICHARD FOSSAKER in his great need and Extremity to save ths said Page
from Prison which loan Page did faithfully promise to repay but now utterly
refuseth .. And now after a full Examination and perusing of all accompts
and their utmost allegations being heard fully by this Court it appears that
there is the sum of two hundred and ninety pounds of Tobacco due upon ballance
of all accounts from William Page to William Brewerton being for that the
said Brewerton did make forth and plainly make appeare that he had paid the
sum of nine hundred pounds of tobacco for the said Page to Mr. Richard Fossaker
Therefore tis ordered that William Page Senr shall make payment of the afsd
sum being in full the ballance of all demands between them ..

Page 98   Court held 10th September 1690

861.   RICHARD GIBSON one of the securities of RICHARD NIXON complaining
       sheweth that the Clerk having returned him one of the securities for
the faithful administration of Richard Nixon (who married the widow of Thomas Holmes) for the said Holmes his Estate and the Estate being totally Em-
bezled and wasted the plt hath Judgment given agst him for two thousand and
seven hundred pounds of tobacco and cask to ROBERT HANK'S one of the creditors
and is Liable to all the rest of the Creditors which this Worshipful Court
well knowing and it having been represented to your worships that unfair and
fraudulent practices have been used in and about the said Estate to the de-
frauding of the Creditors and prejudice of the securities have been pleased
out of Justice and commiseration of the plts sufferings by your order to
him to appoint and Empower him the plt to Search and Enquire after the persons
concerned in the fraud and to bring them regularly before the Court Now may
it please your Worships the plt by his diligent search and Enquiry hath found
out that the principal parts of the Estate of the said Thomas Holmes consisted
in cattle which having been appraised by order of this Worshipful Court before the Inventory and appraisement was returned BURR HARRISON of this County
Fraudulently combined and conspired for avarice sake (with the said Nixon)
to wast and Embezle the said Estate and to that effect did take and accept
from the said Nixon a bill of sale for all the said cattle and did destroy
or otherwise make away the Inventory and appraisement and all the consideration for this bill of sale was for a while to conceal the said Nixon in the
County and then to provide the means of his Escape which the said Harrison
having effected did procure a discharge from the said Nixon so that being
possessed of the cattle and having this private discharge thinks himself discharged and secure in holding of them although all these private Frauds and
ill practices were done in the Space of time betwixt one Court and the next
so that and under all the marks of Fraud Imaginable as the plt is ready to
prove he hath therefore brought his action against the said Harrison and is
ready to prove him guilty of that Fraud beforementioned which being one of
the most hated thing in the Law it being destructive to human Society and
common commerce he humbly prays Judgment for the cattle and all other the Es-

Page 98 (contd)   Court held 10th September 1690

tate of the said Holmes by him so fraudulently taken with costs and Now forasmuch as Richard Gibson could not prove and Justifie and maintain his action as is before alledged against Burr Harrison Therefore tis ordered that Burr Harrison shall of and from this action be dismissed and that Richard Gibson pay costs ..

862. Forasmuch as JOHN MATHEWS did arrest JAMES MAN to this Court and did or could not prosecute his action Therefore tis ordered that John Mathews shall be nonsuit and shall pay unto James Man fifty pounds of Tobacco with costs ..

863. FRANCIS DADE and FRANCES his wife one of the daughters and coheirs of ROBERT TOWNSHEND late of this County deced and JOHN WASHINGTON as Guardian and next friend to MARY TOWNSEND another daughter and coheir of Robert Townsend deced sheweth that FRANCES TOWNSEND Mother to the said Robert in her widowhood did the 7th day of February 1650 procure a pattent from Sr. WILLIAM BERKLEY Knt. for two thousand two hundred acres of land then Scituate and lying in

Page 99 Court held 10th September 1690

Northumberland County and now called Stafford County within the Collony of Virginia which land did descend upon Robert Townsend her son and heir Father to your Petrs which said Robert Townsend dyed in the infancy of your Petrs seised and possessed of the said land after whose decease the same of right descends to your Petrs either as grandaughters and coheirs of their grandmother Frances Townsend (mother to the said Robert their Father) or as coheirs to the said Father Robert Townsend But now so it is that THOMAS DERRICK JUNR. hath for the Space of six months last past entered into and upon one thousand acres of the said dividend of land part whereof is knowne by the name of Rich neck and breaks up the land and cutts downe the Timber to your petitioners damage five thousand pounds of Tobacco for which your Petrs hath brought their action against Thomas Derrick Junr. and craves Judgment for the same with costs of suit as also their Majesties Writ of habere Facias possessionem to put your petrs in Quiet possession thereof And Thomas Derrick Junr. comes in and vouches JEFFRIE JEFFRIES and JOHN JEFFRIES the heirs and Executors of JOHN JEFFRIES late of London Esqr. deced to be the landlords and of whom and by vertue of whose power he was put into the beforementioned premises having legally Rented and leased the same from the said Jeffries Lawful attorney and prays Licence of Imparlance till the next Court to put in their plea and that he may be then discharged from this action which Licence of Imparlance unto him is granted and that then their plea be not wanting.

864. WILLIAM LOXHAM complains against JOHN BLUNDALL in a plea of debt .. the sum of four hundred and thirty pounds of Tobacco won of him in July last past at the house of JOHN COLCLOUGH within this County at the games of cards called Whisk and gleek which he refuses to pay .. But now forasmuch as it appeare to this Court that William Loxham could not aver Justifie and maintain his action as is before alledged against John Blundall Therefore tis ordered that William Loxham shall be nonsuit and shall pay unto John Blundall the sum of fifty pounds of Tobacco with costs ..

865. Capt. GEORGE BRENT attorney of CHARLES ROSE the attorney of BENJAMIN HADDOCK of Charles County in Province of Maryland complaining sheweth that EDWARD HUDGSON stands indebted to the said Haddock for sundry goods wares

862 - 865

Page 99 (contd)   Court held 10th September 1690

& merchandizes sold him the deft in Province of Maryland and in the year 1683
the deft then living there the sum of 1990 pounds of Tobacco and cask as will
appear by the acco. of particulars sworn by the said Haddock before a magis-
trate of that province That soon after the debt was contracted by the said
Hudgson he privately removed himself out of the said province and could never
be found there since to be demanded the same nor ever did Take care to make
any provision for the payment the Plt Wherefore by his attorney he hath
brought his action and prays Judgment for the debt And Edward Hudgson by
ROBERT COLLIS his attorney comes into Court and for plea saith Nil debet And
now forasmuch as Charles Rose could not aver Justifie and

Page 100   Court Held 10th September 1690

maintain his action as is alledged Therefore tis ordered that Charles Rose
shall be nonsuit and shall pay Edward Hudgson fifty pounds of Tobacco with
costs ..

866.   JAMES GALLOHOUGH and MARY his wife as daughter of WILLIAM RUSSELL by
        GERRARD LOWTHER their attorney complaining sheweth that Docter EDMOND
HELDER by his last Will & Testament in writing did bequeath to your Petr all
his cattle with their increase (some of them devised to Legatees in the will
Excepted) and by the will did appoint that your Petr Mary should live with
WILLIAM DOWNING and MARY his wife and that William Downing be named sole Execr.
in the will did prove the same and obtained administration thereupon and
possessed himself of the whole personal estate of Edmond Helder as well
cattle as other goods and chattels and refuses and denies (although often
thereunto requested to deliver to your Petr the Legacy devised to her) Wherefore your Petrs has brought their action against William Downing and William
Downing by RICHARD GIBSON his attorney comes and craves Licence of Imparlance
herein till the next Court to bring in his plea which unto him is granted and
that then his plea be not wanting.

867.   WILLIAM LOXHAM complains against JOHN BLUNDALL in a plea of debt ..
        the sum of twelve hundred and fifty pounds of Tobacco and cask for a
horse sold him .. And forasmuch as it doth appear to this Court that there
is now due but four hundred pounds of Tobacco from John Blundall the deft ..
and that the other eight hundred and fifty pounds of Tobacco due of the sum
being for a horse sold as afsd doth not appear to be due until the Tenth of
October 1691 Therefore tis ordered that William Loxham shall have Judgment
only for the four hundred pounds of tobacco ..

        The remainder of this page and part of page 101 has a resume of
        attorneys and their clients.

Page 101   Court held 10th September 1690

868.   SAMSON DARRELL who married the Sole daughter now living of Capt. JOHN
        NORGRAVE petitions this Court that EDWARD MADDOCK who married the
Relict and Executrix of the said Norgrave deced might give security for the
performance of the said Will according to the Tenor thereof and farther alledged that Coll. Mason in his lifetime and all the time of his life gave
security and that since his decease one of his Sectys is dead also Therefore
prays the said Coll. Mason being dead and his Security dead likewise that
Doctor Maddocks who is since Intermarried and hath by the Intermarriage the
possession and Enjoyment of the said Norgraves Estate may be compelled to
enter Bond with good and sufficient security to be accountable for the same

Page 101 (contd)   Court held 10th September 1690

according to the bequest of the deced & as the Law Injoynes And Doctor Edward Maddock comes into Court by GERRARD LOWTHER his attorney and refuses to
put in Security for these reasons following Vizt. 1. As to the cattle they
are paid 2d the Ring is given the Legatee according to the Will 3. As to the
negroes they are a personal chattel and a remainder Limited in the Will a
Chattel personal is void because if given for one hour they are given forever
they are given to Maddock for her life so that the remainder after her decease
is void therefore from them no security ought to be given 4. noe Exectr named
by the Testator in his will are by Law compelled to find Security for the
performance of the Testators Will but we are Exectrs Therefore unless the Law
will dispose and Intrust his Estate of the Testator otherwise then he designed
we are not obliged to find security for performance of the Testators will and
this appears by the provision made by the Laws of this Countrey that admrs
shall find Security but no Law does oblige Exectrs 65 act of assembly 21 Henry
8. 15 Vid Title Probates of Testaments in Wingates abrigmt. Lastly there has
been Security already found in this matter and if the Court have discharged
them without other we are not every day bound to find new security.

Page 102   Court held 10th September 1690

And the Court having fully and maturelay considered the matter doe unanimously concurr with and approve of Darrells motion and they do accordingly
order and Therefore tis ordered that Doctor Edward Maddock shall give good
security and enter into bond accordingly for the same as the Law doth Enjoyn
and direct with which Judgment of the Court Edward Maddock not being there-
with content doth appeale to the Sixth day of the next General Court to be
held at James City. Mr. SAMUEL HAYWARD became security with Doctor Edward
Maddocks to prosecute his appeale and ROBERT BRENT with Sampson Darrell to
answer his appeale.

> The Court is adjourned to the 2d Wednesday in October next
> God save their Majesties

869.   At a Court held for County of Stafford October the 8th 1690
        Present Lieut. Coll. William Fitzhugh, Mr. Samuel Hayward, Capt. George
Mason, Mr. Mathew Thompson, Mr. Edward Thomason Justices

870.   Ordered that JOHN WHEATCRAFT, ROBERT RICHARDS, ROBERT ALEXANDER &
        CHRISTOPHER RICHARDSON or any three of them shall on Wednesday the
25th day of this Instant October appraise the Estate of THOMAS OD'NEAL deced
and that Mr. SAMUEL HAYWARD swear them accordingly.

871.   Ordered that CHARLES ROSE shall make present payment of eighty pounds
        of Tobacco to EDWARD KENNINGTON and EDWARD TUBB for their attendance
to this Court to prove a Letter from BENJAMIN HADDOCK to Charles Rose with
costs ..

872.   Capt. GEORGE BRENT who was appointed by this Court one of the Surveyors
        of Highwayes in the upper parish of this County made motion to this
Court that he being appointed one of the Surveyors of the Highwayes that he
is not fully satisfied with his precincts and that the Inhabitants within his
precinct refuses to come into the repairing of the highwayes and bridges according to the Summons under a Specious pretence that the Inhabitants are
summoned in by other Surveyors alsoe appointed and the Court taking the same
into their mature consideration doe accordingly order Therefore tis ordered
that the Vestry of the upper parish shall take in the roads in their precincts

Page 102 (contd)   Court held 8th October 1690

unto their consideration and appoint hands accordingly to the repairing of
the Bridges and clearing of the Roads according the length of the ground and
the Quality of the said roads.

873.   THOMAS DERRICK SENR. made an humble motion to this Court shewing that
        he having been a long and antient Inhabiter of this County and now
having attained the age of about sixty three years so that his bodily Labour
is now quite spent and is thereby rendered incapable to get his Livelihood
and doth therefore humbly pray your Worships to discharge and fully exempt
and acquit your Petr from paying any further levy or publick dues which the
Court having duely maturely and charitably considered the same and finding
Thomas Derrick Senr. to be old and unfit or uncapable of getting his livelihood doe accordingly order Therefore tis ordered that Thomas Derrick Senr.
shall after this year be freely and fully discharged and acquitted from paying
any more levies or publick dues.

Page 103   Court held 8th October 1690

874.   Mr. JOHN HARVEY and PHILIP BUCKNER who was appointed by the last Court
        to divide the land Tenement and housing and orchard in dispute between
HENRY MEREST and Coll. WILLIAM FITZHUGH about the said Merests wifes thirds
made a return to this Court of their dividing the orchards in thirds between
the parties and they not knowing well the bounds of the land and being informed by Mrs. ELIZABETH YOUNG that she lays claim to some part of the land
being known by the name of Strife Point do therefore pray either to be discharged and acquitted from the Division or that the Court will please to make
known to them the bounds of the land .. Therefore tis ordered that the tract
of land shall be divided between this and the next Court by John Harvey and
Philip Buckner according to the survey made formerly by Capt. GEORGE BRENT
and Mr. WILLIAM HORTON pursuant to three orders of the General Court for the
Survey of the said Land.

875.   JOHN BREWTON came into Court and confessed Judgment to Mr. MATTHEW
        THOMPSON for the sum of eighteen hundred and sixty nine pounds of To-
bacco in cask Therefore tis ordered shall make payment ..

876.   GEORGE ANDREWS was this day Sworn undersherif of this County and Capt.
        MALACHI PEALE became Security for the True and Faithful performing of
his office.

877.   GEORGE CALVERT complaining against JOHN TARKINTON in plea of debt ..
        in sum of fifteen hundred pounds of Tobacco in cask due per bill under
his hand and seale bearing date the 15th day of July 1690 and that the said
Tarkinton having fugitively absented himself out of this County so that the
Ordinarie Proceedings at Law cannot be had against him .. And George Calvert
having Justly made appear his debt to be due Therefore tis ordered that George
Calvert shall have Judgment for eight hundred pounds of Tobacco against Estate
of John Tarkinton soe attached with costs ..

878.   WILLIAM TODD comes into Court and made oath upon the holy Evangelists
        of almighty God that he did see THOMAS ODENEALL sign seale and deliver
the said Will here in Court produced as his Last Will & Testament being a
witness to the Will subscribed.

879.   Mr. EDWARD THOMASON came into Court and made oath upon the holy Evange-
        lists of almighty God that he did see EDWARD MASON sign seale and de-

Page 103 (contd)   Court held 8th October 1690

liver the said will here in Court produced as his Last Will & Testament being a witness to the Will subscribed.

880.   Ordered that Capt. GEORGE BRENT shall make payment of the sum of forty pounds of Tobacco to WILLIAM TODD for his attendance one day at Court to prove the Last Will and Testament of THOMAS OD'NEALL deced with costs ..

881.   JOHN BEACH came into Court and confessed Judgment to Mr. SAMUEL HAYWARD for the sum of five hundred and seventy eight pounds of Tobacco Therefore tis

Page 104   Court held 8th October 1690

ordered that John Beach shall make payment .. being in full the ballance of all demands between them with costs ..

The Court is adjourned till the Second Wednesday in November
God save their Majesties

882.   At a Court held for the County of Stafford at the house of THOMAS OWSLEY November the 12th 1690

Present Coll. William Fitzhugh, Mr. Samuel Hayward, Capt. George Mason, Mr. John Withers, Mr. Edward Thomason, Mr. William Buckner, Mr. Matthew Thompson, Justices

883.   Whereas it was presented to this Court that HENRY COLDSTREAM of this County had mortally wounded a man with giving him a stab with a Rapier in the groine Therefore tis ordered that Henry Coldstream shall be by the Sheriff taken immediately into custody and by him secured or else to be discharged upon good and sufficient Bail or Mainprize until it is discovered whether JAMES THEARLE the man wounded will live or die.

884.   Ordered by this Court that RICHARD HOLMES shall be Trustee to the Estate of NICHS. MANIERE who lately deced in his said house within this County and that he shall render a Just and true accompt of his said Estate to the next Court.

885.   Ordered that RALPH SMITH, THOMAS BARTON and WILLIAM HANSBRIDGE doe between this and next Court appraise the Estate of EDWARD MASON late of this County deced & that Mr. MATTHEW THOMPSON swear them accordingly.

886.   JOSHUA DAVIS Attorney of JOHN HOARE Execr of KATHERINE WEBB late of the County of Westmoreland deced complaineth against DAVID DARNELL of this County in plea of debt .. sum of five hundred and eleven pounds of Tobacco due as appears per a former order bearing date the 8th of August 1688 .. and David Darnell the deft did appear in this Court and confessed Judgment to Joshua Davis .. Therefore tis ordered David Darnell shall make payment ..

887.   Ordered by this Court that MARY MURRAH Servant to Mr. JOHN WAUGH shall be free at the beginning of December next notwithstanding the assignment (which is made from Mr. RALPH ASH her master who transferred her to Mr. John Waugh) by reason that Mary Murrah did prove in this Court and that the Court is informed that Ralph Ash who brought her in and the ship came in about the beginning of December and that John Waugh shall pay her Corn and cloaths according to the Custom of the country and pay costs.

Page 105   Court held 12th November 1690

888.   Ordered that JOHN WILLIAMS shall be Trustee to the Estate of JOHN
        PORTER late of this County deced who was casually found dead upon the
Kings Road and that he shall render a Just and true accompt of the Estate
upon his Oath to the next Court.

889.   Ordered that Doctor EDWARD MADDOCKS who intermarried with FRANCES the
        widow and relict of Coll. GEORGE MASON late of this County deced who
was formerly the widow and Executrix of Capt. JOHN NORGRAVE late of this
County also deced shall be by the sherif summoned to next Court to give security Touching the Estate of Capt. John Norgrave deced pursuant to an order
of the last General Court and that he bring good security with him to Enter
into Bond for the true and faithful performance of the said Will of Capt.
John Norgrave.

890.   Whereas ELIZABETH MINITHORNE did in open Court assume and promise to
        pay five hundred pounds of Tobacco and caske for the fine of SUSAN
BARRET her Servant for having a bastard child Therefore tis ordered that she
shall make present payment of the same unto the Upper Parish of This County.

891.   RICHARD BROAD humbly complaining sheweth that your Petr having Truely
        & faithfully served his time by Indenture with THOMAS OD'NEALE late
of this County deced and as yet was never paid his corn and cloaths according
to Custom of the County wherefore he humbly prayes that your Worships would
be pleased to grant an order against admr cum Testamento annexed of the Estate of Thomas Od'neale late deced for to pay his corn & cloaths with costs
and the Court having fully and maturely considered the premises doe accordingly order Therefore tis ordered that HENRY COLDSTREAM in Qualification
afsd shall make payment of his freedom corne and cloaths according to the
Custom of the Country.

892.   PETER DAVISON humbly complaining sheweth that your Petr did in Febru-
        ary last past enter into covenant Service by Indenture to serve THOMAS
OD'NEALE late of this County deced until the last day of this Instant November for which your Petr was to be paid by Thomas Od'neale the sum of seventeen
hundred pounds of Tobacco clear of Levy and all other charges Wherefore your
Petr Exhibited his petition to this Court and humbly prays order against
HENRY COLDSTREAM as admr cum Testamento annexed of the Estate of Thomas Od'neale
deced for his wages and pay this costs And the Court having fully and maturely
considered the premises doe accordingly order Therefore tis ordered that
Henry Coldstream in Qualification shall make full and present payment of the
sum .. according to agreement by Indenture with costs.

893.   RICHARD LEE humbly complaining sheweth that your Petr did enter into
        covenant service with THOMAS OD'NEALE late of this County deced from
the middle of March last past until the last day of October for which your
Petr was to have the

Page 106   Court held 12th November 1690

sum of two thousand pounds of Tobacco and cask for his service clear of all
charges if the levy did not amount to more than one hundred pounds of Tobacco
Wherefore your Petr humbly prays Judgment against HENRY COLDSTREAM admr cum
Testamento annexed of the Estate of Thomas Od'neale deceased and now after a
full hearing of the matter on both sides and the Court having fully and maturely considered the premises doe accordingly order Therefore tis ordered the
said Henry Coldstream in Qualification shall make present and full payment
of the afsd sum ..

Page 106 (contd)   Court held 12th November 1690

894.   THOMAS LUND made humble petition to this Court that he having not yet
        attained to the age of one and twenty years doth humbly present Mr.
JOHN WITHERS as his Guardian and prayes that he may be administrator to the
same And forasmuch as Thomas Lund and Mr. John Withers did both appear in
this Court and John Withers did accept Thomas Lund free and voluntary offer
and did willingly take the said charge and forasmuch as Thomas Lund and John
Withers his Guardian did aver and justifie to this Court that HENRY COLDSTREAM
admr cum Testamento annexed of the Estate of THOMAS ODENELE late of this County
deced doth detaine and withhold from him his Estate which was bequeathed to
him by his Father CHRISTOPHER LUND late of this County deced Therefore tis
ordered that Henry Coldstream in Qualification afsd shall deliver up unto
John Withers in Qualification all the Estate which doth properly belong unto
Thomas Lund by vertue of Christopher Lund will his deced Father.

895.   GEORGE BRENT complains against FRANCIS DADE in plea of debt .. the
        sum of six pounds Sterling by Protested bills of Exchange with all
damages as also by account of Tobacco the sum of fourteen hundred and fifty
pounds of Tobacco and caske for both which he brings his suit .. And now forasmuch as Capt. George Brent the plt did by his protested bills of Exchange
make appear the said sum due as aforesaid and that Francis Dade did utterly
deny the payment of the sum of fourteen hundred and fifty pounds of Tobacco
except seventy five pounds of Tobacco and Capt. George Brent could not aver
and justifie the same Therefore tis ordered that Francis Dade shall make present payment of the six pounds Sterling and seventy five pounds of Tobacco
with costs of suit ..

896.   Whereas JOHN LYNDSEY Servant to JOHN HAWKIN did come into this Court
        and did acknowledge his free and voluntary willingness to serve John
Hawkin for the Space of six years from the date of this order for that John
Hawkin had bought him from WILLIAM CLARKSON his Master in Maryland and had
redeemed him from the penalty of Law that he was to have suffered for absenting himself out of his Masters service in Maryland Therefore tis ordered
that John Lyndsey shall serve John Hawkin his said Master the full Term and
Time of six years as aforesaid.

Page 107   Court held 12th November 1690

897.   RICHARD GIBSON humbly sheweth that JOHN CORNISH late of this County
        stands indebted to him the sum of seven hundred and fifty three pounds
of Tobacco and cask due to him by acco. who having absented himself out of
this County the plt took out an attachment against his Estate which was accordingly served in the hands of WILLIAM HARRIS according to Law .. And now
forasmuch as Richard Gibson by his account here in Court produced Justly make
appear his debt to be due Therefore tis ordered Richard Gibson shall have
Judgment against the Estate of John Cornish soe attached in the hands of
William Harris for the said sum ..

898.   Ordered that the action Inter RICHARD GIBSON and HENRY MEREST the deft
        which was referred to be audited at the house of Mr. SAMUEL HAYWARD
and that Mr. Samuel Hayward and Mr. WILLIAM BUCKNER was to audit it accordingly upon the Monday before October Court last past and Richard Gibson and
Henry Merest did not appear timely enough for the audit Therefore tis ordered
that the action shall be referred to Audit till the Eight day of december
next being the Monday before the next Court and that Mr. Samuel Hayward and
Mr. William Buckner shall at the house of Mr. Samuel Hayward audit it accordingly.

894 - 898

Page 107 (contd)   Court held 12th November 1690

899.   Ordered that the sheriff bring the body of ROBERT HANKS to the next
       Court to answer the suit of Mr. SAMUEL HAYWARD or else be Lyable ac-
cording to act of assembly and pay costs. Attachment according to act of
assembly is granted the Sheriff against the Estate of Robert Hanks for his
nonappearance at this Court to answer the complaint of Samuel Hayward with
costs.

900.   SAMUEL POLLARD humbly sheweth that your petitioner having had a long
       and languishing distemper upon him Viz the flux running on him whereby
he is disabled and rendered incapable of getting a further livelihood and
whereby to subsist Wherefore your petitioner humbly prays to grant him an
order to discharge from paying any further Levy or Publick dues and the Court
having fully and maturely considered the premises and charitably taking him
into their consideration doe accordingly order Therefore tis ordered that
Samuel Pollard shall be fully and freely discharged from paying any further
Levy and Publick dues.

901.   JOHN BEACH complains against THOMAS NEWS in a plea of debt .. the sum
       of two hundred and fifty pounds of Tobacco by accompt and for clerks
fees eighty three pounds and sheriffs fees one hundred and eighteen pounds
which makes in all four hundred fifty one pounds of Tobacco which he refuseth
to pay altho often of him demanded .. And now forasmuch as John Beach Justly
made appear to this Court the sum of two hundred and fifty pounds of Tobacco
as per account produced Therefore tis ordered that Thomas News shall make
payment of said sum ..

Page 108   Court held 12th November 1690

902.   SIGISMOND MASSEY attorney of NICHOLAS HAYWARD Notary Publick in Lon-
       don complaining sheweth that Mr. ROBERT KING late of this County did
at the time of his death stand indebted to your petitioner in Qualification
the Just sum of two thousand pounds of Tobacco due per bill under his hand
and seale dated July the 16th 1689 Wherefore your petitioner has brought his
action against MARY KING the widow and relict and Executrix of Robert King
and prays Judgment against her And now forasmuch as Sigismond Massey did here
in Court produce his Bill Therefore tis ordered that Mary King Executrix
shall make payment of the sum ..

903.   SAMUEL HAYWARD complaining sheweth that ROBERT KING late of this county
       deced did at the time of his decease stood indebted to the plt the sum
of fifteen hundred and twenty eight pounds of Tobacco due to him by accompt
for clerks fees for which he hath brought his action against MARY KING the
relict widow and Executrix of Robert King and prays Judgment .. And now forasmuch as Samuel Hayward did here in Court produce his account so that the
same did Justly appear to be due and that the account being clerks fees was
adjudged by this Court to be a debt of record and Therefore doth take priority
in Law before other debts Therefore tis ordered that Mary King shall make
payment of said sum ..

904.   EDWARD THOMASON humbly complaining sheweth that ROBERT KING at time
       of his death stood indebted to the plt the sum of eleven hundred ninety
and nine pounds of Tobacco and caske by bill under his hand given for Levies
and Quit rents for the year 1683 for which your petitioner hath brought his
action against MARY KING Executrix of Robert King and prays for Judgment for
the same and now forasmuch as it doth appear to this Court that there is due

of the account the sum of eight hundred and fifty four pounds of Tobacco
Therefore tis ordered that Mary King in Qualification shall make payment of
the said sum ..

905.   RICHARD GIBSON complaining sheweth that VINCENT YOUNGE at the time of
         his death stood indebted to the plt the sum of ten thousand one hundred
and thirteen pounds of Tobacco due per a former order of this Court appeale
and damages with other costs .. Wherefore he hath brought his action against
ELIZABETH the widow and Executrix of Vincent Younge deced and prays Judgment
and now forasmuch as it appears to this Court that there is due only the sum
of nineteen hundred and five pounds of Tobacco in full the ballance of all
assets due from Vincent Younge Estate Therefore tis ordered that Eliza. Younge
shall make payment of the said sum .. Mr. JOHN WITHERS and Mr. MATTHEW
THOMPSON absent.

Page 109   Court held 12th November 1690

906.   ANNE the widow and relict of THOMAS ODENEALE late deced complaining
         sheweth that HENRY COLDSTREAM who obtained letters of administration
cum Testamento annexed of the Estate of Thomas Odeneale doth contrary to all
manner of Justice Law Equity and Charity keep and detain from your petitioner
all the corn which was made of the Last crop with the Tobacco on the ground
growing thereon so that your petitioner hath not means left for the support
and maintenance of her and her family Wherefore your petitioner hath Exhibited
her humble petition to this Court and humbly prays your Worships order Henry
Coldstream to deliver the full third part of the crop of corn and Tobacco for
the support and maintenance of her and her family with a full third part of
the residue of the Estate which is yet undivided and pay this costs And the
Court having fully and maturely considered of the premises doe accordingly
order Therefore tis ordered that Anne Odeneale shall have a full third part
of the corn and wheat which did grow and was made upon the ground and belonging
to the Estate of Thomas Odeneale deced shall be immediately delivered to her
in kinde and Quantity at the places and most surest conveniences it was made
in also it is further ordered that the residue of the Thomas Odeneale Estate
which is yet undivided shall be immediately divided in Quantity and Quality
and that a full third part of the Estate soe divided shall be delivered to
Anne Odenele she giving bond with good security unto Henry Coldstream for the
full performance and True payment of a full third part of the debts which
shall be legally brought in against Henry Coldstream as admr cum Testamento
annexed of the Estate of Thomas Odenele deced. Mr. JOHN WITHERS and Capt.
GEORGE BRENT came into Court and became security with the said Anne Odenele
for the true performance and full payment of one full third part of the debts
of Thomas Odenele and entered into bond accordingly.

        The Court is adjourned till the morning eight of the clock.

907.   At a Court held for Stafford County at the house of THOMAS ELSEY the
        13th of November 1690

    Present Coll. William Fitzhugh, Mr. Samuel Hayward, Capt. George Mason, Mr.
    Edward Thomason, Mr. Matthew Thompson, Mr. John Withers, Mr. William Buckner,
    Justices

908.   JAMES HEARSE attorney of SUSANA KELLY of Maryland complaineth against
         RICHARD WILLIAMS in a plea of debt .. the sum of sixteen hundred and
six pounds of Tobacco due per Bill .. and Richard Williams deft came into

Page 109 (contd)   Court held 13th November 1690

Court and confessed Judgment .. Therefore tis ordered Richd. Williams shall make payment of the same to James Hearse or Susan Keene (sic) or her assigns with costs ..

Page 110   Court held 13th November 1690

909.   JAMES BURNARD complaining against THOMAS COROESUN in plea of debt .. the sum of five hundred pounds of Tobacco due per bill under his hand and seale dated the 19th day of October 1689 as per bill here ready in Court to be produced .. And Thomas Coroesun came into Court and confessed Judgment .. Therefore tis ordered (he) shall make payment ..

910.   Ordered by this Court that the sheriff shall between this and next Court Impanel a Jury to Lay out the land in dispute between JOHN MATHEWS and Mr. JOHN WAUGH and that it be alsoe surveyed accordingly to the end that all controversies may be decided between them.

911.   Ordered that the sheriff shall bring the body of ADAM ROBINSON to the next Court to answer the suite of Mr. EDWARD THOMASON or else be Lyable according to act of assembly & pay costs. Attachment according to act of assembly is granted the sheriff against the Estate of Adam Robinson for his nonappearance at this Court to answer the suit of Edward Thomason and pay costs.

912.   EDWARD THOMASON late high sherif complaining sheweth that in the year 1683 one of your petitioners deputies Vizt PATRICK HUME arrested PETER DAWSON on a suit of Capt. GEORGE BRENT which said Dawson escaped out of the officers hands before the Court whereby an order went out against the sherif and the second Court Judgment according to act in that case for three hundred thirty seven pounds of Tobacco which debt your petr was forced upon to allow to the said Brent and the said Dawson being returned again into this County your petitioner hath brought his action and prays Judgment for the said sum .. and Peter Dawson appeared in Court and could say nothing to barr or preclusion of the Debt .. Therefore tis ordered Peter Dawson shall make payment ..

913.   SAMSON DARRELL who married the daughter of Capt. JOHN NORGRAVE deced and is the only Sister living of WILLIAM NORGRAVE son and heire of John Norgrave complaining sheweth that John Norgrave did by his last will & Testament in writing under his hand and seale dated the 23d of January 1669 gave and bequeathed his lands in this county to his loving wife FRANCES Vizt six hundred acres more or less Scituate lying and being on the South side Potomack Creek where he lived and died for and during her natural live which said Frances afterwards married with Coll. GEORGE MASON by which means during her Coverture George Mason and Frances stood seized for the life of Frances of and in the premises until the 10th day of September 1684 the said George Mason and Frances by their deeds under their hands and seals released the Estate for life and all other their claim or demand in or to the six hundred acres of land and William Norgrave by the deed of release dated as above and acknowledged in Court the 8th of October 1684 will at large appear by virtue of which release William Norgrave as heir to the said Father was seized

Page 111   Court held 13th November 1690

of and in the said six hundred acres with all its appurtenances in his demesne as of fee and of the same died seized without making any disposition thereof

Page 111 (contd)   Court held 13th November 1690

Wherefore the land descends to the said MARGARET your petitioners wife and that your Petr in right of his wife is Justly seized thereof But soe it is that one SIMON STACEY hath illegally entered upon the land and daily commits trespasses wast and spoiles by cutting downe the Timber breaking up the soile and to your Petrs damage ten thousand pounds of Tobacco Whereupon he brings his suit and prays he may be Ejected and pay costs And Simon Stacey the deft appears in this Court by GERRARD LOWTHER his attorney and confesses and justifies the trespass in the declaration alledged And now forasmuch as Simon Stacey did here produce a Lease of the land from THOMAS WATTS late of this County deced who purchased the deed of sale of the one moiety of the said six hundred acres of land sold and conveyed Whereby it doth appear to this Court that the right of the three hundred acres of land being the moiety of the Quantity of six hundred acres of land comprised in the Lease doth properly belong unto Thomas Watts heirs Therefore tis ordered that the portion or moiety of land shall be divided immediately surveyed and laid out between the heirs of Thomas Watts and Mr. Sampson Darrell according to the direct line and course mentioned in the deed made from William Norgrave to Thomas Watts at the proper costs and charges of the said Watts and heirs and that Samson Darrell pay this costs ..

914.   Ordered that JAMES WAPLE shall make present payment of the sum of eighty pounds of Tobacco unto THOMAS TUSTIN for his two daies attendance at Court in a Suite depending between him and MATHEW MARTYN with costs ..

915.   Ordered that SARAH MATHENY shall pay THOMAS HARRISON the sum of eighty pounds of Tobacco for his attendance two days at Court in suit depending between her and JOHN JONES and pay this costs.

916.   Ordered that JAMES MANN shall make payment of the sum of eighty pounds of Tobacco to JOHN TONEY and ELEANOR FLETCHER the wife of JAMES FLETCHER the sum of eighty pounds of Tobacco per peece for their attendance two daies at Court in a suit depending between him and JOHN MATHEWS with costs.

917.   Ordered that EDWARD MANN shall make payment of the sum of eighty pounds of Tobacco unto JOHN WILLIAMS for his attendance two daies at Court in a suit depending between him and GEORGE LUKE with costs.

918.   Ordered that the sherif bring the body of JOHN REYNOLDS to the next Court to answer the Suite of FRANCIS WADDINGTON or else be Lyable according to act of assembly and pay costs. Attachment according to act of assembly granted to the sherif against estate of John Reynolds for his non-appearance at this Court to answer the suit of Francis Waddington and pay costs.

919.   Ordered by this Court that RICHARD BRYANT shall make present payment of eighty pounds of Tobacco unto JOHN HAWKIN for his attendance two daies at Court in a Suite depending between him and RICHD. ELKIN with costs.

Page 112   At a Court held for County of Stafford at the house of THOMAS ELSEY November the 14th 1690

920.   Present Coll. William Fitzhugh, Mr. Samuel Hayward, Capt. George Mason, Mr. John Withers, Mr. Edward Thomason, Mr. William Buckner, Mr. Matthew Thompson, Justices

921.   Whereas Doctor EDWARD MADDOCKS did bring HUGH MULLEKEN his Servant to this Court to be judged for thirty four days Fugitively absenting himself out of his service and Doctor Edward Maddocks did fully prove and justifie

Page 112 (contd)   Court held 14th November 1690

the same Tis Therefore ordered that Hugh Milliken shall serve his master four
months after his service by Indenture or custom of the country is Expired ..
and forasmuch as Mr. WILLIAM BUCKNER did vouch to this Court that Doctor Edward Maddocks did promise and Justifie before him that if the servant would
not run away nor absent himself any more he would forever forgive him this
Judgment Therefore this ordered that the clerk shall enter his masters promise upon record.

922.   WILLIAM HUTCHINSON of Maryland by Capt. GEORGE BRENT his attorney com-
        plaineth against GEORGE RASCARLY in a plea of debt .. the sum of thir-
teen hundred and sixty six pounds of Tobacco and cask due per account .. and
George Rascarly by GERRARD LOWTHER his attorney comes into Court and for plea
saith Nil debet which plea was overruled by the Court and now forasmuch as
Capt. George Brent having produced in Court an accompt proved by his oath
before two commissioners .. it appears George Rascarly stands justly indebted
.. Therefore tis ordered George Rascarly shall make payment. William Hutchi-
son of Charles County in the province of Maryland by George Brent his attorney humbly complaining sheweth that George Rascarly late of Charles County
afsd the 18th of October 1690 did covenant and agree and with the plt as his
overseer to take charge of such servants as the plt should put under his
charge and command at his plantation at the Eastern branch in Charles County
and with them to make crops of corn and tobacco raise stocks of cattle and
hogs and sundry other things by and for the space of three years to commence
from the date abovesaid as appointed by the articles of agreement under his
the defts hand and seale dated as above Expressed and now in Court produced
in which articles the plt did covenant with the deft to provide corn meat and
stock and other things in the same contained which he punctually performed
and it only remained for the deft to perform his part and charge in the articles contained Vizt to make crops raise stocks of hogs and cattle and the
like and then to have reaped the profits and advantages to him granted but
on the contrary the deft minding to prejudice the plt and him to ruin and
destroy in

Page 113   Court held 14th November 1690

his Estate after he had exposed him to the great charge and Trouble of pro-
viding in the articles contained neglected his contract and fugitively run
away leaving the plts plantation Servants and stock to the loss of his crop
and the greatest part of his stock notwithstanding the deft had bound and
obliged himself to the plt in the sum of 5000 lb of Tobacco and cask to stand
to and perform the same .. and George Rascarly by GERRARD LOWTHER his attorney comes into Court and for plea saith oyer of the deeds and articles and
for Tryal puts himself upon the county the plt likewise Therefore tis ordered
that the Jury Enquire the fact: JOHN HAWKIN, JOHN GOWREY, FRANCIS WADINGTON,
DAVID STRAWHAN, EDWARD WATTS, JOHN TONEY, DAVID WAUGH, RICHARD MARTIN, SIMON
THOMASON, JOHN STOREY, GEORGE SHEPARD and JOHN MATHEWS which Jurors Elected
Tryed and Sworn do say upon their oaths we find for the plt four hundred
pounds of Tobacco damages with costs of suit. Therefore tis ordered that
Judgment shall be entered upon the verdict of the Jury ..

923.   Capt. GEORGE BRENT humbly complaining sheweth that RICHARD MINTHORNE
        of this County deced at the time of his decease stood indebted to the
plt for ballance of accounts due upon several bills the sum of six hundred
eighty three pounds of Tobacco and caske .. he hath brought his action against

Page 113 (contd)   Court held 14th November 1690

ELIZA. MINTHORNE the widow and administratrix of the said Richard deced And now forasmuch as Capt. George Brent did here in Court Justly make appear the debt to be due Therefore tis ordered that Eliza. Minthorne shall make payment ..

924.   Ordered that the horse Turk which was appraised amongst the Estate of THOS. OD'NEALE deced at price of nine hundred pounds of Tobacco shall be deducted out of the appraisement and be put in possession of HENRY COLD-STREAM being in Lieu of a horse which was bequeathed by XTOPHER LUND to KATHERINE his wife and Thomas Odeneale having married the widow of Xtopher Lund obtained a probate of his last will and Testament who not having paid the horse to Henry Coldstreame Therefore tis ordered that the horse Turk shall be deducted out of the appraisement and he accounted the proper estate of Henry Coldstream. ANNE the widow and relict of Thomas Odeneale humbly sheweth that Henry Coldstream who hath obtained Letters of Administration cum Testamento annexed of all singular the estate of the said Odeneale and is daily leasing and parting out of the lands of the deced the consequence of which is to your plts great losse and damage Therefore prays there may be a stop put to such proceedings and that she

Page 114   Court held 14th November 1690

may have her dower assigned to me the full third part of the said Odeneales lands set apart and divided to Law in that case provided And the Court doe accordingly order and Therefore tis ordered that a full third part of the lands of Thomas Odeneale deced shall be laid out and assigned by Mr. WILLIAM BUCKNER and Mr. ROBERT ALEXANDER Vizt the right of dower properly belonging to the widow and that the same being laid out and assigned shall immediately be put into the possession of Anne Odeneale ..

925.   ARTHUR SPENCER Attorney of MOSES HUBBERT by JOSHUA DAVIS his Attorney complains against STEPHEN SEBASTIAN in plea of Debt .. the sum of nine hundred pounds of tobacco in caske as per bill .. and now forasmuch as Joshua Davis did Exhibit his Bill whereby it doth plainly appear the debt is justly due Therefore tis ordered Stephen Sebastian shall make present payment ..

926.   Ordered by this Court that until the new Courthouse be erected and set up that the Courts for this County shall be held at the house of THOMAS ELSEY within this County.

927.   FRANCIS DADE v THOMAS DERRICK JUNR. upon Imparlance from the 20th day of July Anno Dom 1690. The action Inter Francis Dade the plt and Thomas Derrick Junr. the deft is humbly offered by this Court to the honour-able the Lieut. Governour and Councel for to have their opinion in it and the whole deciding the matter.

928.   EDWARD MANNE complains against GEORGE LUKE in plea of Trespass for that the said George Luke did on or about the 24th or 25th of July last past take up out of the wood in this County and within the jurisdiction of this Court a black mare branded in the near buttock with a figure of three being your petrs owne proper goods which mare George Luke did take up and ride to several places without your Petrs leave knowledge or consent since which time the plt could never find his mare tho having made diligent search and Enquiry .. and the Court doe accordingly order Therefore tis ordered that George Luke shall between this and the 20th of February deliver unto Edward Mann his mare or else pay him twelve hundred pounds of Tobacco with costs.

924 - 928

Page 114 (contd)   Court held 14th November 1690

929.   RICHARD BRYANT complaining sheweth that RALPH ELKIN late of this County
       deced did in his last sickness and not longe before his death did or-
der his son RICHD. ELKIN to pay or deliver to the plt one good stear of five
years old for his care medicines and attention of him in his Ralph Elkins
last sickness

Page 115   Court held 14th November 1690

which Richard Elkin refuses to pay.. prays Judgment of the stear or eight
hundred pounds of Tobacco and now forasmuch as Richard Bryant did Justly
make appear his debt to be due Therefore tis ordered that Richard Elkin shall
make payment of the stear or else five hundred pounds of tobacco ..

930.   RICHARD GIBSON humbly complaining sheweth that ROBERT KING in his life-
       time stood Justly indebted to him the sum of nineteen hundred and six-
teene pounds for public dues fees and Tobacco paid for him which he in his
lifetime hath not paid .. hath brought action against MARY KING relict and
Executrix of Robert King .. And now forasmuch that it doth appear to this
Court that there is due the sum and quantity of five hundred pounds of Tobacco
due from Robert King deced Therefore tis ordered Mary King the relict and
Executrix shall make payment ..

931.   SAMSON DARRELL complaineth against JOHN PENNEWALL in plea of debt ..
       sum of five hundred and fifty pounds of Tobacco and cask by account ..
And forasmuch as it doth appear to this Court that John Pennewall doth stand
Justly indebted the sum of three hundred pounds of Tobacco .. Therefore tis
ordered that he shall make payment of same ..

932.   Forasmuch as JOHN BLUNDALL brought his action in this Court against
       JOHN STOREY of this County and could not make appear any just cause
Therefore tis ordered that John Blundall shall be nonsuit and pay John Storey
fifty pounds of Tobacco with costs. Whereas John Blundall did summons JOHN
and BENJAMIN COLCLOUGH of this County to this Court to give in Evidence of
the Truth of what they knew in an action depending between him and John Storey
in a plea of trespass and forasmuch as John and Benjamin Colclough did faile
to appear to give in their evidence and John Blundall was nonsuited by reason of their nonappearance Therefore tis ordered that John and Benjamin Colclough shall be fined according to act of assembly and that each of them shall
pay unto John Blundall three hundred and fifty pounds of Tobacco with costs.
John Blundall complains against John Storey in a plea of Trespass for that
John Storey by force and armes hath taken away the plts horse and from the
time that he so Tooke away the horse

Page 116 Court held 14th November 1690

which was about a month ago since which time the said Storey hath buried rid
and abused the horse by which at present he is rendered unfit for any service
and hath detayned the horse out of the plts possession to his damage at least
two thousand pounds of Tobacco .. And now forasmuch as John Storey did appear
prove and justifie that John Blundall stands indebted to him the sum of eleven
hundred and ninety pounds of Tobacco in cask Therefore tis ordered that John
Blundall shall make present payment of the said sum unto John Storey and that
the said Storey upon payment of the same deliver to Blundall his horse and
that each party pay their own costs. Ordered John Blundall shall make payment of eighty pounds of Tobacco unto RICHARD HENWOOD for his attendance two
daies at Court in a Suite depending between him and John Storey with costs.

                                                                 929 - 932

Page 116 (contd)   Court held 14th November 1690

933.   WILLIAM BUCKNER Attorney of THOMAS STARKE and NICHOLAS HAYWARD Merchants in London complains against EDWARD THOMASON of this County Gent in plea of debt .. the sum of four hundred and eighty pounds of Tobacco as by the audit between Mrs. MARY MASSEY and the plt will appear .. and forasmuch as William Buckner did aver and justifie that Edward Thomason did in the time of his Shreivalty take and carry away and convert to his own proper use one hhd of Tobacco and cask Quantity four hundred and eighty pounds of Tobacco which did properly belong to Thomas Starke and Nicholas Hayward and which was paid by RALPH ELKIN late of this County deced unto WILLIAM BUCKNER but seized by Edward Thomason then high sherif being in the house of Ralph Elkin and for (his) proper and Just debt Therefore tis ordered Edward Thomason shall make present payment of the said sum ..

934.   ABRAHAM FARROW complains against SAMPSON DARRELL in plea of debt ..
        the sum of six hundred and eighty pounds of Tobacco in caske due per bill and accompt .. And now forasmuch as it doth appear to this Court that Sampson Darrell stands justly indebted to Abraham Farrow the sum of six hundred pounds of Tobacco Therefore tis ordered that Sampson Darrell shall make payment ..

935.   JAMES HEARSE complains against RICHARD WILLIAMS in a plea of debt ..
        the sum of one hundred and ninety five pounds of Tobacco due per note under the hand and seale and thirty pounds of Tobacco due per account ..

Page 117   Court held 14th November 1690

which he refuseth to pay altho often fairly demanded .. And Richard Williams by RICHARD GIBSON his attorney came into Court and confessed Judgment .. Therefore tis ordered the said Williams shall make present payment of same ..

936.   Whereas JOSHUA DAVIS did arrest JOHN ATTERTON to this Court and the sherif returned him non est inventus Therefore tis ordered that Joshua Davis shall have an attachment against Estate of John Atterton according to act of assembly and with costs.

937.   Ordered that the sherif bring the body of JONAH REVET to the next Court to answer the suit of JOHN AMEE or else be Lyable according to act of assembly and pay costs. Attachment according to act of assembly is granted the sherif against the estate of Jonah Revet for his nonappearance at this Court to answer the complaint of John Amee and pay costs.

938.   Ordered that the sherif bring the body of ROBERT HAMBLETON to the next Court to answer the suit of WILLIAM WILLIAMS or else be Lyable according to act of assembly. Attachment according to act of assembly is granted the sherif against the estate of Robert Hambleton for his nonappearance at this Court to answer the complaint of William Williams and pay costs ..

939.   Ordered that the sherif bring the body of ROBERT LEATHERLAND to the next Court to answer the suit of DAVID STRAHAN or else be Lyable according to act of assembly and pay costs. Attachment according to act of assembly is granted the sherif against the estate of Robert Leatherland for his nonappearance at Court to answer the complaint of David Strahan and pay costs.

940.   Ordered that the sherif bring the body of WILLIAM COCKE to the next Court to answer the suit of DAVID STRAHAN or else be Lyable according to act of assembly. Attachment according to act of assembly is granted the

933 - 940

Page 117 (contd)   Court held 14th November 1690

sherif against the estate of William Cocke for his nonappearance at Court to answer the complaint of David Strahan and pay costs.

941.   Forasmuch as JOHN BLUNDALL brought his action in this Court against WILLIAM WILLFORD deputy sherif of this County and could not aver Justifie prove and maintain his action Therefore tis ordered John Blundall shall be nonsuite and shall pay William Willford the sum of fifty pounds of Tobacco with costs.

> Remainder of page 117 and part of page 118 summary of attorneys and their clients.

Page 118   Court held 14th November 1690

> The Court is adjourned till the 2d Wednesday in Xber next
> God save their Majesties

942.   ANNE the widow and relict of THOMAS ODENEALE Late of this County deced made humble petition to this Court that she might have her paraphenalia granted her out of her deced husbands Estate according to act of assembly set apart these things which followeth being as she conceives proportionable to his Estate and her Qualification doth humbly pray that these things which were not appraised but set apart out of her husbands Estate may be allowed her for her paraphenalia Vizt in her room one feather bed and furniture, one chest and one small trunk three pewter dishes and six plates six spoons and one Iron pot one brass kettle and a skillet one warming pan Two pair of sheets half a dozen canvas napkins 2 Towells one case and five knives one box iron one small silver drain cup one iron pestle one little trunk one old pewter tumbler one old pewter tankard and the Court having taken it into their most serious charitable and mature consideration doe accordingly order Therefore tis ordered that Anne Odeneale according to her Qualification shall have the abovementioned and Expressed goods allowed her out of her deced husbands Estate for her paraphenalia.

943.   At a Court held for County of Stafford at the House of THOMAS ELSEY december the 10th 1690

> Present Coll. William Fitzhugh, Mr. Samuel Hayward, Capt. George Mason, Mr. John Withers, Mr. Edward Thomason, Mr. Matthew Thompson, Justices.

944.   DOROTHY HAMBLETON complaining sheweth that your Petrs Husband being lately runaway out of this County hath left behind him your Petr and two small children all sick and unable to get their Living or Subsist at present

Page 119   Court held 10th December 1690

the Creditors having taken by attachment all and everything in and about the house and plantation as Corne and three head of Cattle belonging unto your petitioners youngest Sonne as a gift given by WILLIAM LANE his godfather wherefore your petitioner most humbly desires your worships order to Vacate the said cattle soe attached and the Corne and other small absolutely necessary things without which your petitioner can no ways Subsist And the Court having charitabley and maturely considered the premises doe accordingly order Therefore tis ordered that the said Dorothy the wife of Robert Hambleton shall have all the Corn with the Beans which was lately attached by RICHARD MARTYN for a debt due from the said Hambleton for the support and maintenance of her

Page 119 (contd)   Court held 10th December 1690

and her children and that the Sheriff shall put her into the immediate possession of the same. ROBERT BRENT the attorney of the said Richard Martin
came into Court and craved an appeale from the foresaid order Which this
Court would not allow by reason the appeale was not Lawfully to be granted till
the whole cause is determined. Ordered that the three head of cattle Vizt
one cow a three year old heifer and a two year old heifer which was attached
by Richard Martin as a debt due from Robert Hambleton late of this County
shall by the Sheriff be put into the immediate possession of Dorothy the wife
of the said Robert Hambleton provided that she give good security and enter
into bond if she doth not prove at the next Court that the foresaid cattle soe
attached doth not properly belong to one of the said Dorothy children as a
gift given by William Lane formerly of this County deced being as godfather
to the said child in his Last will and Testament.

945.   Ordered that JOHN HOTHAM be Summoned to this Court by Tomorrow morning
        at Ten of the Clock to make his personal appearance and to bring into
Court articles of agreement formerly made between EDWARD WHEELER of Westmoreland County and ROBERT HAMBLETON and was then put into the Custody of the
said John Hotham by consent of both of the said parties.

946.   SAMSON DARRELL complaining sheweth that JOHN BASFORD late of this
        County stands indebted unto the plt the Sum of three thousand eight
hundred pounds of Tobacco due to him by account who having absented himself
out of this County the plt took out an attachment against his Estate according to Law Wherefore the plt humbly craves Judgment against the Estate of
John Basford soe attached with costs attached in the hands of HENRY COLD-
STREAM admr Cum Testamento annexed of THOMAS ODENEALE Late of this County
deced And now forasmuch as Sampson Darrell did Justly in this Court make appear his debt to be due Therefore tis ordered that Sampson Darrell shall
have Judgment against the Estate of John Basford for the sum of four hundred
pounds of Tobacco soe attached in the hands of the afsd Henry Coldstream in
the Qualification aforesaid being due as a Legacy given to John Basford by
the afsd Thomas Odeneale in his Last will and Testament.

947.   Ordered that WILLIAM LYNNE, JANE LYNNE and WILLIAM HAMBLETON shall by
        the sherif be Summoned to the next Court to give good Security and
Enter into bond that they shall faithfully keep and preserve the Cattle and
mares with their Increase for the use and benefit and behoof of BARBARY the
daughter of WILLIAM MASON late of this County deced according to the true
intent purport and meaning of the aforesaid William Mason last will and
Testament.

Page 120   Court held 10th December 1690

948.   ISAAC ALLERTON Esqr. humbly sheweth that your petitioner Stood bound
        to JOHN COLLOM Late of Plymouth deced to NICHOLAS SPENCER late Collec-
tor of Potowmack district for the payment of Twenty Seven pounds fifteen shillings and three pence by bills of Exchange the same being due for port duties
of Tobacco belonging to Mr. JOHN ADDIZ of Plymouth Mercht. and ABRAM BEALE
shipped on board the Ship King David which said bills came in protested which
with damage and Cost amounts to Thirty two pounds one shilling and the said
Collom not having Effects here to answer the same your petitioner humbly prays
an attachment against the Estate of the said Addiz and Beale for Satisfaction
of the said Debt And the Court having fully and maturely weighed and throughly

Page 120 (contd)   Court held 10th December 1690

considered the premises doe accordingly order Therefore tis ordered that
Coll. Isaac Allerton Esqr. shall have attachment against the Estate of the
afsd John Addiz and Abram Beale now in the hands of JOHN WITHERS in this County
provided that Isaac Allerton give good Security and Enter into bond to render
what part of the Estate the afsd Abram Beale hath in the hands of John Withers
if it doth not appear that the afsd John Collom was not in the Employ of
Abram Beale at the time of the drawing the afsd bills of Exchange. Capt.
GEORGE MASON became Security with Mr. ROBERT BRENT attorney of Isaac Allerton for the True performance of the same..

Mr. William Buckner present

949. EDWARD THOMASON late high sheriff complaining sheweth that in the year
      1683 one of your petitioners deputies Vizt PATRICK HUME arrested ADAM
ROBINSON in an action of debt at the Suit of Capt. GEORGE BRENT which said
Robinson Escaped and out of the officers hands before the Court Whereby an
order went against the sherif and the second Court Judgment according to act
in that case for five hundred fifty one pounds of Tobacco debt and charges
which said debt your petition was forced upon acco. to allow to the said Brent
and the said Robinson being since returned into the County doth alledge that
he hath alsoe paid the said debt to the said Brent wherefore your petitioner
hath brought this Complaint and humbly craves this Worshipful Court consideration of the matter and Judgment therein against the said Robinson Except his
Allegations be True and that he pay costs And ADAM ROBINSON came into Court
and confessed Judgment to the aforesaid Edward Thomason for the sum of five
hundred and fifty one pounds of Tobacco unto Edward Thomason Therefore tis
ordered that Adam Robinson shall make present payment of the same ..

950. HENRY COLDSTREAM made humble petition to this Court that whereas your
      petitioner was ordered by your worship's last Court to give Security
and Enter into bond for and concerning JAMES THEARLE which was unfortunately
wounded and forasmuch is well recovered and gone home about his Lawful occasions Wherefore your petitioner humbly prays your worships order for to be
released and that he with his Security may be discharged from their bond And
now forasmuch as Dr. EDWARD MADDOCKS did appear in this Court and aver and
Justifie that James Thearle which was so wounded by Henry Coldstream was well
recovered and healed of his wounds Therefore tis ordered that Henry Coldstream
with his Security shall be released and freely and fully discharged from
their bond and that the sherif shall immediately deliver up the same unto
them.

951. JOHN BREWTON complains against ADAM ROBINSON in plea of debt for that
      he stands indebted to the plt the sum of five hundred pounds of To-
bacco and cask due per bill under his hand and Seale and Two hundred and fifty
pounds of

Page 121   Court held 10th December 1690

Tobacco due per account for which the plt craves Judgment with costs And Adam
Robinson came into Court and confessed Judgment unto John Brewton for the sum
of six hundred pounds of Tobacco Therefore tis ordered that he shall make
present payment of the same with costs ..

952. FRANCIS WADDINGTON complains against JOHN REYNOLDS in a plea of debt
      .. the sum of four hundred and fifty pounds of Tobacco and cask and
Ten Bushels of wheat due by Two bills dated under his hand and Seale the 26th

Page 121 (contd)   Court held 10th December 1690

day of January 1689 which the said Reynolds refuseth to pay altho often
fairly and Legally demanded Wherefore the plt hath brought his action and
craves Judgment .. And now forasmuch as John Reynolds did by ROBERT BRENT his
attorney make appear to this Court that he hath paid Two Bushels of wheat out
of the debt and could not say nothing in Barr or preclusion of the sum of
four hundred and fifty pounds of Tobacco and Eight Bushels of wheat Therefore tis ordered that John Reynolds shall make payment of the same ..

953.   ADAM ROBINSON came into Court and confessed Judgment unto STEPHEN
       SEBASTIAN for the sum of Two hundred and forty pounds of Tobacco due
per Bill Therefore tis ordered that Adam Robinson shall make present payment
of the same ..

954.   Whereas CHARLES BALDRIDGE brought his action in this Court against
       JONATHAN BUCKLEY and could not Justify aver and maintain his action
Therefore tis ordered that the said Charles Baldridge shall be nonsuit and
shall pay Jonathan Buckley the sum of fifty pounds of Tobacco with costs ..

955.   DAVID LINDSEY made humble petition to this Court that he being Sixty
       four years of age and having served in the Wars under King Charles the
Second both in England and in Foreign Countreys and having served the full
time of four years in this Country with THOMAS GREGG Wherefore your petitioner
humbly prays that your worships may be pleased to Exempt him out of and
country duties And the Court having fully and maturelay considered the premises doe accordingly order Therefore tis ordered that David Lindsey shall
be fully and freely discharged and Exempted from paying for the future any
Publick duties or Levys.

956.   Ordered that CHARLES BALDRIDGE shall make present payment of the sum
       of Forty pounds of Tobacco unto BENJAMIN WEBB for his Attendance one
day at Court in a Suit depending between him and JONATHAN BUCKLEY with costs ..
Charles Baldridge complains against Jonathan Buckley in a plea of debt ..
the sum of three thousand two hundred pounds of Tobacco and cask by Two bills
(Vizt) one for Two thousand four hundred and another for eight hundred pounds
of Tobacco for which the plt hath brought his action And the said Jonathan
Buckley the deft by ROBERT BRENT his attorney came into Court and prayed over
of the said Bills And now forasmuch as it appears to this Court that the debt
of three thousand two hundred pounds of Tobacco due from Jonathan Buckley unto
Charles Baldridge by the Two bills the Court having allowed

Page 122   Court held 10th December 1690

Bills to be good in Law Therefore tis ordered that Jonathan Buckley shall
make present payment of the same .. And Robert Brent Attorney came into Court
and prayed Injunction in Chancery against the said Baldridge for his two Bills
which unto him is granted he the said Buckley the deft giving good security
and Enter into bond to performe what the Law requires. And now forasmuch as
Jonathan Buckley did not appeare and give Security and Enter into bond according as the Law directs Therefore tis ordered that Judgment shall issue
upon the afsd order with costs ..

957.   Ordered by this Court that if JOSEPH SUMNER of this County will accept
       of five hundred pounds of Tobacco for the future yearly for the mending
and keeping of Pasbitanzy bridge per annum in repair that then Joseph Sumner
shall be annually allowed the same out of the County Levy soe Long as he shall
keep the bridge in repair.

958.   Whereas Capt. MALACHI PEALE high sherif of this County did publickly
        in this Court refuse the collection of the County Levy for this pre-
sent year he alledging for his reason that the upper Parish of this County
had taken the Collection of the parish Levy out of his hands and that Mr.
SAMPSON DARRELL the Cheif undertaker for the Erecting and building of a new
Courthouse for this County did here likewise in Court offer and Tender himself to Levy and Collect the County Claims and Levys Therefore tis ordered
that Sampson Darrell shall collect the County Levy for this present year he
giving good security and Entring into bond for the True performance and paying
all the publick claims to Each respective person where they became due at the
Laying of the said Levy. Mr. JOHN WITHERS became security with Sampson Darrell for the true performance of the same.

959.   Ordered by this Court that RICHARD BANKS Servant to Mr. RICHARD GIBSON
        shall be from this day freely and fully discharged and set at Liberty
from his master for that Mr. Richard Gibson hath not performed and Taken the
care and pains towards the Effectual means of curing Richard Bank's Scald
head and for not putting him to Learn to read and write according to a former order of this Court.

960.   GEORGE BRENT humbly sheweth that the 14th of November last past your
        petitioner obtained Judgment in this worshipful Court against Mr.
FRANCIS DADE for the sum of Six pounds Sterling money and Seventy five pounds
of Tobacco with Cask on which Judgment he Took out Execution against the
said Dades Estate and delivered the same to WILLIAM WILLFORD Subsheriff of
this County who Levied the same upon one CHARLES MINGO a negroe boy of the
said Dades and had not only order to bring the boy to appraisement but also
your petitioner had Taken such care to provide ready money to have paid the
Overplus if any that the Negroe should be valued at according to Law. Yet
he the said Wilford not minding his Bath and office but Craftilly to deceive
your Petr without your petrs order released the Executed Negroe and Takes
Tobacco according to his own will and pleasure without every bringing the
said Negroe to appraisement as his Oath office and direction of Law is
bounde which false and Illegal proceedings of such an officer as it is to
your Petrs greatly detrimentall soe it is of most pernicious Consequence and
publick inconveniency by such falacious actions rendring Judgments ineffectual
Wherefore he humbly prays that the said Wilford may be punished for his breach
of Oath and office as your worships shall adjudge his crime deserves and that
your worships will order the high sheriff to take the Negroe boy and have him
duly appraised and delivered to your Petr upon paying the overplus if any that
the Negroe shall be appraised at. And now forasmuch as it doth appear to this
Court that the said Wilford had Levyed an Execution on the said Charles Mingo
a negroe boy belonging to the said Dade and did afterwards release and discharge the negro boy contrary to Law his Oath and office and that it doth appear to this Court that the Tender of the said Dades in Tobacco for the negroes
discharge was not good in law and that the said Wilford Subsheriff his receipt
and discharge to Francis Dade was not according to Law Justice and Equity but
contrary Illegal and retrograde to his oath and office Therefore tis ordered
that Charles Mingo the negroe boy belonging to Francis Dade shall be Immediately
be taken and seized by the high Sherif of this County and that he shall Summons lawful appraisers to appraise him according to act of assembly ..

        The Court is adjourned till the 2d Wednesday in February next
        God save King William and Queen Mary

RUSH. William 21, 36.
RUSHTON. William 91.
RUSSELL. Nicholas 85, 86, 343, 401;
  William 866.
RUST. Mr. 257; William 212, 229.
RUSTALL. William 548, 637, 696, 749,
  757.

SALLAWAY. William 358.
SALLEE. Herman 661.
SAMSON. Robert 448.
SAMWAIES (SAMWAIDS). John 100, 115,
  119, 162, 163, 166, 172, 196, 213,
  222, 224, 230, 268, 269, 270, 280,
  300, 315, 327, 329, 333, 337, 339,
  394, 424, 491.
SANDERS. Edward 113, 146, 161, 273,
  331; Mr. 169.
SANDS. Edward 598.
SANDYS. Elizabeth 358; Robert 358.
SCARLET. Martin 509, 616, 819;
  Mr. 752.
SEAS. Mathew 581.
SEBASTIAN. Stephen 572, 629, 637,
  696, 858, 925, 953.
SHARPE. Thomas 36, 376, 380, 477.
SHAW. Thomas 539.
SHELTON. Robert 296.
SHEPPARD. Anne 144; George 580,
  637, 650, 749, 757, 763, 922.
SHUTE. Thomas 623.
SIMMS. Anne 718, 809.
SIMONS (SYMONS). John 652, 659;
  Mary 417.
SIMSON. John 559, 560, 561, 562,
  571, 588, 789.
SISSON (CISSEN). Daniel 152;
  Henry 451; Mr. 188.
SLEDGE. Charles 719, 720, 802.
SLYE. Gerrard 668, 678.
SMITH (SMYTH). Ann 555; Danah 757;
  Edward 512, 628; John 314, 359,
  389, 555, 718, 809; Ralph 527,
  533, 606, 609, 611, 614, 626, 885;
  Samuel 679; Stephen 593, 698;
  Thomas 359, 783; William 528, 688.
SNEAD. Henry 110.
SOLEY. Thomas 76.
SORRELL. John 358; Joseph 358.
SPEED. Ralph 546.
SPEEDY. Thomas 8, 120, 400.
SPENCE. Martin 711.
SPENCER. Arthur 925; Colo. 564;
  Nicholas 275, 825, 948.

SPILLAR. George 696.
SPINCE. William 555.
SPOONER. Samuel 78, 237, 286, 441.
STACEY. Simon 511, 549, 572, 636, 650,
  693, 854, 913; Timothy 330.
STANLEY. Robert 572.
STANTON. Anthony 144; James 696, 855.
STAVES. John 330.
STEPHENS. Stephen 752.
STOELL. William 330.
STONE. John 90, 224, 320.
STONING (STONEING). Roger 607, 654,
  804, 828.
STARKE (STORKE). Mr. 77; Thomas 933;
  William 79, 87, 97, 98, 157, 213,
  246.
STORY. John 922, 932; Mary 358.
STRAWHAN (STRAHAN). David 572, 618,
  650, 777, 922, 939, 940.
STREET. Robert 45, 93, 116, 344, 364,
  376, 477, 482, 513, 607.
STURDY. William 623.
STURMAN. John 354; Richard 354, 421;
  Robert 421.
SUMNER. James 322; Joseph 813, 815,
  956.
SUMPTNER (SUMPNER). James 304, 375,
  426, 452.
SWAINE. Thomas 615.
SWAN. Susanna 534, 622.
SYNNETT. Alexander 305, 323.

TALLWOOD. Hum: 358.
TARKINTON. John 877.
TAYLOE. William 359.
TAYLOR. Edward 617; Edward Junr. 744,
  745, 796, 800; Henry 749; Jane 393.
TENANT (TENNENT). James 239, 359.
THEARLE. James 664, 799, 883, 950.
THOMAS. David 196, 792; Simon (Symn)
  444, 537, 638, 740; William 129, 130,
  131, 169, 196, 212, 229, 257, 283,
  288, 330, 339.
THOMASON. Edward 507, 516, 594, 640,
  686, 782, 794, 811, 819, 836, 858,
  869, 879, 882, 903, 907, 911, 912,
  920, 933, 943, 949; Simon 714, 832,
  854, 922.
THOMPSON (THOMSON)(TOMSON). Ann 359;
  Capt. 274; Fras: 359; Henry 576,
  580, 712, 714, 740, 749, 757, 763,
  778, 779, 832, 845; James 359;
  Mathew 507, 516, 519, 541, 542,
  543, 550, 554, 569, 592, 594, 601,

(contd)

www.ingramcontent.com/pod-product-compliance
Lightning Source LLC
Chambersburg PA
CBHW080615270326
41928CB00016B/3066